God Calling...
please pick up!

To Brad,
You have been an instrument of God's grace to my family. Thank you for your witness & inspiration~
Gratefully
Patty Ward

Patricia G. Ward

Published by
Bezalel Books
Waterford, MI
www.BezalelBooks.com

Printed in the United States of America

ISBN 978-0-936453-01-6
Library of Congress Control Number 2010942075

Foreword

"A faithful friend is a sturdy shelter; he who finds one finds a treasure. A faithful friend is beyond price, no sum can balance his worth. A faithful friend is a life-saving remedy." – Sirach 6:14-16

I remember the first time I met Patty Ward as a little girl in January of 1964. I was the new student in the first grade at Gesu School in Detroit. Thanks to the classroom policy of alphabetical seating lists I was placed behind Patty. Our last names began with K and we became instant friends. She often jokes that she liked my voice, my laugh and my shoes in those early years of our friendship. I was attracted by her incredible singing abilities and her exceedingly large family. She had the blessing of big sisters and brothers which gave her access to all the wisdom and ideas of older siblings. As the second eldest in our growing family I felt slighted that I only had one older brother. Patty is the 11th of 13 children. Perhaps that accounts for another quality I have appreciated since the outset of our friendship - her urgent desire to excel at everything. While that can sometimes lead children into unhealthy rivalries, I found myself delighting in Patty's abilities and accomplishments, and looking for ways we could creatively combine our interests and talents. I organized backyard May crownings complete with readings and songs that Patty would lead. In fourth grade we collaborated on a St. Patrick's Day musical theatrical production performed on the stage at our school. I narrated, Patty performed the female lead and our teacher allowed us to cast our friends in the supporting roles. To my great horror, her family moved across town the following year. Although we briefly lost contact with each other, God brought us back together for high school.

Patty's musical talents blossomed at our all girls high school, where she sang in the choir and starred in school plays. Her constant pursuit of excellence continued to impress me. Once again I took great joy in her accomplishments. But we also shared some less than admirable exploits as we ventured into the world of parties, dating boys and sharing a dorm room at the University of Michigan. During that phase of our friendship, the faith we shared as children often took a back seat to the mutual goal of achieving the elusive labels "cool" and "popular." We took quite different routes toward that goal in early adulthood, discovering only later that neither label could bring the happiness and peace offered by the faith of our youth. Once again our friendship went temporarily dormant while God began preparing us to reconnect on a more spiritual level.

Since returning to Michigan nearly 20 years ago I have been privileged to accompany Patty on her quest to know Our Lord more deeply and follow His Church more faithfully. Her life-long pursuit of excellence and her sometimes impatient urgency for clear explanations led us into complicated and long discussions, particularly since she knew I had been actively pursuing adult faith formation while living in Florida. Patty wanted to know how to answer the doubts about Catholicism she increasingly encountered. New Age spirituality had begun attracting some of her loved ones away from the Church. And her ongoing participation in community theater had provided many friends who lived lifestyles inconsistent with the teachings of the Catholic Church. The murky discussions among priests and theologians about following one's conscience rather than formal Church teachings regarding married life often disturbed her. Like no one else I have ever known, Patty has no use for grey areas when it comes to making decisions. With an open mind she seeks the truth and when she finds it she firmly grabs hold. Simply put, Patty wants to know what is wrong and what is right, and why. She seeks understanding and she wants to please God.

I am eternally grateful to God for her friendship. By seeking answers from me, Patty inspired me to strengthen my own understanding and love of the Catholic faith. Just like back in grade school, we began looking for ways to creatively combine our talents, but this time with a desire to serve God in the process. The informal Catholic study group I led in my home was the precursor to several more formal collaborations. We co-founded an apostolate called 'Stage of Faith Productions.' We have produced several meditational CDs that feature Patty's original songs. We created spiritual programs for retreats and parishes. In the years I hosted a daily morning show on a Catholic radio station in metro Detroit, I developed a segment called "Book Lights and Footlights" so that Patty could join me on the air each Friday to discuss literature and entertainment through the lens of faith. We continue to look for more ways to serve God together.

Patty is one of the most talented and faithful people I have ever known. The list of her theatrical roles is long and impressive. She has played the lead role in some of the most famous and beloved musicals. She has choreographed many shows. Although she does not play a musical instrument, Patty has written dozens of wonderful songs celebrating faith and family life. She has created a thought-provoking pro life reader's theater program. Her enthusiasm for Catholicism has also led to facilitating Catholic scripture study groups and regularly singing at liturgies.

But none of this compares to her outstanding accomplishments at home. Patty's marriage to her high school sweetheart, Bill, is a true love story. Together they have raised three remarkable, committed Catholic children. Their family demonstrates that it is indeed possible to be both Catholic and "cool." Now, Patty presents us with this wonderful book. With great humility and a lot of humor, Patty shares her many adventures of trying to live the faith in real life situations. You will get to know Patty as I know her. And that means you will get to love the Patty I love. I pray this will lead us all to love Christ and His Church more deeply.

-Mary Dudley
Prolife Speaker & former radio host of 'Live From the Shrine'

Part One: Finding God at the Country Club and Other Unlikely Places

Introduction: Suburban Housewife Seeking Loving, Personal God

1) **The Country Club**
   Why do you notice the splinter in your brother's eye, but do not perceive the wooden beam in your own? Luke 6:41
2) **Mall-Walking**
   Preach the gospel always, if necessary use words. St. Francis of Assisi
3) **The Golf Course**
   I've got that joy, joy, joy, joy down in my heart. George Willis Cooke
4) **The Bridge Table**
   We know that all things work for good for those who love God, who are called according to His purpose. Romans 8:28
5) **The Mix-up**
   And forgive us our debts, as we forgive our debtors. Matthew 6:12
6) **The Clinic**
   For human beings it is impossible but not for God. All things are possible for God. Mark 10:27
7) **The Other Political Party**
   Do to others whatever you would have them do to you. Matthew 7:12
8) **The Soccer Field**
   For I know well the plans I have in mind for you, says the Lord, plans for your welfare, not for woe! Plans to give you a future full of hope. Jeremiah 29:11
9) **The Hot Moms**
   Stop judging and you will not be judged. Luke 6:37
10) **The Theatre**
   Always be ready to give an explanation to anyone who asks you for a reason for your hope but do it with gentleness and reverence. 1 Peter 3:15-16
11) **The Problems**
   Are not two sparrows sold for a small coin? Yet not one of them falls to the ground without your Father's knowledge. Even all the hairs of your head are counted. Matthew 10:29-30
12) **The Voice Lesson**
   Sing to the Lord a new song. Psalm 149:1

13) **The Corvette**

It is easier for a camel to pass through the eye of a needle than for one who is rich to enter the kingdom of God. Mark 10:25

14) **The Wedding List**

Blessed are those who have been called to the wedding feast of the Lamb. Revelation 19:9

15) **The Pulled Hamstring**

The Lord lifts up all who are falling and raises up all who are bowed down. Psalm 145:14

16) **The Jigsaw Puzzle**

Deprive not yourself of present good things, let no choice portion escape you. Sirach 14:14

17) **The Knitting**

Indeed, like clay in the hand of the potter, so are you in my hand. Jeremiah 18:6

18) **The Accident**

He will make straight your paths. Proverbs 3:6

19) **The Ah Moments**

Are they not all ministering spirits sent to serve, for the sake of those who are to inherit salvation? Hebrews 1:14

20) **The Holy Medium**

So, because you are lukewarm, neither hot nor cold, I will spit you out of my mouth. Revelation 3:16

21) **Kicking and Screaming**

What you did not do for one of these least ones, you did not do for me. Matthew 25:45

22) **A Typical Quandary**

The fruit of the spirit is love, joy, peace, patience, kindness, generosity, faithfulness, gentleness, self-control. Galatians 5:22-23

23) **Worrying**

Cast all your worries upon him because he cares for you. 1 Peter 5:7

24) **The Playing Field**

Where there's despair in life let me bring hope. The Prayer of St. Francis

25) **The Breakups**

Our hearts are restless until they rest in you. St Augustine

26) **The Gifts**

Where are the other nine? Luke 17:17

Part Two: God Calling, Please Pick up!
Introduction: The Doubts

27) **Exfoliation**
    Whatever you loose on earth will be loosed in heaven. Matthew 16:19

28) **Drifting Away**
    Persevere in running the race that lies before us. Hebrews 12:1

29) **Share Your Toys**
    All who believed were together and had all things in common. Acts 2:44

30) **Dilemmas**
    Think of what is above, not of what is on earth. Colossians 3:2

31) **Procrastination**
    The foolish ones, when taking their lamps, brought no oil with them. Matthew 25:3

32) **Waiting**
    Let's think of something to do while we're waiting. Fred Rogers

33) **The God Box Project**
    For us there is one God, the Father, from whom all things are and for whom we exist. Corinthians 8:6

34) **Feelin' Groovy**
    We believe in God, the Father almighty, creator of heaven and earth. The Apostles Creed

35) **The Fun Contest**
    With three things I am delighted, for they are pleasing to the Lord and to men: harmony among brethren, friendship among neighbors, and the mutual love of husband and wife. Sirach 25:1

36) **Beyond Breakfast**
    I will enter his house and dine with him, and he with me. Revelation 3:20

37) **Sassy Spray**
    They will know we are Christians by our love. Carolyn Arends and Peter R. Scholtes

38) **Time**
    There is an appointed time for everything. Ecclesiastes 3:1

39) **Messages**
    When you send forth your breath, they are created, and you renew the face of the earth. Psalm 104:30

40) **House Chardonnay**
    Do whatever he tells you. John 2:5

41) **Think Little**

Amen, I say to you, unless you turn and become like children, you will not enter the kingdom of heaven. Matthew 18:3

42) **Sense and Sensible Shoes**

Frequent the company of the elders; whoever is wise, stay close to him. Sirach 6:34

43) **Nice Matters**

Whatever you do, do everything for the glory of God. 1 Corinthians 10:31

44) **Inner Beauty**

Although our outer self is wasting away, our inner self is being renewed day by day. 2 Corinthians 4:16

45) **Opening Doors**

I have given you a model to follow, so that as I have done for you, you should also do. John 13:15

46) **Losing**

Whoever loses his life for my sake will find it. Matthew 10:39

47) **Treasures**

For where your treasure is, there also will your heart be. Luke 12:34

48) **Grow up**

I could not talk to you as spiritual people, but as fleshly people, as infants in Christ. I fed you milk, not solid food, because you were unable to take it. 1 Corinthians 3:1-2

49) **Shock and Awe**

A clean heart create for me, God; renew in me a steadfast spirit. Psalm 51:12

50) **By Myself**

There are many parts, yet one body. 1 Corinthians 12:20

51) **Just Right**

This porridge is just right! Goldilocks and the Three Bears

52) **Looking Back**

Since you have taken off the old self with its practices and have put on the new self, which is being renewed, for knowledge, in the image of its creator. Colossians 3:9-10

Part 1

Finding God
at the Country Club
and Other Unlikely Places

Writing essays on where to find God will seem ridiculous to some people, I am sure. We all know that God is everywhere and that we can find Him in everything. The problem is that most of the time we forget to look. We tend to separate our "God time" when we are in prayer or at a liturgy or participating in one of the sacraments from our "normal time" which is when we are doing everything else.

A few years back I began to pray an examination of conscience each day which was broken into Gratitude, Petition, Review, Forgiveness and Renewal. The "Review" section, at the prompting of my spiritual director, focused on where the action was in my day. I would review what really brought me joy, anger or confusion and try to find God at work in that. I kept journals of these "Examens" and eventually thought I had some stories to tell. I was finding God at work in my life in so many unexpected places that I wondered if someone else could possibly relate to my observations.

I know that I have led a blessed life. When I speak of "problems" I know that in the grand scheme of things mine are very small. When I speak of "rich" and "poor" I also know that these are relative terms and that there will always be richer and poorer than those to whom I am referring. In these pages, I am revealing a great deal about my life and the people and activities that comprise it and I am sure some will simply roll their eyes and say "no wonder she has time to write essays...she doesn't really DO anything!"

So be it. For some reason I feel compelled to share my faith journey and hope that others might see themselves in my journey and walk along with me. I have tried to practice the presence of God in my daily life, but, many times it has been only in the "looking back" that I have found that He was there all along.

Thank you for reading my stories. I have tried not to mention anyone by name if I thought they would be offended by anything I had to say about them. The person that I am convicting over and over again in these observations is me. This is my own version of reality which may or may not agree with someone else's version of the same circumstance. I apologize, in advance, to anyone who may feel called out by anything that I have to say. My intentions are certainly, first and foremost, to do no harm.

Join me in a suburban housewife's quest for God.

I was raised in a family of thirteen children in a little white bungalow with three bedrooms and one and a half baths. The upstairs was a dormitory where we kept adding trundle beds and triple bunks as each new child arrived. We had one car which my mom used to drive the kids around. My dad took the bus to and from work. We had a roof over our heads, food on the table and got "chips and pop" on Saturday night while we watched *The Jackie Gleason Show* featuring *The June Taylor Dancers*. We considered ourselves blessed as we were rich in love, although clearly not familiar with any type of luxury. I explain this merely to help you understand what a transition it was for me to join the local country club after my husband became established in his medical practice.

The first time I showed up to golf with the girls, a woman told me that my wedding ring was too small, my golf clubs needed to be upgraded and my visor did not match my outfit. She is actually a friend of mine now. She was not trying to be mean or hurtful but merely instruct me on what I needed to do to fit in there, knowing that I was new. I spoke with my spiritual advisor at the time about distancing myself from activities at the club since I was so uncomfortable with the materialism and superficiality of it all. Her response to me was "But then who will minister to the rich?" Her advice was to "bloom where I was planted." She assured me that God uses all of us with our unique backgrounds and circumstances to bring about His purposes on earth. We will find Him in the unlikeliest of places if we take the time to look.

As a graduate of an all-girl Catholic high school I was not used to getting dressed up for girls. We would show up for school without make-up, our hair in messy pony tails under bandanas, wearing shirts that did not match our socks or our uniforms and frequently sporting unshaved legs. We saved dressing up for any and all contact with members of the opposite sex when we would go for the "full court press" including jewelry, perfume and nail polish. So when I was first invited to join a group of women friends at the club for golf and was told we had the earliest tee time, 7:30 in the morning, I crawled out of bed, washed my face and brushed my teeth, put my hair in a pony tail under my golf hat, grabbed the clothes closest to the closet door and headed to the club. Well, it was a situation akin to "one of these things is not like the other, one of these things just doesn't belong" from Sesame Street.

Club women dress well consistently, whether for play or for socializing, for women or for men. They can afford the best and generally sport the best. A typical golf outfit will include shoes that match the color of the visor and the ensemble and occasionally even the glove and golf balls. When everyone shows up to play, the first five minutes of discussion tends to revolve around where someone got the latest polo shirt, shorts, sweater or whatever. After listening to a few of these exchanges, I finally decided to fess up and report that I purchased the golf shirt I was wearing for $19.99 at TJMaxx. Well, this definitely got a rise out of the crowd, (I think more for admitting it than having actually done it) but then walking up to the tee another woman whispered to me that she bought her top at *Target*. A fashion soul mate was found!

Frequently after golf in the morning I like to head to 12:00 Mass at a neighboring parish. I tried to keep this under wraps for a while, not sure how it would be received. Mainly because I do not always act as holy as I should and once people know that you are a daily Mass attendee they tend to have higher expectations of your behavior. So, yes, I was a coward for not admitting this sooner but eventually I did explain why I wasn't staying for lunch. Two interesting things happened. First, some of the women started to ask me to pray for their special intentions. I thought this was very cool. It initiated conversations about things going on in their families and their lives that I might not have known about otherwise. Secondly, a few of them asked me if I had ever seen Mrs. X or Mr. Y at Mass since they also frequented the neighboring parishes. I discovered that I was not alone in my spiritual practice and realized that many of my fellow golfers and club members, men and women, attended daily Mass as part of their weekly devotions. I was finding lots of faith-filled people at the club, a place I had not even thought to look.

When my husband was on the board of the country club the board wives (jokingly referred to as "bored" wives) were required to go to new member cocktail parties and get to know the prospective members' spouses while the prospective members were being interviewed. It didn't take me long to realize that I was way out of my league here. While many of the conversations were enjoyable, I was not prepared for the jewelry assessments, purse assessments and outfit assessments. When one woman noticed that I still wear my original wedding ring she commented on how that was so "sentimental." I told her that I still have my original husband and since I would not replace him just because he was showing signs of wear I would not replace the ring either. Another board wife confessed to me that her friends had gathered to inform her that she was in need of a "purse intervention." Her purse simply did not meet the standards of her group of friends and out of concern for her they wanted to take her shopping to update her accessories.

I found myself becoming a reverse snob. This means that before I would let anyone look down their nose at me I would decide that their priorities were all in the wrong place and that they were simply not my kind of people. I would have to look elsewhere for friends. But around that time an interesting thing happened. I became active with some local charities and church groups and began to notice the names on the letterheads that reveal the advisory boards and the honorary committees. Here I found many of the country club folk who, unbeknownst to me, were spending a great deal of time and money giving back to the community. I became aware of how many women work at soup kitchens and are involved in tutorial programs and quietly donate to crisis pregnancy centers and build wings at hospitals. There were many charity golf outings sponsored at the club as well as scholarship programs and breast cancer awareness events. These people were spreading their wealth around in ways that put me to shame. I realized that I needed to spend a lot less time praying for conversion of the hearts of others and a lot more time activating my own.

Quite simply, before concerning myself with the splinter in my neighbor's eye I needed to remove the plank from mine. It is much easier to seek and find God once the blinders are removed. I began to see Him in the kindness and dedication of the staff and their efforts to always make us feel like family. There is something about going to a place where everyone knows your name. We had all three of our children's high school graduation parties at the club and received a "thumbs up" from the attendees. Once the kids got past the no cell phone and no denim policies and the requirement that men wear a collared shirt, they realized that fun could still be had without your cell phone attached to your ear while wearing decent clothing. The karaoke DJ was kept very busy all three nights. Our daughter's wedding reception, also held at the club, was another joyful celebration with an equally crowded dance floor. My golf girlfriends were the first to head out to dance and the last to leave the party at the end of the night.

I recently attended a funeral celebration for a man I knew casually from the club. I knew him only as someone who seemed to be at every function and appeared to be the "life of the party" type. At his memorial it became clear that he was very active in his church. His minister knew exactly where he sat with his family each week. I also learned that he had two special-needs sisters who had been the recipients of his care and a brother who had fallen on tough financial times whom he was assisting. I ran into a few people there that I did not know were friends with the deceased. One said he had been the best man at their wedding. Another told of wonderful trips their families had taken together. This man had touched many people's lives in many ways and yet I only knew him as someone who took a lot of pictures at parties and lived well at the country club.

Living well at the country club is something that you tend to want to share with others. Whenever you have something special you find it is all the more special when shared with those you love. Just as I appreciated being invited to friends' clubs when I was growing up, never dreaming that I would someday belong at one of those places, I know our guests always appreciate being invited to our club and enjoy the beauty and hospitality provided. The idea is to make people feel welcome and at home and, above all, comfortable, when you are entertaining. I can honestly say that once I began to relax and be myself it became easier for me to help others do the same. I had to learn to be comfortable in my country-club skin. Since it is actually the same skin I had back in my old neighborhood it really should not have been that hard. I simply had to do something with the wooden planks in my eyes first. Once they were removed it was much easier to find God in my surroundings, especially at the country club.

Day 1.) Do you have any preconceived notions about the wealthy? Have you ever been proven wrong about these notions? Is there someone who has these preconceived notions about you? Reflect on how dollar signs or price tags may have gotten in the way of potential relationships.

Day 2.) Can you think of a wooden beam in your own eye which may be preventing you from seeing your neighbor as he or she truly is? Do you have a tendency to focus on the splinter in your neighbor's eye and overlook the plank in your own? Does the term "hypocrisy" always seem to best describe someone other than yourself? Ask Jesus to remove any blinders you may have and give you eyes to see and ears to hear.

Day 3.) How do you feel about the expression "Clothes make the man?" How concerned are you about what you wear or what others wear? If you have recently considered yourself overdressed or underdressed for an occasion did that disturb you? Have you ever been chastised for inappropriate attire? Reflect on the role of appearances in your life.

Day 4.) Have you ever had a "God moment" when you were least expecting it? Have you ever felt that you were planted in a particular circumstance to minister to those around you? Have you ever become suddenly aware that God has spent years orchestrating a particular encounter? Consider the gifts of the Holy Spirit and how you might use them to build up the body of Christ.

Day 5.) Does a sign saying "Members Only" arouse any particular reaction from you? Can you think of a time when you were on the outside looking in or the inside looking out and were not comfortable with your position? How often do you put yourself in situations that are outside of your comfort zone? Reflect on barriers, either real or imagined, which prevent you from seeing someone as your neighbor.

Day 6.) Have you ever tried to downplay or draw attention to your holiness? Does your holiness factor change depending on your company or environment? Are you comfortable with faith-sharing or do you feel that discussions about religion should be avoided in public? Ask Jesus to enlighten you about how your words and deeds might bring Him glory.

Day 7.) Is the life you are now living very different from the way in which you were raised? Do you see your life now as an improvement upon your former life or as a regression in some way? Do you feel that your lifestyle is moving you towards God or away? Take time to reflect on your faith journey and ask God to guide your steps.

I love to power walk and when the weather prevents walking outside I head to the local mall and do my laps. It's actually not a mall. According to the sign in front, it's a "collection" meaning a potpourri of upscale stores that does not like to be referred to as a "mall." (It is way above that!) I generally walk with my friend Sal and we have been nicknamed the "road runners" because we clip along at a pretty good pace. One older gentleman tells us daily that he is going to give us a speeding ticket if we don't slow down, chuckling to himself at how funny this is, as if he's never told us this before. We chuckle back and look at each other and smile because we can't believe that he doesn't realize that he says this to us every day.

The "collection" in the hours before it opens is like a little village with a unique and interesting cast of characters. There is one woman who is always there, no matter what time of the day or evening I decide to walk. She is incredibly thin and generally wears the same outfit (white shorts and black tank top). She looks more like she needs a cheeseburger than a workout but, like the energizer bunny, she just keeps going and going. She seems to know a lot of the other walkers and will occasionally silently mouth a "hi" when she passes us.

This brings me to my point, which is how utterly amazing it is to Sal and me that there are people that we pass at the mall almost every day who will not make eye contact with us or say "hello." We have been doing this now for about ten years. We see pretty much the same people every day. Yet, there are some who simply refuse to look at us or smile. I have taken it as a personal challenge to smile at certain individuals relentlessly until they look at me and smile back. But there are some really stubborn non-smilers out there who just won't let the corners of their mouths turn up.

I have made this my mission thanks to one walker that I have dubbed "smiley lady" because of the beautiful smile she always has on her face as she walks by us. She is not to be confused with other regulars: "oxygen man," an older gentleman who only walks the overpass with a walker and oxygen tank for his lungs, ten times; the "arm swinger," a woman who swings her one arm out so far to the side that you need a lot of clearance to pass her or else you get bonked; "smart baby," a little toddler being pushed by her mother in a stroller who has the most intense and inquisitive look on her face that she seems to be able to see through to your very soul; and the "hand holders," an elderly couple who stroll along looking entirely in love and at peace after all their years of marriage, just happy to be able to walk together and enjoy another day.

There are many other married couples who walk every day, but due to a preference for a different pace some choose not to walk together. Pace matching is very important when choosing a walking partner. The couples work this out by beginning together and ending together but splitting apart somewhere in the middle. This seems to work well for them as it does for another group of ladies who walk in two groups, the faster in the front and the slower in the back, rotating so as not to miss conversation with anyone. This is a polite choice as people walking five abreast would be very difficult to pass. Every village has its rules whether spoken or unspoken and faster walkers passing on the outside is an unspoken rule. Some people simply hate to be passed however, and one woman even threw an elbow at Sal once when we sped by her group. We try to give a heads up that we're on the right or the left but some folks just don't like being left behind in the marble, tile dust. Just as every village has its rules, it also has its villains. But, fortunately, heroes trump villains, and that brings me back to the "smiley lady."

The lesson here for me was how much joy this one woman was bringing to others every morning through the simple act of wearing a smile on her face as she walked by them at the mall. (The "collection" will hereafter be referred to as the "mall" for the sake of simplicity.) I realized when she smiled at me, and I smiled back, that many times I was not smiling before I saw her and, as a matter of fact, I was deep in my own thoughts and most likely scowling like those other non-smilers I referred to previously. She inspired me to simply try to look happier and to share that happiness with others I passed. It is amazing how good that little change felt. I now seek out other smiley faces and try to return their positive attitude with gusto as a result of this one woman's example. We choose the face that we want to present to the world each day and just as a scrunched up, angry face says "Don't mess with me, I am ticked off!" a radiant, joyful face draws others to you and encourages them to smile and share your joy.

This is just one of the ways that I have found God at the mall. Another is in the example of an obese, middle aged man who is slowly but deliberately attempting to walk off the pounds. I don't know him but I literally want to say "You go, buddy!" every time I pass him. I do ask God to bless him and be with him in his efforts to get in shape. Another woman, obviously recovering from a stroke, walks with great difficulty very close to the storefronts, increasing her distance by just a few steps each day. She is a lesson in perseverance and inspires me to say a quick prayer of gratitude that I have legs that work and have actually chosen to use them that particular morning. Another group of three women began to slow their pace down as one of the three suffered through breast cancer, chemo, hair loss and eventually passed away. I saw God in their friendship and their willingness to accommodate each phase of her illness. I don't see them at the mall anymore. It may be too painful for the other two to walk without the company of their dear friend.

It is strange when someone that you see regularly at the mall stops coming. Since you don't really know these people you have no idea if they have moved away, passed away or simply chosen to stop walking for one reason or another. Sometimes people don't come for a long time and then suddenly reappear. You are quite relieved to see them again. When Sal and I returned last fall after a summer of golf and walking outside, several people commented on how it was good to see us again and that they were glad we were back. We don't even know these folks but it was still nice to be missed.

While mentally taking attendance of the "regulars" one morning, Sal and I noticed a tall, burly man walking briskly through the mall with several shopping bags full of shoes. We both commented on how we had seen him several times before and became intrigued with his story. We hypothesized that maybe he had a women's shoe obsession, though he didn't look the "type" (whatever that "type" is) or that he was a professional shopper for some very wealthy woman who had a thing for shoes. One day when I was walking without Sal, and very bored doing my laps alone, I approached him. I said I couldn't stand it anymore and had to know why he was always buying shoes at the mall and wondered who was the lucky recipient. (This is unbelievably nosey, I know, but true!) He actually had a perfectly legitimate reason for carrying around bags of shoes. He is a shoe repair man! He goes to shoe stores in the morning before they open to collect any damaged shoes, takes them to his shop for repair and later returns them to the storeowners to sell. This may not be as much fun as dressing super models (one of our other fabricated occupations for the mystery man) or wearing the shoes himself, but it certainly taught me a lesson in choosing simple explanations over seedy ones.

We are all being observed and appraised by others daily as we go about our business. Yet, we are generally unaware of these appraisals and observations. I was surprised once when walking at the mall alone, how many people commented on how I was "going solo" that day asking "where's your sidekick?" People I didn't even recognize were aware that a part of my routine, my friend Sal, was missing and yes, I told them it was harder walking alone and I missed my buddy. Another morning, Sal and I brought her grandson in a stroller on our mall walk and one of the people we passed yelled out "Oh, you two had a baby!" We smiled and certainly hoped that she was kidding. But, just as I am carefully observing those around me and wondering about their stories, so too those I encounter are making mental notes about my behavior and writing their own stories about me. How I would love to be privy to a few of those chapters! What an incentive and opportunity for each of us to preach the gospel always and use words only when necessary. We can start by simply walking the walk, following the rules, and wearing a big smile...at the "collection."

Day 1.) Have you ever had someone comment that they always see you doing a certain thing at a certain place when you had no idea you were being observed? Did it make you uncomfortable that you were being observed? Are there people in your community that you observe regularly and have an interest in getting to know? Do you feel comfortable approaching these people? Reflect on the people you encounter daily and ask God if there is a particular reason why they have been placed in your life.

Day 2.) Have you ever caught a glimpse of yourself in a mirror and been surprised by what you saw? Do you tend to scowl or frown without realizing it? Have you ever had someone ask you if you were alright because of a worried expression you did not know you were wearing? If the eyes are a window to the soul consider what you would like your eyes to say about you.

Day 3.) How important is exercise to you? Do you attempt to exercise regularly and maintain good physical health? Is this something of which you tend to do too much or too little? Do you view your body as a temple of the Holy Spirit? Discuss any concerns about your physical health with the Lord and ask for guidance in caring for your temple.

Day 4.) Is there a particular person in your life whose behavior or demeanor is exemplary? What is it about this person that makes him or her stand out? Do you consciously try to emulate this person? Do you consider yourself to be a positive person? Place any character flaws of which you are aware before the Lord and ask for help in eliminating or minimizing these flaws.

Day 5.) Is there a "village" of which you are a part? Are you an active or passive member of this community? Are you comfortable with the role you play and the extent of your involvement? Do you derive a sense of identity from being a member of this village? Reflect on the many hats you wear and roles you play and try to see yourself as God sees you.

Day 6.) Assess your daily rituals. Is there a proper balance of work and play, noise and silence, companionship and solitude? Do you invite God into your daily activities? Is your spiritual health as important to you as your mental or physical health? Rest before the Lord and ask Him to show you how to balance concerns of mind, body and spirit.

Day 7.) Do you feel like you are constantly in motion? How would you describe the pace of your life? Do you feel the need to rev it up or slow it down? Do you ever feel like you are moving so fast that you are missing things along the way? Take a few moments to be still, basking in the presence of the God who loves you...and listen.

I tend to do everything fast. I walk fast, talk fast, eat and drink fast and am constantly in motion. I am a "leg shaker" which means that I bounce my knees up and down when most people are sitting still or if my legs are crossed I am flinging the crossed leg up and down rhythmically. I sometimes chew the insides of my mouth and my cuticles. I am kind of hyper or "tightly wound" as they say. This is why my attempts to learn a game that requires tempo and balance, takes four hours to play and provides benefits to those who can demonstrate a fair amount of patience, has been challenging—to say the least. Welcome to the world of high-strung woman meets the game of golf.

My husband is an avid golfer and when we began dating in high school I realized that my choices were either to learn to play or be left home. He really has a passion for the game and I could see that golf was always going to be a part of our lives. So, I have tried over the years to master something that does not come naturally to me. I wish I had cold, hard cash for every time I have heard someone say "You really need to slow that swing down!" because my purse would be overflowing. But, alas, I have persevered because there are many life lessons to be learned from this game.

Golf is a game of integrity. You are required to keep your own score, know and follow the rules, call penalties on yourself, maintain an accurate handicap and practice golf etiquette among other things. You can really learn a lot about a person by the way he or she approaches the game and, conversely, that person can really learn a lot about you. There are people that you would like to meet for coffee and people that you would like to meet for golf and they are not necessarily the same people.

Golf is a game which allows people of varying abilities to play together without adversely affecting the enjoyment of either party. It is not like tennis where the person who hits the ball to you requires you to hit it back in order to keep the rally going. In golf your ball just sits there until you hit it (and hit it and hit it!) until it goes in the hole and you move on to the next. (Sounds simple, right?) My husband's handicap is around a "2" and I am around a "20" which simply means that I am supposed to hit the ball about 18 more times than he does on a good day. We find ourselves to be pretty compatible golfers and similarly enjoy playing with our kids and their spouses despite a wide range of golfing abilities. We have all learned to simply keep it moving!

Golf is a game you can play when you are old. As long as you can still walk and still see, you can probably still swing a club. You may not hit it very far and you may have to ride in a cart rather than take a caddy but you can still enjoy the game. I have seen many a long ball hitter outscored by an old guy who can chip and putt. Long after the football cleats, hockey skates, running shoes and lacrosse sticks have been sold at your garage sale your golf clubs will still be in use. There is a greater return on your investment for golf equipment than for most other things you might buy at a sporting goods store if you simply choose to keep using them.

Golf is a game which allows you to enjoy the beauty of God's creation. The greenness of the grass contrasted with the blueness of the sky and even the splash of the sand or the water when it greets your ball can be magnificent to behold. Alright, I admit the trees, sand and water are more beautiful when your ball is sailing past them rather than finding them, but truly many of the views from the fairways to the greens on a typical golf course are spectacular.

This brings me to how I find God on the golf course. I find Him in the joy I see on my husband's face when he approaches the first tee after a long week of work, escaping to his happy place with his buddies. I find Him in the perseverance of the little caddy, not much bigger than the bag he is carrying, shuffling along to keep up with his group and hopefully earn a good tip from his assigned member. I find Him in the eternal hope of the older golfer, who can barely see and has colored spots on his golf ball to help him identify it, still attempting to beat his wife of 50 plus years. I find Him in the daughter steering her elderly father around the course, when he doesn't know where to park the cart and can no longer keep pace, still cherishing these golf opportunities with family.

Golf is a game which allows you to actually have a conversation with the people in your group while you are playing. A typical round of 18 holes of golf should take about four hours. This provides ample opportunity to discuss something that might be on your mind or to listen to what may be laying heavily on someone else's heart. I have frequently witnessed someone getting frustrated with their game only to have them eventually blurt out that there is something bothering them and the something has nothing to do with golf. I will then generally invite the person to share whatever it is that is on their mind if they feel so inclined. Not many sports allow opportunities for this kind of sharing.

I decided a few years back that since I probably was never going to be a great golfer I would make it my mission to try to bring joy to the game. This is a hobby after all, a pastime, and we are actually paying to have the opportunity to play it. It is supposed to be fun! I am not referring to serious, competitive golf here, but the social variety which comprises the majority of my golfing experience. How often we forget about the fun in the midst of our struggles to score, swing properly, sink putts and keep the ball in play. Sometimes we need to have someone remind us to lighten up!

I announced my mantra of "nothing is going to steal my joy today" to my husband last year before heading out to play with him and our two sons. I had been struggling with my game and taking lessons, trying to smooth out my swing and slow it down. I was fighting my tendency to muscle the ball and was getting so caught up in the technicalities of the swing that I simply could not hit it. We were on vacation in Florida, however, and it was an absolutely gorgeous day. I was determined to enjoy every minute with my family and not let my lack of progress with the game interfere with our trip to the links.

This relaxed and joyful approach of "not thinking" worked well for me on the front nine. Then, of course, I began to fall back into my old habits of swinging faster and harder. On the 12th hole I dribbled my ball off the tee, kerchunked one into the rough, bladed one into the water, dropped another and hit it into a shrub, chipped back and forth over the green a few times and then picked up my ball and walked angrily to the next hole. I heard my husband say to my sons as they were approaching the next tee "Why don't one of you go ask Mom what happened to her joy?"

"I heard that!" I snapped. And then I began to laugh. I began to laugh because I saw the boys trying to contain their belly laughs so as not to anger me further. I needed to lighten up and was grateful for my husband's sense of humor and reminder about what my goal had been before heading out to golf that day. "Don't let anything steal your joy" has now become the family reminder to not take the game too seriously.

Of course this does not apply to playing tournament or competitive golf. I know the importance of not being a distraction when the game really matters. But as one who did not grow up belonging to a club and who never guessed I would have the opportunity to play these beautiful courses, I really try to appreciate it. I am allowed to escape the responsibilities and pressures of the outside world for four hours while walking a fabulous course with a loved one. What's not to like?

Frequently when we are on our home course we hear sirens from the major intersection nearby. My Catholic school training kicks in and I silently say a "Hail Mary," "Our Father" and "Glory Be" for whomever it is that might be suffering. Then, of course, I begin to think that I am enjoying a game of golf at a beautiful club while others are struggling to get through their day. The recent double bogey, missed putt or errant shot that had just seemed so frustrating suddenly becomes a non-issue. I have legs. I am healthy. I have the opportunity to play golf at one of the most prestigious clubs in the country. I should be smiling!

I often think that unhappy Christians are a bad advertisement for Christianity. There is a line from the musical "Mame" that I love that goes something like this, "Life is a banquet and most poor fools are starving to death!" This is not to minimize the suffering of people that are literally starving but merely to remind those that are surrounded by abundance and immersed in blessings to have an attitude of gratitude. Put a smile on your face for goodness sake. Enjoy the game. Thank God every day for your health and the opportunity to participate in what has been referred to as the greatest game ever played. Slow down, take a look at that gorgeous club house, thank God you are here and let your swing and joy flow freely.

You are at the banquet and need to savor these moments and be a gracious guest. This does not mean that you have to stop hoping to outplay your opponent or even give up on winning that "press" on the 18th Hole. But win or lose keep smiling, offer that handshake and don't let anything steal your joy. This includes having to pay off all of those bets in the clubhouse.

Fast pay makes fast friends and God loves a cheerful giver.

Day 1.) Is there any particular hobby or pastime which you find yourself taking too seriously? Has anyone ever told you to lighten up? Have you been the bearer of this message to another? Reflect on your pastimes and how much importance you give to them. Ask God to help you to assess your priorities.

Day 2.) Have you ever taken something up to spend more quality time with a loved one? Has someone in your life done this for you? Have you benefited from these common experiences? Is there something you have refrained from trying for fear of failing? Reflect on your recreational activities and how they have enhanced or diminished your relationships.

Day 3.) Is God a part of your recreation? Do you invite God to join you as you play as well as when you work? Do you recognize that all of your talents and athletic abilities are gifts from God? Consider the many gifts that God has given you and contemplate how you might better use those gifts.

Day 4.) How much do you allow your bad days to affect others? How do you handle your own poor performance? Do you know someone whose moods have a way of souring an experience for all participants? Reflect on a time when poor sportsmanship soiled an experience and consider how that situation could have been avoided.

Day 5.) Do you remember to bring joy to your endeavors? Do you understand the difference between joy, which can't be taken from you and happiness, which is fleeting? Do you work at trying to be an "upper" rather than a "downer" amongst your peers? Pray for an awareness of the joy that God has placed in your heart and ask for continued reminders to share that joy.

Day 6.) Do you agree with the notion that life is a banquet? Do you have an attitude of gratitude for the offerings at the banquet of your life? Do you tend to overlook the banquet that God has prepared for you and feel hungry in the midst of a feast? Take a few moments to sit at table with the Lord pondering all of the delights He has prepared for you. Be an appreciative guest.

Day 7.) Ponder the phrase "God loves a cheerful giver," (2 Corinthians 9:7) which follows verse 6 explaining "whoever sows sparingly will also reap sparingly, and whoever sows bountifully will also reap bountifully." Each must be done without sadness or compulsion. Are you planting seeds of joy or seeds of bitterness? Reflect on the quality and quantity of your harvest.

It can be very difficult as an adult, especially a middle-aged adult, to be willing to try something new. This is particularly true if you are used to being pretty good at most things you do. My husband, who was a three letter varsity athlete in high school and is an avid golfer, refused for a long time to join our local couples bowling league. He simply did not want to stink at something. But the winters are long in Michigan and there are only so many movies you can see on "date-night" so eventually he relented. We are now thoroughly enjoying our Friday night bowling league. It was a similar story with me and the game of bridge. I fought the idea of learning how to play for a very long time.

Fortunately, I have a very persistent friend who loves bridge and really wanted her non-bridge friends to learn how to play the game. She repeatedly mentioned to me that she had this friend who was giving bridge lessons whom she thought that I would really like. She insisted that I would enjoy learning from her. She also knew that I had expressed interest in the game because my recently-turned-90-year-old mother loved the game. I had hoped to be able to play with her one day. Obviously, this is a woman who does not buy green bananas so what was I waiting for?! I put the bridge teacher's phone number in my cell phone and eventually made the call.

Bridge is a complicated game and it takes a long time to feel comfortable at the bridge table. It combines bidding knowledge with knowing how to play the cards, keeping track of the cards, partnership agreements, conventions and knowing what you are allowed to say and not say. You must be willing to make mistakes and occasionally feel dumb (even when you are not the dummy!). It can be very humbling, especially in the beginning ascent of the learning curve. It is also incredibly addictive.

What I love about bridge is that it is a great equalizer. Unlike golf, where your equipment can be assessed as well as your clothing and club membership and even the car you drive into the parking lot, bridge players only care about how good of a bridge player you are. Really. All that is required is two decks of cards, paper and a pencil. Your financial background, religious background, political beliefs, neighborhood, possessions, size or shape does not matter. As long as you know the basic rules and can be relied upon not to misrepresent your hand, people will play with you.

I have met so many nice and amazing women since I have learned to play bridge. The surprise for me here was getting to know quite a few moms from the "other" school. My sons went to an all-boy Catholic school in the city of Detroit and most of the boys that live in our suburb went to the "other" non-city school. Our school got beaten up pretty badly in sports by the suburban schools most of the time and since my sons were involved in these rivalries for over a decade, I became very much entrenched in the story of "us" versus "them."

However, it has been moms from the "other" school that have been the most welcoming and inclusive to me in these early months of not really knowing what I am doing at the bridge table. When I have lost track of the number of trump that were out or neglected to pull them, or forgotten "high from the short side" or even trumped my own trick (really bad!) one of these most forgiving moms who was my partner said, *"Who cares? It isn't like you lost a kidney! Don't worry about it."* She and her sister laugh and chirp at each other the entire time they are playing and will even sing such ditties as "Going out of my hand, over you..." to remind themselves that the next card played should come from their hand and not the board.

Now prior to the opportunities to play bridge with these gals I had been invited to one of their "cottages" (a lovely lake home, really) to celebrate a mutual friend's 50th birthday. While there I had been privy to admissions of some being "wine snobs" (only liking the finest wine) "sheet snobs" (only purchasing the highest thread count sheets) and even "silverware snobs" (liking the way better silverware feels in their hand and seeing it neatly displayed in a drawer). In my typical "I can't compete with this" fashion I had begun making mental notes about the cheap wine I drink, the discount sheets I buy and the messy silverware drawer in my home. I felt totally inadequate and like I didn't fit in.

But back at the bridge table none of this is important. At the bridge table everyone who knows how to play and is willing to learn fits in. I usually arrive in my baseball cap and exercise clothes with no make-up on, having just come from power-walking. No one seems to care. I recently found out that my bridge teacher is active with "Mother and Unborn Baby Care," a local organization that I also support, and we have jointly begun attending their programs. My teacher and I also recently attended a luncheon for a local "Community Dispute Resolution Program" since another woman in our class is active in this organization. Still another group is helping me plan a golf outing next summer to support breast cancer research. Good things are happening at the bridge table every day.

There are many cliques (for lack of a better word) at the club I belong to and in the town in which I reside. I have been gingerly trying to sidestep full immersion in any of them and float around the perimeter of all of them. This is a very tricky business, in case you have never tried it, because while attempting to float in and out of many groups you end up really belonging to none. It can be lonely. But the beauty of bridge is that it has allowed access to many different groups of women which I did not have access to before. This is because bridge players are always looking for a fourth. You need four people to play the game and if you have ever tried to find a sub, you know how relieved you are when someone says "yes."

There is a blonde bombshell at our club who drives a Harley, occasionally smokes cigars, has the hottest moves on the dance floor and basically lives large. She did not go to college but has dabbled in a variety of activities ranging from becoming a Jehovah's Witness who was proficient at sign language to working as a cleaning lady and teaching exercise classes. She met her husband (a father of four) in one of her aerobics classes. She is perfectly put together and can be both intimidating and refreshing because she is not like the other club ladies. I recently had the opportunity to play bridge with her and get to know her a little better.

She was frustrated when I arrived because she had thought bridge was from 10-12 and eventually realized it was from 12-2. She had made plans to do something with her mother after bridge and felt badly that she ended up having to renege. *"Oh well,"* I told her. *"Your mother was probably meant to do something else today. God has a funny way of redirecting our lives sometimes when He needs us to be in a certain place."*

"Wow, that's really funny that you say that!" she responded. *"Because when I couldn't find anyone and realized I had to just sit and wait here until noon I began to talk to Linda, the locker room attendant. Did you know that her husband died last year in her arms? She gets down this time of year and told me how she misses him and was having a really blue day. She ended up crying on my shoulder while I hugged her. We sat and talked for a long time and I feel grateful that I was able to be here for her."*

Exactly. She was exactly where God needed her to be that day to answer Linda's prayer to please send someone to listen and offer compassion for her loss. We continued to have a little discussion about being open to God's plans for us each day and how the coincidences are really "God-incidences." Then, this gal who never went to college, and considers herself under-educated compared to other club women, proceeded to beat the pants off of my partner and me. She is a good bridge player but, also, I can't help thinking she was blessed with good cards that day because she had performed such a kind deed for another hurting soul.

God is at work everywhere, all the time, in each of our lives in so many ways. The next time you get a call to sub for bridge (and you know how to play!) go. You may be asked a question that day that only you can answer or encounter someone that God wants you to meet for a very special purpose. Similarly, if you attempt to respond *"yes"* and they have just found their fourth, be open to whatever else God has in store for you that day.

God's plans for us are always better than our own. Remember, He sees the big picture. And finally, don't be afraid to learn something new just because you think you are too old. The new activity may be part of the script God is writing in which you play a critical role.

The scene may take place at the bridge table and the main character may be you.

Day 1.) Have you been hesitating to try something new because you feel you are too old to start? Is it difficult for you to be a beginner at something when others are advanced? Is there something you would try if you knew you couldn't fail? Lay your fears before the Lord and ask for guidance with respect to this new endeavor.

Day 2.) Is there a nudge from a friend to try something new that you have been ignoring? Have you been encouraging another to pursue a particular activity with you? Do you recognize the importance of shared interests and common ground in your relationships? Have you considered how a new activity may expand your friendship circles? Ask Jesus to enlighten you about any opportunities He has provided that you may be resisting.

Day 3.) How welcoming are you to new people who desire to join your circle of friends? How accommodating are you to people who are at the beginning of the learning curve when you are proficient at something? Do you have a tendency to take people under your wings or push them out of the nest? Reflect on a time when you were welcoming to someone else or someone else made an effort to welcome you.

Day 4.) Have you ever had your day altered only to realize that you ended up exactly where God needed you to be? Are you open to God redirecting your steps? Do you acknowledge and thank Him for these opportunities to serve? Reflect on any recent "God-incidences" in your life and pray for the courage to respond to His call.

Day 5.) Do you attempt to find God in all things? Do you try to see the face of God in every person? Do you try to let God's light shine through you? Are you tuned in to the sacred moments which occur during the ordinary events of the day like running errands, doing household tasks or playing a game of bridge? Contemplate being yoked to Jesus as you go through the motions of your day and be attentive to where He is leading you.

Day 6.) Has being placed in a new situation with a particular person ever opened your eyes to qualities you did not know he or she possessed? Were you willing to change your opinions about this person? Has someone ever admitted that they had a change of heart about you?

Ponder how limited our human vision is and pray to see as God sees and love as God loves.

Day 7.) Ponder the expression "Play the hand you're dealt." You don't have any control over the cards you're dealt but you do have control over how you play them. You also have control over your attitude and demeanor as you play them. Take any concerns you've had with recent "bad hands" to the Lord and seek consolation and direction.

A few years ago on a chilly November morning I drove to pick up my friend Sal to head to the mall for our usual power-walk. When I pulled into her driveway to pick her up she came to the door with our local paper in her hand. *"Did you read this?"* she asked looking somewhat concerned. *"Uh...no,"* I confessed, *"I did not get to the paper this morning."* My husband, Bill, usually brought the paper in and left it on the counter for me, but he had gone on a highly anticipated golf trip with his buddies a few days prior, and our morning paper was still on the front porch.

"Well, I think you need to take a look at this" Sal insisted with an unusual sense of urgency and brought the business section of the paper out to the car.

The headline of the business section in bold print on that Tuesday, November 6, 2007 announced "Knee, hip docs got payments." In smaller print under the headline followed "Names made public after companies settle kickback cases." The first sentence reported that "Michigan orthopedic surgeons and health systems performing hip and knee replacements received more than $1 million from five medical device companies, according to a landmark settlement of allegations of kickbacks by the companies."

"Whoa, this isn't good!" I blurted out. *"Yeah, turn the page,"* Sal said.

On the next page, under "WHERE THE DEVICE COMPANIES' PAYMENTS WENT," was my husband's name at the top of the list in the second column. It read: Dr. William Ward, Pontiac, $25,000-$50,000. I knew something was wrong immediately because the device company the article was claiming Bill had received a kickback from was not even a company whose devices he used. In fact, I had never even heard of the company. In addition to that, I knew that my husband had expressed disgust and disappointment over the fact that doctors he knew were receiving these payments. There was definitely a mistake and I needed to contact him right away.

I proceeded to call his cell phone and leave a message. I could not reach him because he was on an airplane flying home from his "relaxing" getaway. (He had no idea how quickly this relaxation was going to come to and end!) He later told me that both his cell phone and office voice mail were jammed with messages that morning.

My next call was to his office manager to ask her if she had seen the article. *"Oh yes, the phone has been ringing off the hook all morning,"* she replied. *"Well, there is no validity whatsoever to Bill's involvement in this, right?"* I demanded. *"No, there has been a huge mistake and Dr. Ward is investigating it as we speak,"* she assured me. He had called the office that morning to simply "check in" and had gotten quite an earful.

It turns out that the article confused Dr. William S. Ward, a Pontiac orthopedic surgeon with a Winston-Salem, N.C. doctor with the same name but different middle initial. It took quite a few phone calls from my husband to the paper to get the journalist to listen to him. He kept telling her *"You have the wrong guy!"* but because the information had been picked up off of a company website—where it was also WRONG!—the journalist was quite confident that her information was correct.

Now I need to interject here that my husband is one of the "good guys." I mean he is squeaky clean. He has been audited several times by the IRS and Blue Cross and Blue Shield of Michigan and they have found nothing the least bit suspect. He has been in the same orthopedic surgery practice for 25 years in approximately the same area where we grew up and has a vast network of friends. In addition to being an excellent surgeon he makes every effort to run on time and still be extremely personable with patients. He has been honored several times as a "Top Doc" in a local high end publication. He has a pristine professional reputation and his patients love him.

But it took several phone calls to the newspaper, the medical device company and a law firm before the newspaper finally agreed to write a retraction. On Thursday, November 8, 2007, a much smaller article than the original appeared in the lower, left corner of the business section entitled "Wrong doctor listed in data on payments." The opening line of this article very simply stated, "The Website for a medical device company wrongly listed a Pontiac doctor among orthopedic surgeons receiving compensation from the company." It went on to explain that names from a list of surgeons in the United States were somehow merged "in a sorting error" with names the company compiled for the Web page. It deemed this a "mix-up" and a "tragic error."

Although the article did state that my husband was not a consultant for this medical device company, never performed services for their company or received payment from them at any time, an apology for this mistake from the company or the newspaper was not forthcoming. It was all attributed to some computer mix-up. But, obviously there are human beings at the company that feed information into the computer and human beings who edit the Web page and human beings who collect information from Web pages to write their articles. Surely, someone along the way was responsible for ensuring that the information presented on the Web page was correct. It can't just be the "Website's fault."

At least the newspaper printed a retraction. It was an attempt to set the record straight.

It included a quote from "Ward of Pontiac" which said "It is unfortunate that my integrity, credibility and reputation have been misrepresented. I've spent 24 years building a practice based on the highest ethical standards." Of course, we will never know how many people only read the first article which was so boldly displayed across the top of the front page of the business section and never saw the smaller second article tucked in the lower left hand corner. This is the problem with gossip, slander, bearing false witness against thy neighbor or a website mistake. The ripples on the water of the "damaged reputation pool" are far reaching and try as you may, you cannot stop the continuation of those destructive waves.

There were definitely some good things that came out of all of this, however. We are instructed to praise God in "all things" and it is certainly easier to do so when we see reminders of Him in the kindness and compassion of others. Many people came forward to support my husband through this ordeal with an outpouring of concern, love and loyalty.

One friend of my husband's marched into his office at 8:00 am the morning after the first article was printed, holding the newspaper in his hand, and telling Bill that this required a full court press. He knew, without asking, that the article was erroneous because he knew the kind of man my husband is, and proceeded to map out a strategy of rebuttal and setting the record straight.

Later that afternoon when my husband arrived at the men's grill of our club it was momentarily silent when he walked through the door. He had been the president of the club the year before and was well known and respected. This bad press leaking out on their doctor, friend and former president was alarming to all. One well known member, who was a former news anchor, walked right up to Bill, put his arm around him and said, *"Billy, I've had my share of bad press in this town and I know what it feels like to be thrown under the bus. I want you to know that you are my friend. You were my friend before this story broke and you will still be my friend when it's just a bad memory."*

My husband then pulled a letter out of his pocket from the medical device company clearing his name and admitting that the information in the story was in error. This former news anchor asked the men in the room for their attention, got up on a chair and read aloud the latest news report indicating that my husband was innocent of any wrongdoing. The place erupted with applause.

That Friday when I was attending a spirituality class at the Mercy Center, next to Mercy High School where I had been a student, a little nun left a handwritten note on my desk. It said, "Wm Ward, MD" on the front "via kindness of Patty." My husband opened it when I got home and shared it with me. It is dated November 9th, 2007 and reads "Dear Bill, I am very sorry to hear that you have been the victim of misinformation. It was very difficult for me to believe that you would have been involved in the kickbacks. You and your family are in my prayers. In Mercy, Sister Charlotte."

This letter prompted me to buy a wall hanging that is displayed very near the front door of our home. The advice in the framed reminder is "Live in such a way that if anyone should speak badly of you no one would believe it!" Sister Charlotte's admission, and that of so many others, was that they could not believe that Bill could have been involved in something scandalous. His well-earned reputation of being a man of integrity overrode the website error naming him as a man who could be bribed. Bill has lived his life as a man for others and these many others came forward to lend their support when he needed it. God who uses all for good was clearly working overtime covering this website "mix up" with His blanket of goodness.

Several weeks later some of Bill's closest friends at the club presented him with a clock engraved with the words "Nobody does it better." They had seen how much this entire situation had saddened and disappointed him. Bill had even overheard another orthopedic surgeon in the doctor's lounge say, on the day after the first article came out, that he had always figured Dr. Ward must be on the "take" as he was so financially successful. The jealousy of some of the other surgeons made them want to believe that there was something questionable about Bill's success. But, in fact, Bill's success had come about in the old-fashioned way. He had earned it.

Bill sat our young adult children down, and explained that the blessing in this situation was that the allegations were clearly, and without a doubt, false. He had not received kickbacks, been paid a "consulting" fee for work not performed or been reimbursed in any way for using a certain company's product. He had, in fact, been offered the opportunity to switch to another medical device company previously, and would have been financially rewarded for doing so, and he had vehemently declined the offer. He instructed our kids to live their lives in this same way, to choose the "greater good" which in this case was to do what was best for his patients and not what was most lucrative for him.

Even though we certainly would not have sought out this "teachable moment," we were grateful for the opportunity to share and discuss this situation with our family. We are just passing through this world and are living our lives to hear *"Well done, my good and faithful servant"* when we meet our Maker in the next. We will not have to explain to Him that the newspaper article was a "mix-up" because He knows all and sees all and from Him nothing can be hidden. He will forgive us our trespasses "AS WE" have forgiven those who trespass against us. We may not be able to believe everything that we read but we can definitely believe everything that God has promised.

Therefore, we will forgive those responsible for the "mix-up," move on to life's next chapter and continue to look for God in the unlikeliest of places. I trust that we will continue to find Him.

Day 1.) Have you ever been the victim of slander, gossip or misrepresentation? Did you attempt to right the wrong or set the record straight? Are you still holding on to anger you experienced as a result of this? Ask Jesus to help you to rid yourself of this anger and to relieve yourself of all negativity associated with this.

Day 2.) Do you have a tendency to believe everything that you hear? Are you willing to accept that there are generally two sides to every story? Do you keep an open mind when presented with damaging information about another person? Have you heard some disturbing news lately that is weighing heavily on your heart? Ask Jesus to give you a heart that seeks truth and is not quick to condemn.

Day 3.) Do you secretly enjoy a good gossip session? Do you derive a certain satisfaction from being in the know? Is it difficult for you to resist passing on newly acquired information about another person which may be potentially harmful? Ask the Holy Spirit to give you the gifts of wisdom, discernment and self control.

Day 4.) Are you willing to accept responsibility for your actions? If you have wronged someone is it difficult for you to apologize? Do you understand the relationship between actions and consequences? Ask the Holy Spirit to enlighten you about someone you have wronged, knowingly or unknowingly, and to give you the courage to ask for forgiveness.

Day 5.) Is there someone you are unwilling to forgive? Is there a hurt you cannot seem to get past? Do you replay a painful scenario or conversation over and over again in your mind? Tell Jesus about the difficulty you are having forgiving this offense and enlist His help in changing your heart.

Day 6.) Is there someone who owes you an apology or is indebted to you? Are you reminded of this debt every time you encounter this person? Is this person's unwillingness to apologize, make amends, show remorse or admit culpability preventing you from being able to forgive? Spend a few moments contemplating the innocent Jesus on the cross suffering for the sins of all asking "Father forgive them, for they know not what they do." Lay this debt at the foot of the cross.

Day 7.) Do you have difficulty forgiving yourself? Do you have trouble grasping that we are all going to fall many times on our journey in our human condition? Do you beat yourself up for your shortcomings, weaknesses, unkindness and tendency toward sin? There is no sin too big for Jesus to forgive. Come to Him with a repentant heart and bask in the glow of His mercy.

Our parish participates in a "40-days-for-life" prayer vigil outside of a local abortion clinic called *Womancare*. Each parish takes a 24 hour shift and members sign up for an hour to pray the Rosary and be a presence for the unborn and all those considering an abortion on a given day. We have strict instructions to stay on the public sidewalk and pray quietly, not confronting anyone. I have done this several times in the past but was going to pass this year because of the many things I had scheduled to do on our assigned day. I have never been totally comfortable doing this, a little fearful actually, and was secretly relieved that October 21st was simply not going to work for me this year.

I was attempting to sneak past the sign-up table after Mass when the woman in charge, who happens to be a friend, grabbed me and said she was desperate for my help since she had many shifts to fill. She would have to cover them herself if parishioners did not fill the time slots. I should explain that this very woman, several years prior, had asked me to put a program together to commemorate the anniversary of the Roe vs. Wade decision, which prompted me to begin songwriting and start an enterprise called *Stage of Faith Productions* featuring a pro-life program called *Life Stories*. She is also the person who introduced me to the accompanist at Mass who provided me the opportunity to become a cantor at our parish and is a lifelong friend. Frankly, this was one woman I could not say no to in good conscience. Our God is not only awesome but a very, very intelligent designer.

I went home to write this commitment on my calendar and realized that the 8 to 9 am shift that Wednesday was going to conflict with my leaders' session for Bible study which begins at 8:30. I was really resenting the fact that I had said yes to this and even made some phone calls to see if someone would split my shift or take it for me. Believe me, the number of people you can call to fill in for you to pray the Rosary at an abortion clinic is a very short list. Not many people really want to do this. I even called one friend on my birthday, October 19th, thinking she would have a hard time saying no to my request on such a special day. She said no anyway, but did wish me a very happy birthday.

My plan was to arrive at the clinic early and then leave early so as not to miss too much of my next appointment. I was hoping someone else would be there praying also, so that I would not leave the site unattended and break the prayer chain. The man on the shift ahead of me was most happy with my early arrival and asked if he could leave early to get to 8:00 Mass. *"Fine,"* I replied. I would be okay on my own, grumbling inwardly that my own early exit plan was being foiled. A group of adolescent males on their way to school approached me, which scared me just a little, but I kept my head down and prayed fervently. One of them tapped me on the shoulder and asked in a very sweet voice if that was my baby over there. I followed his gesture to a car seat, sitting next to a parked van with a sign that read "Pray to End Abortion," with an apparent infant tucked inside.

"Oh gosh, no," I said. "That's just a doll to remind people that every baby has a right to life." He looked relieved and went on his merry way. I thought how odd it must have looked to him that I was praying for unborn children while my own "child" was shivering on the ground in an old car seat. I was glad that he asked me his question so that I could clarify. Things are not always as they appear.

A woman approached at this time from the van and struck up a conversation with me. I guess she had been praying either in the van or near it and I was just not aware of her presence until now. She was a praying "regular," I gathered, and was very enthusiastic about recent "saves" that had occurred. She began to share some of her stories with me. She had some special salt that was blessed and she said when she placed some on the parking lot a few weeks ago no one had come to have an abortion that day even though it was a Saturday and generally the busiest day at the clinic. Also, a woman that worked at the clinic had asked her for a Rosary and told her that she had begun praying the Rosary recently. I asked her if she would spread some of the salt today since it had been so effective the other day. She said yes and did so.

After this I began praying again and two women showed up to join me. The first was my friend from the parish who had asked me to sign up and obviously sensing my hesitation had felt compelled to accompany me. The other was a woman in charge of "Mother and Unborn Baby Care," a local organization that lends support to women who choose not to have an abortion. Things were definitely looking up and I was grateful for their company and voices joined in prayer. I did not know yet just how appreciative of their presence I was going to be.

In the midst of our Rosary a tan SUV pulled into the lot in front of the clinic. A nicely dressed man about my age got out of the car and approached our group inquiring if he could ask us some questions. "Sure," we replied, though I was thinking that this had never happened to me any of the other times I had prayed in front of the clinic and was immediately doubting my ability to provide intelligent answers to his questions. The conversation went something like this with all three of us interjecting as almost one voice.

"So you really think that abortion is murder."

"Yes."

"So you really think that the people performing abortions in there are murderers."

"Well...yes."

"So if I have assisted on an abortion procedure then I am a murderer."

"Well, you are choosing the terminology here, but, yes, you are assisting in ending the life of a child."

"So, if you fell down on the sidewalk right now and were dying you would not want me to save you because I am a murderer."

"Well, no, I would want you to save me."

"But you just said that I am a bad person."

"Whoa, I said the actions of the abortionist and the industry are bad, not the people. We can judge actions but we cannot judge hearts. Only God can judge hearts."

"So, you're saying when I die I am going to be damned to hell."

"When you die you will have a personal encounter with Jesus Christ, who is all truth and all life and everything that is now concealed will be revealed. You will rely on God's mercy as we all will. That is why we are praying out here...for conversion of hearts now, in this world."

"So, you are saying that those women in there who are having abortions are damned to hell even if they think that what they are doing is right. What about render unto Caeser what is Caeser's? What they are doing is legal you know."

"Just because it is legal does not make it right in the eyes of God. Actually I was one of those women (this is the woman from 'Mother and Unborn Baby Care'). I had an abortion when I was 18 and I tried to tell myself that what I was doing was right, even though my conscience kept hounding me and telling me otherwise."

"So, how do you know that you are not damned to hell for your sin?"

"I know because I have repented and immersed myself in the forgiving love of Christ and am committed to try and prevent other women from making this same mistake."

"What about the health of the mother? Doesn't the doctor have the responsibility to save the mother's life over the baby's life?"

"You know, I am married to a physician (me speaking) and I have asked him that very question and he has responded that with advances in medicine and prenatal care it is possible now to deliver the baby early and then tend to the mother's needs, attempting to save both lives. Having to abort a baby to save the life of the mother is one of those propaganda things that the feminists rally around to make it sound as if pro-lifers don't care about the mothers. Actually, we care about both."

"Your husband is a doctor? So what do you think about stem cell research? Is that murder also?"

"I support adult stem cell research which happens to be where the real progress for cures is being realized."

"So all those doctors meeting in Ann Arbor for the conference on embryonic stem cell research this Saturday are murderers also? Why would these intelligent professionals be pursuing something that is morally wrong?"

This guy would really not get off the murder theme! My friend interjected at this point that you really need to follow the money. She is a public health nurse and is very well versed on the flow of public funding. The abortion industry, embryonic stem cell researchers, cloning and genetics experts, drug companies developing the morning after pill and so on are all in business. It is big business and there are major profits involved. Greed is certainly not the best motivator for making moral decisions.

"Well, I just wish that your husband would call up to the conference this weekend and let his voice be heard and tell them that what they are doing is wrong! Maybe since he is a doctor they would listen to him."

At this point I saw tears in the man's eyes and I began to sense that he is involved in the abortion industry somehow and yet has reservations about his line of employment. He was obviously conflicted about the moral implications of what he was doing and was sincerely looking for answers to the questions that were haunting him. I told him that I would speak to my husband about this but since he was an orthopedic surgeon I wasn't sure how much weight his voice would carry. Many former abortionists and OB/GYN professionals have converted to the pro-life side and given their testimonies of regret and it has not deterred the choice side much.

He then asked us why we stand out there day after day. He says he drives by and sees the Rosaries rattling and wonders what we think we are accomplishing.

We replied that we believe in the power of prayer. If our presence can deter one woman from having an abortion then we have saved one life. Many women are not choosing abortion freely and are being coerced by boyfriends or husbands or parents. Maybe the presence of someone who can provide an alternative is the answer to their prayers that day. Basically, we are not throwing stones but throwing prayers (and sometimes a little salt!). We told him we would pray for him. He thanked us and drove off.

We all stood there kind of stunned and expressed profound gratitude for what each of the women had contributed to the conversation. The combined backgrounds of a woman who had procured her own abortion, a public health nurse and a pro-life activist who happened to be married to a doctor, all brought credibility to our attempts to respond to the man's questions. Maybe it was my baseball cap and workout clothes and the fact that we looked "like him" that made him decide we were approachable. Maybe it was the blessed salt that the women had spread on the parking lot. Most likely it was simply God orchestrating an encounter between His children on opposite sides of an issue. We were all meant to be there that morning to have an exchange of ideas in an atmosphere of gentleness and respect. I had fought God's plan for me all along the way to fit that hour into my busy schedule. Once again, God's plan for me was perfect and I found Him in the unlikeliest of places.

Day 1.) Where do you stand on this issue? Are you comfortable with where you stand? Have you taken the time to educate yourself about this issue so that you can explain your stand? Reflect on your position in a prayerful way and ask God to enlighten you about any aspect of this issue where your knowledge may be lacking.

Day 2.) Do you have a disdain for "pro-lifers?" Does the whole movement turn you off in some way? Is there an aspect of the movement you would like to change? Do you avoid discussion, interaction or confrontation with pro-life people because of preconceived notions? Ask God to make any biases you may have clear to you and to give you a heart willing to overcome these biases.

Day 3.) Are you generally willing to stand up for your beliefs? Are you comfortable voicing your opinion or do you prefer to keep your opinions to yourself? Have you had a negative experience with conflict or confrontation in the past which is causing you to remain silent? Lay your concerns before the Lord and ask for help in discerning when to speak and when to remain silent.

Day 4.) Are you aware of the Holy Spirit prompting you throughout the day? Do you listen to those prompts or try to ignore them? Have you ever given in to a nudge to do something and realized later how important it was to follow that directive? Ask God for a heart that is open to His will and ears to hear and respond to His voice.

Day 5.) Have you or a loved one been personally affected by the wounds of abortion? Is there a need for physical or emotional healing? Is there a need for repentance and forgiveness? Ask God if He can use you in some way to be the balm for these wounds and to give you the courage to make yourself available where needed.

Day 6.) Do you believe that God places people in our lives for a particular reason? Is there a certain person who has led you into a particular cause you would not have joined otherwise? Have you led others to involvement in causes that are close to your heart? Are you comfortable using your influence in this way? Ask God if there is someone you are in a unique position to influence or if you have been resisting someone He has put in a unique position to influence you.

Day 7.) Do you believe in the power of prayer? Do you believe in a loving, personal God who is listening as you pour out the concerns of your heart? Do you hesitate to come to God with your needs feeling you are either asking too much or your prayers are inconsequential? Can you name specific instances when your prayers have been answered? Come to Jesus with a grateful heart for all of the ways He is at work in your life and continue to lay your needs before Him as He loves you personally.

I recently got together with an old sorority sister of mine who lives out of town. We were at the University of Michigan together in the 70s, lived on the same floor of the same dorm, moved into the same sorority house and eventually rented another house on campus with four of our closest friends. She is one of the first people I met at college and we were drawn to each other immediately. We looked and dressed alike and were together so much that people often confused us for one another. We had a very similar sense of humor and always had lively discussions about politics, religion and culture.

This is where the similarities stopped as she was an only child from the country and I had twelve brothers and sisters and grew up in the city. Her parents were divorced; mine were married. She was an Episcopalian; I was a Catholic. She was raised in a household that supported one political party; I was from a family deeply entrenched in the "other" party. In fact, she was the first person who encouraged me to cross political lines and check out the message on the other side of the political fence.

When she first suggested that I go with her to hear Gerald Ford speak on campus I was a little leery. I thought about what my father's reaction would be if he knew, and really felt that I was somehow betraying my family and my upbringing by attending a rally for the "other" party. The "John F. Kennedy Catholic" blood ran pretty deeply in my veins and I had repeatedly been told that the "other" party was the party of the rich and that they did not care about the little guy. More specifically I had been told that they were always trying to put the "screws" to the little guy. Yet, I was also trying to form my own political opinions and allegiances and was not personally that committed to either side at this young age. I decided to go and hear what the man had to say. These were the first steps I took toward becoming a conservative.

I reminded my friend that she had introduced me to the "other" party during those college days in Ann Arbor, shortly after she and her husband arrived at our home in Birmingham this past fall. I don't think it made her feel particularly proud. She had been telling me that her eldest son had worked for the John Kerry campaign and had then listed several other organizations that her family supported and it became pretty clear to me that her political loyalty had shifted. When I told her that I had co-hosted a program on Michigan Catholic Radio, had written and recorded original Christian music and had a pro-life program that I had taken on the road, her face began to register horror and she asked, *"You're not like right wing are you?"*

I could tell by the tone of her voice and the look on her face that being "right wing" was not something she considered to be good. I began to stammer a little and said, *"Well, I don't consider myself to be a right wing zealot or an extremist or anything (like I have never thrown bombs at an abortion clinic or tried to shoot anyone) but I definitely lean toward the conservative and traditional side of things."* Weak, I know, but we hadn't gotten together as couples in over twenty years and this was the beginning of the evening.

She suggested that this was probably due to the fact that my husband is a doctor and we are anticipating being adversely affected by national health care. I agreed that this was a factor among many, especially the thought of taxpayer funded abortions under the plan, but attempted to divert the conversation from our desire for less government by asking when her politics had shifted.

She began making comparisons of Ronald Reagan, who in her opinion was not that bad, with George Bush, who she of course thought was stupid. I really hate it when people get into the Bush-bashing thing so again tried to redirect the conversation. I asked her if she was happy with Barrack Obama now that he was president. She said that she was certainly happy with his willingness to enter into dialogue with other countries. I started to say something about how dialogue should not include bowing to other world leaders when she interjected that she liked the concept of a moderate politician. I mentioned that I thought John McCain was moderate and then she went off on Sarah Palin and what a bimbo she was. I've never really understood the Palin hatred so at this point shifted to, *"So, how about those Tigers?"*

This is frequently how I segue off of sticky subjects and onto neutral ones. Here, in Detroit, people love their Tigers, their Red Wings, (even their Lions!), classic cars and "Motown" and these are always safe and enjoyable topics. We kept the conversation light while we put away the appetizers and joked about how I still don't like to cook and consider hummus and pita bread and salsa and chips culinary delights. Then we headed out to dinner and had a wonderful time.

As the wine flowed we began to laugh at old stories and play off of one another as only old friends can do. We both happen to be pretty good conversationalists with decent timing and have the ability to come up with the same punch lines in unison like a vaudeville team. We confessed to each other how good the belly laughs felt and how often we are stuck socially with someone who makes you do all of the work. There is nothing like history between people. You don't have to explain to them what you were like in college or before kids because they were there. We were at each other's weddings and knew each other during the thinnest, firmest days of our lives.

Our husbands were getting along splendidly despite the fact that one is a doctor and the other is a lawyer. This can be like mixing oil and water in case you have never tried it. They both discussed changes in their professions in recent years and their hopes and dreams for their sons and daughters and their chosen career paths. We lingered over dinner, not wanting the evening to end. At last we commented on how thoroughly enjoyable and "easy" the time together had been. We found it surprising that we still had so much in common other than that one little problem of each belonging to different political parties. We vowed to get together again the next time they came to town.

I have thought a great deal about how and why this evening turned out so well. Especially since I have liberals and conservatives in my own family and no matter how calmly we begin discussing a political or moral issue it almost always escalates into something ugly. Similarly, most of the people we have chosen to befriend in town are likeminded individuals and this is not by accident. We take our politics seriously as do most of the people we know and there is a tendency to begin to demonize the other side.

This is exactly what did not happen on this particular evening with our old friends. There was no demonizing of the other party because our friendship was already based on love and respect. We knew that our old friends were good, solid, intelligent people who wanted similar things for their loved ones that we want for ours. I was suddenly the face of that right wing pro-life zealot that they read about in their publications and they became the faces of those Bush-bashing, Sarah Palin-haters that I hear about on Fox News. Except that this time we knew the heart and soul of the individuals behind the labels and we already liked them. We had shared many life experiences. We had shared many laughs. We were alike except for that one little political party affiliation issue.

I begin my journaling time each morning praying for light, to see God at work in my life as I reflect on my prior day in praise and thanksgiving. This particular day I could clearly see God at work in opening my eyes toward the goodness in my dear friend and her husband, despite the fact that they happen to be card-carrying members of the "other" political party.

Day 1.) How tolerant are you of opposing political viewpoints? Do you have a tendency to demonize the other side? Have you been made out to be the demon by someone you know on the other side of the political fence? Reflect on the role politics plays in your life and in your relationships.

Day 2.) How educated are you on political issues? Do you tend to form your own opinions or are you influenced by those close to you? Are you willing to do the research necessary to make informed choices? Give yourself an "effort" grade for your study of politics with supporting comments.

Day 3.) Are you willing to discuss politics in public? Can you recall a time when a political discussion went well or turned sour? Reflect on why and how this discussion had either a happy or sad ending.

Day 4.) Do you have any political heroes? Name a person you consider to be exemplary in a leadership role and reflect on what makes this person head and shoulders above the rest. Pray for the wisdom and the courage to follow this person's example.

Day 5.) Have your political loyalties shifted? If yes, can you recall a specific turning point on your political path? Have your faith journey and your political journey paralleled each other? Ponder the role that your faith has played in your political leanings.

Day 6.) Do you pray for our government officials? Do you believe in the power of prayer to influence those running our cities, states and country? Do you pray for guidance when making your political decisions? Pray for an informed conscience and ask the Holy Spirit to guide our elected officials.

Day 7.) Do you tend to choose like-minded friends? Do you have a tendency to categorize and label people and then leave entire groups of people outside of your circle of friends? Have you ever felt left out because of your political beliefs? Examine your behavior for signs of bias or bigotry and pray for an open and receptive heart.

All three of my children played a variety of sports while they were growing up. My husband had been an athlete and felt that not only was exercise beneficial but the lessons to be learned from being part of a team and being involved in healthy competition were critical. Most of our sporting experiences were positive until our first born decided to try out for travel soccer.

Our town had an "A" team and a "B" team for the boys at this level. The "A" team was supposed to get the better players, travel more and be a bit more competitive and the "B" team was supposed to get the next tier of players. Our son's current coach had been designated the coach of the "A" team and since we had always had a very positive experience with him we were hoping that our son would have a successful tryout and get to work with him again.

However, resentful that they had not been assigned the "A" team, the "B" team coaches began to recruit all of the better players. We discovered this when our household was one of the many that was called by these coaches in their efforts to encourage the better players to ask to play on the "B" team that year. At the tryouts, regardless of the child's ability, the parents were supposed to say that they wanted their son to travel less and play on the less competitive team.

The phone lines were buzzing and all of the parents and the boys in the community were discussing the advantages of playing on the "B" team rather than the "A" team. The "B" team coaches happened to have two of the biggest soccer talents in town as sons and they were also very popular and persuasive. Playing on the "B" team became the cool thing to do that year and their team was definitely going to be stacked.

We sat down with our son and had a long discussion about doing the right thing in this situation. We knew the coach of the "A" team to be an exemplary man. He was a man of integrity who had always treated his players and their families with respect. He was clearly being undermined here. We felt strongly that we could not support the sabotaging tactics of the other coaches. We encouraged our son to do the best tryout that he could and if he made the "A" team he would play on the "A" team the way the system had been designed. He made the team and made the commitment.

Not surprisingly, numerous parents of the better players decided that they wanted their sons to have a "less intense experience" that year and opted for the "B" team. The "less intense" team ended up being a powerhouse, traveling a great deal and drumming up lots of victories.

They kept inquiring about playing the "A" team just for "fun" to see which team was truly better. This challenge was avoided for a while but eventually the "A" team coaches agreed to play the "B" team in a scrimmage.

These boys were in the fifth and sixth grade and many of them went to the same school. That transfer to middle school is an awkward enough stage already without the added divisiveness and pressure caused by this increasingly intense rivalry. The kids were involved. The parents were involved. It was not friendly. There was much build up and "in your face" taunting leading up to this dreaded scrimmage that was supposedly "just for fun."

We lost. I don't remember the score now or many of the details but seem to recall a lot of break-away goals and momentum consistently building on their side. We played like the underdogs that we were. On the way out to the parking lot, as I walked past the cheering throng of "B" team players and their parents, one of the dads from their side that I knew said, "So, what'd you think about that game? Fun, huh?" "Not really," I replied in a terse tone walking briskly to my car and racing out of the lot.

I found myself getting really worked up over this and spent the evening trying to put it all into perspective. These were eleven-year-old boys playing a game, a scrimmage actually. The better team won. I should have put a smile on my face and walked up to the parents and winning players, after the contest, and congratulated them on their fine performance. It should not have become a battle over right and wrong with eleven-year-olds as the foot soldiers. I decided that I needed to apologize to the dad to whom I had been so abrupt.

Knocking at the door of his home the next day I was a little nervous but had carefully rehearsed what I planned to say. It would be short and sweet (but sincere!) and I would be out of there in a few minutes. He was surprised to see me but invited me into the kitchen where his wife and daughter were gathered around the table. The audience was growing. Great.

"I feel I owe you an apology for the way I behaved toward you after the game yesterday. I was not friendly and must have looked ridiculous speeding out of the parking lot. I am embarrassed that I did not show better sportsmanship and I hope you will accept my apology. I was making this into a game about good guys and bad guys and forgetting that it was just about kids kicking a ball."

Well, the "good guys and bad guys" line really hit home with him and he began to explain that their victory was so important to them because they saw us as the "bad guys." They felt that the "B" team coaches had been terribly wronged by the local sports commission when they were not assigned the "A" team. The whole mission of the kids and the parents on that team had been to rally around their coaches, the "good guys," and be victorious to prove to the powers that be that they had made a big mistake. He went on to explain what a special "espirit de corps" existed on their team and contrasted this with the "sourness" he sensed from our side.

This was quite interesting. We had both divided the forces into good guys and bad guys but had a completely different view on who was good and who was bad. He proceeded to talk about nasty things that had happened and had been said by our side and I listened attentively because this was the first time I was honestly willing to see things from their point of view. We shook hands and parted on good terms and both vowed to display better sportsmanship in the future.

This dad actually followed up this conversation with a four page hand-written letter sent to me in the mail. He was clearly relieved that the walls preventing communication about this incident had been removed and had much more to explain. Mainly, now that he was aware that they had been viewed as the "bad guys" in this scenario he had more to say in defense of his team and their motivations and experience. We, however, were definitely ready to move on.

Our son decided to switch to football. The nickname "big foot" he had been tagged with in soccer led him to become the kicker and punter on his grade school team and eventually to other positions in high school. He also moved to a Catholic academy in the city for his seventh grade year. It was time to make some changes. The whole soccer debacle had carried over into basketball, as one of the "B" team soccer coaches was also the boy's basketball coach at the local Catholic grade school which was a feeder for a boy's travel basketball team. We could not seem to avoid him. He was not particularly fond of us or our son but if our son wanted to play sports in our town—and he did—we had to make every effort to get along.

Looking back, this all seems like very small stuff now, because it was. But I can also see God's plan for my son unfolding in all of it. Our son went on to become the captain of his high school football team and an all-state kicker. This led him to play football in college at an Ivy League school which provided him with the opportunity to do medical research for an alumnus, a former football player, who happened to be a world renowned orthopedic surgeon. This played a critical role in my son's acceptance to a Catholic medical school where he met the woman he is about to marry, another Catholic doctor to be, whom we love dearly. How good is God!

The soccer experience was just one step on the rungs of the ladder of life which my son had to climb to get to where he is today. The fact that it was not the most positive experience is what led him to try something else. The something else was actually a much better fit for him and opened doors of opportunity that would not have been open to him otherwise. God took an apparent failure and transformed it into something that we consider a very blessed success. He is the potter and we are clay. We need to allow Him to do His molding without kicking and screaming and complaining about the indentations in our pots along the way.

God was at work in our minds and hearts in many ways during those early days of sports. My conscience was constantly reminding me to see the face of God in every person, even in our opponents—or especially in our opponents! I needed to silence that mean voice that would somehow escape from my lips on the sidelines. God gives us all of these wonderful opportunities to run, leap, jump, kick, throw, develop coordination and make our bodies strong and we tend to find ways to muck it all up.

But, as the referee exclaims with his arms lifted up as the football sails through the goalposts, *"It's good!"* And it truly is.

Day 1.) What kind of a fan are you? Have you ever let your emotions take over and said or done something you later regretted? Have you ever felt the need to apologize for an outburst or inappropriate comment from the stands? Reflect on the issue of sportsmanship and the role it has played in your life.

Day 2.) Have you seen God at work in the decisions you or a family member have made about which activities to pursue? Have you seen an apparent failure transformed into a blessed success? Are you open to the hand of God guiding you toward the greater good or the path that uses your talents to bring Him glory? Contemplate the many times you have come to a fork in the road and reflect on the Divine guidance you have received.

Day 3.) Have you ever divided a group into good guys and bad guys only to realize later that the line was not so clear? Have you ever been made aware that you were placed in the bad guy category and unjustly so? If you had an opportunity to set the record straight did you do so? Ask God to enlighten you about a time you have wrongly determined who was a friend and who was a foe.

Day 4.) Can you think of a circumstance in your life that you thought was a really big deal at the time but in retrospect realize it was not so big? Can you now see how things got blown out of proportion? Consider how your behavior may have aggravated this situation and ask forgiveness for those you may have hurt knowingly or unknowingly.

Day 5.) Do you have a difficult time trusting in God's plans for you or your children? Can you accept that God loves your children more than you do? Do you believe that God has "plans for your welfare, not for woe, plans to give you a future full of hope?" Take a few moments to surrender and unite your will to God's will.

Day 6.) How competitive of a person are you? How much do you involve yourself in the competition of your children? Do you let them fight their own battles or head right to the front lines for them? Reflect on the difference between being a "helicopter parent" or an advocate for your child.

Day 7.) Consider the expression "do as I say not as I do." Think about a time your instructions and your behavior were incongruous. Contemplate a time you were a positive role model as opposed to a time your behavior was not exemplary. Pray for the ability to learn from your mistakes and to continue to ask "what would Jesus do?"

Several years ago when my sons were playing grade school football, there was a football mom who was definitely a "head turner." I mean she was an absolutely gorgeous creature with long, thick, chestnut hair and the kind of figure that you see in a "Victoria's Secret" catalogue but rarely in real life. I would be sitting up in the stands with the other "lesser" moms and she would walk by with her hair blowing in the wind, sunshine hitting her highlights just so, flashing a perfect teeth smile to someone in the stands below me. This is when the nasty thoughts would begin.

The thoughts could be summed up in the "Who does she think she is?" or "Well, she certainly thinks she is something!" category, but, for purposes of this exercise, I will break them down. I would decide that her shorts were too short, her tank top was too tight and that her body parts were manufactured. I would also decide that she was trying to attract attention to herself and was way too into her looks and probably not much else. Then, I would conclude that we could probably never be friends because we would have absolutely nothing in common. All this without a single greeting exchanged.

Fast forward about fifteen years when I was asked to facilitate a Catholic Scripture Study for the women in my parish. You are probably wondering how someone as spiritually immature and judgmental as I would be asked to facilitate a Women's Scripture Study. The answer is simply that they only have sinners from which to choose. I had grown in my faith somewhat at that point but still had a long way to go. I am handed my class roster on the second week of class and lo and behold there is the "head turner" along with several other younger attractive moms from the neighboring parishes.

I happened to mention this line-up to a mutual friend and her comment was, "*Whoa! You have all of the 'hot moms' in your group!*" Great. I am hoping to grow in faith by studying God's word with other spiritual seekers and now I am suddenly feeling junior high school pangs of not being cool or pretty enough and thinking just a little too long about what I am going to wear to Bible Study. Not good. Not a great way to start the year of deepening my faith but the "God of the impossible" had some surprises in store for me. I was about to find God amongst the "hot moms."

One of the fears of being a facilitator is that you will get a group that does not "share" or participate. You will ask one of the study questions and be greeted with silence and heads staring down at their papers not wanting to make eye contact with you. Well, these fears quickly dissolved as the women in my group were eager to share their answers and personal experiences. They were all very respectful of one another despite a vast range of age, socio-economic backgrounds and scriptural knowledge. And the woman who surprised me the most with her level of commitment to the class was the "head turner" from grade school football.

This woman would check the Catholic Scripture Study website for various commentaries on the subject matter each week. She would delve deeper into the questions than was even required by the study sheet and bring the supplemental material to class to share with everyone. In addition to her degree from a prestigious university, and a full-time prior career, she was now substitute teaching and working at a local clinic. She was also incredibly funny, quick-witted and highly energetic, starting a weekly walking group on Wednesdays after class. She took the initials CSS for Catholic Scripture Study and named the walking group Catholic Spiritual Sisters. She even hosted a going-away party at her home for one of our class members who moved out of state at the end of the year.

On the last day of class this dedicated pupil brought her camera to take a picture of our group. She asked if she could say something to the class and proceeded to tell us that this had been a life-altering experience for her. She explained that she had been "down" the year before, not in a good place, and the Scripture Study and faith sharing had truly had an uplifting effect on her soul. We were all teary-eyed as other members began to share how the class had impacted their lives also. The "unhot moms" as well as the "hot moms" were now truly burning from the same flame. They were on fire with the Holy Spirit and it was powerful and contagious.

The head of CSS at our parish told me that she prays in front of the Blessed Sacrament when deciding who will be assigned to what core group. She relies on the Holy Spirit to tell her which participant would benefit most from which core group facilitator. Her choice is not at all random. We are placed in each other's lives for a reason, all in God's perfect timing. I learned a great deal from each and every woman in my core group that first year, but I especially learned a lesson in not judging a person's interior from their exterior and not letting my own insecurities prevent me from making a friend.

A woman I know recently told me that she used to refer to me as "Miss Birmingham." Birmingham is the Michigan suburb where I reside and is typically associated with affluence and considered a little snooty. I stood there thinking about being the eleventh of thirteen children and growing up in a tiny, white frame house in Detroit. My father made $17,500 a year when he retired. I had to share bath water, amongst other things, with the siblings closest to me in age. I was aware that the "doctor's wife" this woman was viewing, with the professional highlights in her hair and country club logo on her warm-up suit, was a far cry from the little girl in that bungalow on the west side. Man, I thought, she doesn't know me at all.

Bingo! She did not know me at all in exactly the same way that I did not know the women in my class until we let down our guards and allowed others to see what was lying behind the walls we put up. We have started a new year of Scripture Study and most of these women have now been assigned to new facilitators who will have the opportunity to look beyond those walls and help each other to grow in their faith. Many have even brought friends to the study hoping they will have a similarly positive experience. The walking spiritual sisters continue to pound the pavement with new members who are walking the walk and talking the talk. The circle of friendship is growing, and the Holy Spirit is alive and well at the center of it, burning brightly in the flame of these very hot moms.

Day 1.) Is there someone that you have been judging harshly? Can you simply not find it in your heart to give this person the benefit of the doubt? Is it possible that you are intimidated by this person and the harsh judgments are a defense mechanism? Ask Jesus to help you to see as He sees and love as He loves.

Day 2.) Have you ever found that you have been completely wrong about someone? How or why was your opinion changed? Can you see in the "looking back" how or why the misinterpretation of their behavior or character came about? Ask Jesus for forgiveness for your hardness of heart and for His help in seeing the face of God in every person.

Day 3.) How concerned are you with the way others look? Do you choose your friends based on their outward attractiveness or their inner beauty? Have you ever steered clear of someone because of how attractive they are? Have you ever felt scorned because of your lack of physical beauty? Ask Jesus to help you to choose your friends based on inner beauty rather than outer beauty and to seek companions for your faith journey.

Day 4.) How much of a priority is the state of your soul versus the state of your body? Are you a person of the flesh or a person of the spirit? How do you balance "mind, body and spirit" and what importance do you give to each? Ask Jesus for direction and clarity with respect to balancing physical health with spiritual health.

Day 5.) Do you have a tendency to compare yourself to others? Do you see life as a contest or competition with a scoreboard in your head reminding you of where you stand? Are the winners and losers based on heavenly criteria or earthly criteria? Ask Jesus to help you to have an appreciation of your own unique gifts and purpose. Enlist His help in turning off the scoreboard and celebrating who you already are: a child of God.

Day 6.) Do you set aside time to study God's Word daily or weekly? Is Christian fellowship a priority in your life? Do you have a longing for faith sharing with your friends? Place this longing at Jesus' feet and ask Him to provide opportunities for intimacy with Him and fellow believers.

Day 7.) Do you have a mentor in the faith? Are you or would you like to be a mentor to someone else? Do you understand the concept of winning souls for Christ? Ask Jesus today how you might bring souls to the kingdom and if there is a particular soul you are in a special position to influence.

Walking the walk of faith in the performing arts is a very challenging enterprise. This is especially true for the aging or "mature" actress. Younger women play the ingénues, the sweet innocent characters in the boy-meets-girl-conflict-resolution scenarios. The middle-aged women more typically play the character roles, the women who have been around the block and have become tough and jaded. The town prostitute, barmaid, gypsy or witch comes to mind. At any age trying to find roles that do not require running around on stage scantily clad, using obscene language or hopping in and out of the sack is difficult.

Musical theatre has been a big part of my life since high school. I truly love "the smell of the greasepaint and the roar of the crowd" and have a passion for immersing myself in a good character role. The problem I encounter repeatedly is trying to find material that does not contradict my values. I will not use the Lord's name in vain, for example, and many scripts are loaded with expletives. I also will not put myself in sexually inappropriate situations. Any stage action that would make my husband, my children or my mother squirm is not for me.

Of course, I have been informed that this is very unprofessional. Directors tell me that it is not actually "Patty" saying, doing and wearing these things on stage but my character. But the lines are, in fact, coming out of my mouth, the bumps and grinds are coming from my hips and the navel and the thigh being revealed are mine also. I am a wife, mother, daughter, church cantor, Bible study facilitator and child of God. My body is a temple of the Holy Spirit and I am careful about what I do with this temple.

Once you are labeled a prude it is like the kiss of death in the theatre world. The shows are becoming racier and racier and the material more explicit. There are increasingly fewer roles for which I can audition. I check an audition website regularly for opportunities and did recently perform in a dinner theatre show about motherhood. This sounds mild enough but the production staff decided to hold an essay contest and give a prize to the candidate that best represented their concept of motherhood. I decided to make an entry as I consider my mother to be pretty amazing and wanted to honor her. They chose a woman who used her womb to provide a daddy-daddy couple with a son.

This is pretty typical of the nontraditional mindset of the creative types. I was in rehearsal last year for another musical which dealt with an eccentric woman taking on the evil corporate men in her town. We were rehearsing a scene which involved a mock trial to convict all of the greedy capitalists and send them out into their own world and away from ours. The actors were not responding with enough intensity and the director wanted more anger and emotion and asked the cast to think about the evil people in our world today. This elicited many comments about George Bush, Dick Cheney and many other Republicans for whom I had voted.

There is an unspoken assumption that everyone in the theatre world is a liberal. When casts have gatherings after rehearsals and the conversation turns to politics it becomes very clear that the conservatives are not represented. I have often felt conflicted about whether or not I should speak up and express the opposing viewpoints but it is difficult to be a party of one. When I attempted to explain my pro-life positions to a fellow female cast member once, I was told to "keep my rosaries off her ovaries" and received a diatribe about her body, her choice. Since we were going to be sharing a dressing room for many weeks and needed to get along I simply suggested that we agree to disagree.

I have become braver about standing up for what I believe in because I know how shameful it feels to be silent and go along with the majority. When I lived in Ann Arbor in my twenties I sang in an all-girl band that was asked to be the entertainment for some women's rally. It turned out that this rally was raising money for the local Planned Parenthood center. I ran into some women I knew from home and they indicated how surprised they were to see me there as they were sure I would have been on the other side of the fence on this issue. I replied that I **was** on the other side of the fence on this issue. I had no idea why I had said yes to this and why I was there. I declined to be involved in this the following year which prevented our group from performing and I was very unpopular. But at least I could look at myself in the mirror.

Trying to find shows that do not celebrate marital infidelity, sexual promiscuity, alternative lifestyles or have anti-Catholic themes is challenging. I was recently approached by a director about trying out for a role in a musical about two murderesses.

He promised to take out the "GDs" and dress the females more modestly than usual as he knows that I have issues with this. He argued that the show is a farce and that I need to lighten up and appreciate the humor in the writing and not be so concerned with the seediness of the script. The role he is referring to is a perfect fit for me vocally and with respect to age-appropriateness and physical type. Yet, I have a hard time envisioning my husband and the Bible study ladies in the audience. Temptation abounds.

In my quest to look for God in all things I reflect on when and how I have found Him in the theatre world. My thoughts land on a director I have worked with many times who is an attorney for the ACLU. His day job requires him to work for almost everything that I am against. But he is one of the nicest, kindest, most compassionate people that I have ever known. He is an extremely warm individual who treats everyone he encounters with respect. We have always had an excellent working relationship and though I am sure he knows that I oppose most of the things for which he is fighting, we have our desire for excellence in theatre in common. Our theatrical common ground works.

When I drove up to the theatre recently to purchase tickets for something I noticed a car in the lot that had bumper stickers indicating that the driver was opposed to abortion. I asked the man in the ticket office, who is an acquaintance of mine, if he knew whose car it was that was parked next to the door. He said yes and informed me that it belonged to a woman I knew who is a long time member of our theatre group. I had no idea that these were her political leanings and was really impressed with her bravery to sport such controversial messages on her car at such a liberal place. Her courage inspired me and made me wonder how many other likeminded individuals surrounded me of whom I was not aware. It reminded me to be bolder.

A few years back when performing in a children's musical (as a witch, of course...the young girls play the princesses and the old broads play the witches) the director and the cast members were constantly taking the Lord's name in vain. I would cringe every time this happened and close my eyes and say a silent prayer of forgiveness for this disrespect. One of the cast members, a friend of mine, noticed my discomfort and asked if it was alright if they said "Zeus Damn it." She thought that since Zeus was a pagan god and not my God that this was a good compromise for those who liked to curse but did not want to offend me. I said that this was fine with me and it actually became quite a joke and the impetus for a lot of laughter. It also pretty much eliminated the cursing all together as they realized how it had been overused and now was not as satisfying.

During another children's show an actress with whom I was sharing a dressing room became very upset when I was going to kill a spider on the makeup counter. She is an animal rights activist and rallied for putting the spider on a piece of cardboard and moving it to another location. Another actress would not eat yogurt in the cafeteria because it had gelatin in it which is taken from animal bones. She refused to gnaw on a fake turkey leg as part of a scene, substituting a loaf of bread, and also protested an animal fur rug as part of the set. Out of respect for them I did not kill any spiders and stopped having yogurt for lunch but was also reminded of that bumper sticker that says "How come America? We brake for animals, save the seals, protect the whales and kill our unborn children!"

Most people are turned off by born-again Christians who wear their religion on their sleeves. Coming across as a preachy individual or one attempting to be holier than thou will frequently do more harm than good. There is a time and a place for honest political and religious debate and, generally when we are participating in our pastimes with acquaintances, this is not the time. These discussions do seem to happen at the theatre, however. You can be involved in the same theatrical production for months (even years!) and when you are sharing a dressing room with someone, you end up getting to know them quite well. I never want to miss an opportunity to witness when it is presented. As Saint Peter tells us, we should always be prepared to give an answer for the hope that is in our hearts, but we must do so with gentleness and respect.

I must remind myself why it is that I am drawn to performing in the first place. I am drawn to it because it brings me, and those for whom I am performing, joy. I am drawn to it because God gave me the ability to sing, dance and act. He did not give this ability to everyone and I should not put my talents under a bushel basket or bury them in the ground. The ability to connect with an audience while bringing a character to life is an amazing experience. I think it makes God smile. I know it makes audiences smile. Even though I can no longer play Maria Von Trapp, Eliza Doolittle or Annie Oakley I have to trust that playwrights will continue to create quality bodies of work for the mature actress and I will be sure that I am ready when they appear. I may be the only pro-life, Catholic, conservative woman my fellow thespians ever encounter. I'd better play my role well.

Day 1.) Reflect on your passions and how you see God at work in these activities. Do you tend to separate "God time" from "ordinary time" or are you aware of God's presence in all that you do? Thank God for the passions He has given you and ask Him to enlighten you on how these can be used to bring Him glory.

Day 2.) Do you have a difficult time walking the walk of faith when participating in certain pastimes? Do you avoid certain situations because they tend to contradict your values? Do you struggle repeatedly with decisions to either participate or not participate in certain activities with certain groups? Reflect on situations which may be problematic for you.

Day 3.) Do you have a hard time avoiding discussions of politics and religion? Have you ever attempted to broach a delicate subject and later regretted it? Do you feel stifled or frustrated by the trend toward political correctness? Pray for the wisdom to know when to speak and when to remain silent.

Day 4.) Does the "anything goes" mentality in the performing arts bother you in any way? Do you find the seediness of scripts for plays, movies or television offensive? Do you lean toward more censorship or are you comfortable with complete freedom of speech? Think about your body, and that of others, as a temple of the Holy Spirit and reflect on the maintenance of these temples.

Day 5.) Have you ever set aside your values to participate in something and later regretted it? Is there a person in your life who tends to lead you down paths you do not wish to go? Have you ever confronted a person you consider to be a bad influence or has someone confronted you with a similar concern? Examine the closets in your life and determine if any need a good cleaning.

Day 6.) How careful are you with your speech? Consider James 3:9-10 which says of the tongue: "With it we bless the Lord and Father, and with it we curse human beings who are made in the likeness of God. From the same mouth come blessing and cursing. This need not be so." Ponder your use of language and pray for help in taming the tongue if necessary.

Day 7.) Think about your life as a play. Are you as happy with Act Two as you were with Act One? Who is the author of your script? Who gets top billing? How would you like the play to end? Are there any new characters you wish to introduce? Write an outline of your play in one, two or three acts complete with title and main characters. How do you feel about your story thus far?

My husband is always telling me that there are "breast lumps" and "gravy lumps" and that we need to know the difference. When someone is confronted with a serious illness suddenly everything else becomes small stuff. It actually always was small stuff but now in the midst of medical procedures and hospital stays and the inability to function normally all the other things get really small. Pain and fear drum out the sound of everything else and all one wants to hear is "You are going to be okay."

Swine flu stopped me in my tracks recently and I had plenty of time to reflect on how blessed my life is normally. I generally hate going to the grocery store but once the flu hit I just wished I felt well enough to drive myself there. I thought about how fortunate I was to have money to buy groceries. I thought about my cozy bed and the tea I was drinking and all of the comforts of my home. I thought about how nice it is to have a home. With relief I noted that my being bedridden was temporary. It is not that way for Clancy.

Whenever I need a reality check I call my friend Clancy. This is actually her last name but for some reason that's what she goes by. Clancy has MS and is confined to a wheelchair and can no longer stand alone. Her mother and her brother care for her though she lives separately in her own apartment. They come in the morning to get her out of bed and help her to get dressed and ready for the day and then they come back in the evening to reverse the process. Clancy has an incredible sense of humor and is generally upbeat when I call.

Despite her disabilities Clancy tends to focus on what she is able to do. She is grateful for her legs even though they don't work very well. She is grateful for her eyesight even though it is failing and she is grateful for her mind even though some memories are painful for her. She lost her father recently and gets emotional when she speaks of him which aggravates her MS. She is especially grateful for her TV and her computer. The ability to send and receive emails allows her to stay in touch with the outside world. I usually don't like to get forwards but I enjoy exchanging them with Clancy because I know how much they mean to her.

Clancy pops into my head when I hear someone complaining that their highlights are too brassy, their recent massage was too deep or not deep enough, their cleaning lady isn't up to snuff, service they received at a restaurant was inadequate or any other number of complaints I hear on a daily basis. I hear women exclaim that they need a manicure or pedicure with such cries of desperation that you would think they were in need of insulin for their diabetes. I think it is fair to say that most of these complaints fall into the "gravy lump" category.

I try to stay as positive as possible when I am talking to Clancy because whatever it is that I might be considering a problem will simply pale by comparison to what she confronts every day. I have been fighting mid-life weight gain, for example, but won't discuss this with someone who can't keep weight on and is trying to stay above eighty pounds. I wrestle with being motivated to work out but would not dare complain about that to someone who would give anything to have functioning legs. I sometimes feel that my life lacks purpose but know that Clancy is appreciative for every morning she wakes up in her own bed and greets a new day.

We all need to have a Clancy in our lives. We need something to burst our shiny, pampered, protective bubbles. Clancy always puts things in perspective for me.

She has a way of letting me know that whatever it is that I am fretting over is not that big of a deal and that all will be well. This was especially true during a chapter in our lives which revolved around trying to sell our house.

For several years I was lamenting to Clancy about not being able to sell our house. Twice we had built new homes with the hopes of downsizing. Twice the idea was to sell our big, old money pit of a house for a certain price and buy something smaller for a better price in an attempt to become debt-free. Twice we ended up having to put the new homes on the market and sell whichever one got an offer first. The kids were gone and the timing seemed right to simplify our lives. We even hired a "stager" to come in and make our country home look more desirable. But, no one wanted to buy our 1924 federal colonial with "lots of charm."

The stager told us to get rid of the country stuff, to de-clutter, to take all of the wallpaper down, to paint the woodwork white and change the décor to green. Blue was definitely out. She said that the window treatments had to go and suggested we pull up the rugs. She told us to put white towels in all the bathrooms, put away the collages of pictures and sports trophies and get rid of the teddy bears. It was basically supposed to look like nobody lived there. The look was lots of clean lines and maybe some white roses in a vase. I did it (except for painting the woodwork!) and I hated it and it still didn't sell.

Clancy reminded me that I have always loved my home. She reminded me that my favorite color is blue. She knows that I love my old teddy bears and dolls and antiques and country tins. My children were raised in this house and it was extremely difficult for me to imagine a Christmas in any other place. The house was cozy and creaky and old fashioned and traditional just like us. I didn't really want to sell it anyway. We took the house off the market, reinstated the blue, put the rocking horses back and are living here 'til death do us part.

Not being able to sell our house was definitely a "gravy lump." Clancy helped me to see that. We were still going to have a roof over our heads either way, a new roof or an old roof, and many people cannot say that. Our pride was hurt a little by all of the criticisms we heard about our décor, but we like our décor, and think it will work well for the grandchildren we hope to have someday. Not much is breakable. When the kids come home now they still retreat to their old rooms and with a son and daughter-in-law added to the mix all the rooms seem like a boon instead of a bust.

My mind flashed to Clancy and our housing problem recently when we were at an out of town wedding in Florida. There was a lot of discussion about real estate and how hard it was to unload property in such a down market and the financial drain of maintenance on vacation homes and investment properties. We were seated next to the CEO of some company who was lamenting about the trials and tribulations of owning a home in southern Florida. He explained how the salt air just beats up on the exterior of their place and how there is always something in need of repair and that they frequently return after a long absence to find rodents running about. He also mentioned that he rarely has time to enjoy his southern residence or the leisurely activities associated with it because of the demands of travel and his job.

Our inability to sell our home or another's inability to sell extra homes or the problems they face maintaining them are inconveniences not problems. A person facing foreclosure of their one and only residence has a problem. A person losing their one and only job has a problem. A person confronting a serious medical issue has a problem. Having to live without luxuries when others are struggling to simply live is like comparing gravy lumps to breast lumps. There is simply no comparison.

I thank God that He has put Clancy in my life to remind me of His promises. He will use all for good. No suffering offered up to Him will be wasted. He knows when a sparrow falls to the ground and He has counted the hairs upon our heads. He holds us in the palms of His hands. He will make sense out of all of our lumps. He is the Divine Physician and it is with ultimate authority that He tells all believers and doers of the Word that "Eye has not seen and ear has not heard what

God has ready for those who love Him." That is a most reassuring way of being told that "You are going to be okay," lumps and all.

Day 1.) Reflect on any "lumps" you are confronting in your life right now. Is it possible that some are merely "gravy lumps" that you have placed in the wrong category? Ask the Lord to give you the gift of discernment with respect to these difficulties and the courage to confront and overcome any obstacles.

Day 2.) If you are in fact confronting "breast lumps" or problems of a serious nature lay these concerns at the foot of the cross. Tell Jesus about your fears, worries and sufferings and ask that your sufferings be united with His and used for His purposes. Ask the Lord to renew your spirit and replenish the hope in your heart.

Day 3.) How do you generally react to the expression "Don't sweat the small stuff?" Are you able to view most of the problems you encounter daily as fairly inconsequential? Make a list of all of your present concerns and ask yourself if any of these will matter to you five years from now or even five months from now. Pray about each and then let it go.

Day 4.) Is there someone in your life who seems to have a way of putting things in their proper perspective? Are you this person to someone else? Is this easy for you to do for others yet not for yourself? Reflect on being a good role model or on someone who has been a good role model for you and pray for these qualities.

Day 5.) Consider this Scripture passage: "Look at the birds in the sky; they do not sow or reap, they gather nothing into barns, yet your heavenly father feeds them." (Matthew 6:26) Also consider "Learn from the way the wild flowers grow. They do not work or spin. But I tell you that not even Solomon in all his splendor was clothed like one of them." (Matthew 6:28-29) Take a moment to place yourself in God's hands trusting that He will provide for all of your needs. Pray "Jesus, I trust in you."

Day 6.) Was there a time in your life when you experienced suffering that you can now see as a time when you drew closer to the Lord? Can you see in the looking back that obstacles were really opportunities? Is there a present challenge which may in fact be an invitation to greater intimacy with God? Be still and let God reveal to you how He is at work in your life.

Day 7.) How do you view the role of suffering in your life or in the lives of those you love? Are you willing to offer your suffering up to the Lord and trust that He will use all for good? Do you understand that you are never alone and that Jesus is willing to suffer with you? Meditate on these words from the Anima Christi: "Passion of Christ strengthen me, O good Jesus hear me, within your wounds hide me, suffer me not to be separated from you."

I have been surrounded by and immersed in music my entire life. My mom and dad and brothers and sisters all loved to sing. We sang while we did the dishes, folded laundry, took baths, rode in the car, watched TV or listened to records. As soon as a new musical came out on Broadway my dad would buy the album. We would then sit around the record player and sing the songs from the show until we knew all of the words. We also watched *The Lawrence Welk Show, Sing Along With Mitch* and any and all Christmas specials with The King Family, The Lennon Sisters, Andy Williams or Johnny Mathis.

When I got to high school I performed in all of the musicals all four years. I also joined the show choir as I loved ensemble singing. After high school and college I began to do community theatre, sang in a trio, became a cantor at my parish and even attempted songwriting and recording. I bought the first Karaoke machine that was made as debuted in the movie *When Harry Met Sally* after seeing Meg Ryan and Billy Crystal sing "The Surrey with the Fringe on Top." I sort of took my voice for granted thinking it would always be there for me. I thought I knew what I was doing vocally.

While performing in a local theatre production about a dozen years ago I lost my voice as a result of stress, misuse and illness. I was attempting a "belt" sound in imitation of a particular Broadway actress I admired but I was not doing it correctly. I realized that I wanted a fuller, freer sound and that I needed to expand my range. I was referred to a woman who was a professor of voice at a local university. I had no idea at the time how broken my system was and how much of an overhaul I was about to receive.

At my first lesson I was asked to sing something that I knew well so that my teacher could evaluate my vocal technique and my instrument. I sang about three lines of the song before she said "Stop!" She told me that I was pulling into my throat and engaging all sorts of muscles I was not supposed to be engaging. She added that I was not using my air and that my soft palate was not lifted. I spent the rest of the hour learning how to breathe and use my air, perfecting my posture, making hissing sounds and attempting lip drills. I sang bent over, while throwing an imaginary ball in the air, walking back and forth and using nasal vowels. It was humbling to say the least. I had to decide then and there if I was going to entrust my voice to this woman and if I was willing to do the work that was necessary to be a legitimate singer.

I decided to stay. At my voice lesson recently, a dozen years later, I was reminded of why I chose to hang in there. My teacher suggested that I do it for God. She told me that God made me to sing. He wants me to sing in the same way that He wants my teacher to teach. It is our gift. She told me this in response to my tears of frustration over lack of vocal progress. I went to my last lesson feeling very discouraged because I had listened to a recording of myself recently and had not liked my sound. Yes, I have gotten rid of a lot of my tension and yes, my voice is healthier and freer than it used to be. But I still cannot float a high note or sing through my break as well as I would like to. And I still fight performance anxiety and I am 52 years old.

My vocal journey parallels my spiritual journey in many ways. My voice teacher is always telling me that I have to get out of the way. This means that once your posture and alignment are correct and your soft palate is lifted and you take your air deeply and have all of your ducks in a row then you simply have to get out of the way. You let the sound go. This reminds me of letting go and letting God. You allow God to use you as His instrument. You place yourself in His presence and quiet your thoughts and listen for the still, small voice and get out of the way and let God be God and work through you. I tend to want to control things vocally and otherwise and this is the opposite of being free.

I also have to take my ego out of it. I was told once that "ego" stands for "edging God out." I must remember that I am to do all for the glory of God and not the glory of Patty. Thy will be done—not my will be done. I am attempting to make a joyful noise unto the Lord not a joyful noise unto my fans. Of course, it is nice when others tell me that they enjoy my voice or look forward to hearing me perform but I am certainly not the favorite of every listener. There are many beautiful voices out there and I must fight the urge to compare myself to others and resist feeling hurt when people choose another vocalist to sing at their engagement. Each bird singing in the forest adds its own song to the chorus. I am my own unique songbird with a song in my heart to share even if sometimes another songbird is preferred.

I have found the most appreciative of audiences in the elderly. I sing with a local Straw Hat Band and we frequently perform at senior centers and assisted living communities in the area. Some of the residents are wheeled in their chairs or attached to oxygen or use walkers and have hearing aids. But they wear big smiles and sway and applaud enthusiastically. They also frequently grab hold of my hand on the way out and say the performance was lovely and how much they enjoyed it. This is music at its best. It uplifts and brings joy to others. I share the gift of song and they share the gift of appreciation and we all share a smile.

I do believe that singing is praying twice. When I cantor the weekend Masses my favorite part is the "Holy, Holy, Holy" because we believe that our voices are joined with the heavenly choir. The veil of heaven is pulled back and we join with all the angels and saints and sing that heavenly song of praise. The energy in the church is very powerful at that time and I feel the Holy Spirit at work lifting our voices up to the throne of God. I feel very blessed to have the opportunity to use my voice in worship. I sing with another musician who plays the piano and frequently get to harmonize with him. Achieving a perfect blend with another voice is a truly beautiful way to pray.

I arrived at my recent voice lesson with thoughts of giving up on singing due to despair over a lack of vocal progress. I left feeling recharged and renewed after a hug and some encouraging words from a wise woman who had been down once herself. She knew what to say to encourage me. I expected to find criticism and instead found hope. Once again, when I wasn't looking for Him I ran into God at my Monday afternoon voice lesson.

Day 1.) Have you ever thought you knew exactly how to do something only to find out that you had much to learn? How did you handle this realization? Were you willing to seek and accept help from someone more knowledgeable than yourself? Reflect on a time when your ego may have gotten in the way of making true progress.

Day 2.) Have you been given a certain gift that you have been choosing to ignore? Do you have a tendency to downplay your talents? Have you been given opportunities to share your talents with others and chosen instead to keep them to yourself? Make an honest assessment of your talents and gifts and ask the Lord how you might be able to use them to bring Him glory.

Day 3.) Does music play an important role in your life? Is music an important part of your worship experience? Do you ever find yourself singing songs of praise throughout your day? Reflect on the lyrics of your favorite church hymn and integrate them into a prayer to the Father, Son and Holy Spirit.

Day 4.) Have you recently had an unexpected faith-sharing moment with someone? Do you seek out opportunities to share your faith with others? Are you comfortable with someone desiring to share their religious beliefs with you? Ask God for the wisdom to know when to speak and when to remain silent. Trust that He will give you the appropriate words at the appropriate time.

Day 5.) Reflect on the phrase "Let go and let God." Are you a control freak? Do you have a difficult time giving up control and surrendering your will to God's will? Do you understand that God's ways are far from our ways? Take a moment to offer your day to the Lord: your prayers, works, joys and sufferings. Unite your will to His will.

Day 6.) Is there an aspect of your life that is in need of an overhaul? Is there something that has been getting too much attention or not enough attention? Have you been spinning your wheels in some way and not getting the desired results? Try to make an honest assessment of this problem and ask the Lord to lead and guide you through any required trouble-shooting.

Day 7.) Reflect on the psalm "Sing to the Lord a new song." Name an "old song" that best describes your former self and a "new song" you would hope describes your new self. If you don't know a song that explains this ongoing conversion write the lyrics of the new song you would like to sing to the Lord.

My husband just bought a new Corvette. It is charcoal grey with a black top and all the fancy gadgets. He is beyond thrilled with this new car. He has always loved cars and would linger especially long at the Corvettes on display at the Auto Show or The Woodward Dream Cruise. He reads car magazines and browses E-bay and auction sites looking for good buys on new and used automobiles. He insists on "Buying American" and this new purchase is the best of all worlds for him.

I am not really into cars and do not care what kind of car I drive as long as I have transportation and it is reliable. I prefer simple. I do not like to read manuals so hope that everything in my vehicle is pretty self-explanatory and uncomplicated. I used to have an SUV, but now have a station wagon, which sits lower to the ground, and is easier for my mom to enter and exit when I take her places. My mom and I especially love heated seats and consider this the only important feature when choosing an automobile.

The interesting thing about my husband getting a Vette was people's reactions. Some were very happy and excited for him. They indicated that he had worked long enough and hard enough to be able to drive whatever kind of car his heart desired. Others seemed horrified. Either they thought this was extremely out of character for him, as in "too showy" or were simply jealous. Whatever the reason it was clear they were definitely not happy for my man.

I was a little uncomfortable with the whole idea myself even though it had been at my suggestion that he had seriously begun to investigate the purchase. The models of cars he had been considering seemed to me to be old and stodgy. At the age of 54 if he was ever going to get his dream sports car it seemed like it should happen sooner rather than later. I figured this was the least harmful way he could act out a mid-life crisis and that our marriage would not be threatened by this other, new love.

Still, I have never been into public displays of wealth and anticipated some negative reactions from family and friends. When we had bought our cottage a few years back one of my brothers had called me on the carpet. I had been discussing my concern for the "unborn" when he remarked that I should be more concerned about the "born" particularly the poor and homeless. Here I was with an extra home that sat empty most of the year when some people don't have a roof over their heads at all. He suggested I use it as a home for unwed mothers or for the marginalized. Ouch! He didn't mince words.

It also made me think about the times I have not been happy for someone else's success. My sister used to try out for roles that I wanted in community theatre and got cast instead of me a few times. I was definitely not happy for her when this happened. She had gotten something that I wanted and I was jealous and resentful. I am not proud of this but it is simply a fact. Another time a neighbor purchased a home over by our church that I adored. It was a big, new, but old-looking Victorian home (ala Lady and the Tramp where the Darlings lived) with a swimming pool and a picket fence. I was assaulted by the green-eyed monster when I heard about this move, not really because I wanted to live there, but just because I was annoyed that they were going to live there. Clearly I was "coveting my neighbor's goods."

So, to exonerate myself from my husband's purchase I started to say things like "I don't even know how to drive a stick shift" and explain that I (my humble, simple self) would not be driving this fancy new car. These comments were really unfair as I just don't happen to appreciate cars. But, I have a great appreciation and have spent lots of money on sound systems, karaoke machines, recording sessions, voice lessons, show tickets, a dance room, musical instruments and other paraphernalia that have to do with music and theatre which are my passions. These are hardly necessities, but luxuries, just like getting my hair highlighted every six weeks and having someone clean my bathrooms and kitchen one half day a week.

I have always justified this by telling tales of how I was a "have not" when growing up. I lived in the low rent district of our parish and was very aware of the difference between our home and my friends' homes. Our clothes were from K-Mart and our food was the Ann Page brand from A & P. I know that at least we had a home, food and clothing but on my little girl scoreboard I was losing the game and I didn't like it.

When I first began working and would grocery shop I was so excited to buy Oreos rather than the store brand sandwich crèmes and Lay's Potato Chips rather than the bargain brand. Similarly, I couldn't wait to go to the fine department stores to buy my clothes and search out name brands that I had never had the privilege of wearing. Now, I am no longer impressed by brand names, but did have to experience the freedom of shopping like a "have" before I could admit that in many cases there is very little difference in the products.

My husband also grew up in a modest neighborhood as compared to most of his classmates. He parked cars at a downtown restaurant to put himself through medical school and felt very behind financially when he finally finished his residency and began to earn money. He refers to this as the "delayed gratification" period of his life and was most happy to join the ranks of those with purchasing power and start to play the accumulation game.

Of course this is all "stuff" being talked about here and you certainly cannot take any of it with you when you die. The one who dies with the most toys definitely does not win. We will have to account for how we have spent our lives and how we have used our time and talents. Jesus warned that it is easier for a camel to get through the eye of a needle than it will be for a rich man to enter the kingdom of heaven. I always wonder about the rich man who went away sad, because his possessions were great, when he was told to sell all he had, give the money to the poor and follow Christ.

My hope is that after my husband has driven his Corvette around for awhile he will realize that it is just a car and the novelty will wear off. He will likely sell it and buy something sensible and stodgy like he was inclined to do in the first place. In the meantime I will try hard to be happy for the success and acquisitions of others. I now know how it feels when people do not want to share in your joy. Maybe it's because they already know that this is just "stuff" masquerading as joy, but it still feels crummy.

The problem, of course, is not in the "stuff" itself but how we feel about the "stuff." God does not tell us that we are not to have possessions but that we are not to be attached to our possessions. They do not define us or make us who we are. They are baggage and we are to be unencumbered by baggage. God wants our hearts and wants to be our treasure. We are not to let our love of cars, homes, the latest technology, applause, approval, heated seats or anything else rank above our love of God. He is to be in the driver's seat of our lives and the state of our soul should be much more important to us than the state of our chassis. We are on the ride of a lifetime and we need to have our eyes fixed on our destination. The hottest car is not going to get us there but the right man in the driver's seat will. Give Him the wheel.

Day 1.) Is there any possession in your life right now that you are valuing more than the love of God? What are some of your "idols?" (power, prestige, fame, toys etc.) If you felt God was asking you to sell or eliminate this thing would you be willing to do so? Talk to Jesus about anything that might be standing in the way of your following Him.

Day 2.) Is there someone who has received, earned or purchased something lately that you resent? Do you feel that life is unfair and that you are not the recipient of something you feel you deserve? Can you place this at Jesus' feet and speak to Him about this resentment?

Day 3.) Can you think of a time when someone rejoiced with you over your good fortune? Did you express gratitude to that person for sharing in your joy? Has this same person ever wept with you during a time of sorrow or disappointment? Have you been this kind of a friend to someone else? Ask Jesus to give you a compassionate heart and to point you toward someone who might be in need of your support.

Day 4.) What kind of a consumer are you? Can you easily separate needs from wants? Can you resist the temptation to spend more than you have or buy something you can't afford? Have you ever purchased something that you thought you wanted or "had to have" only to realize later that it was not satisfying? Ask Jesus today to give you a heart that desires Him above all things.

Day 5.) How concerned are you with what other people think about you? How much do you value others' opinions about your clothes, car, home, children, occupation or talents? Are you more concerned with pleasing God or man? Ask Jesus today to help you to be in the world but not of the world and to seek the approval of the residents of heaven rather than the residents of earth.

Day 6.) Who is in the driver's seat of your life? Do you consult your heavenly Father before making plans or forge ahead with your own plans? Do you pray that your will be aligned with God's will for you? Ask God today to help you to discern His will for you and to give you a distaste for things that aren't pleasing to Him.

Day 7.) Do you have too much "stuff" cluttering up your life? Is the buying, selling, maintaining, storing, insuring, rearranging or simply worrying about the things in your life more of a priority than your pursuit of spiritual things? Do you need to de-clutter the physical things to make room for spiritual gifts? Ask Jesus to identify the ways that you might decrease so that He might increase.

Most of us have heard horror stories about "bridezillas" and wedding plans gone awry. When my one and only daughter got engaged a few years back I was a little nervous about what was to come and what was expected of me as mother of the bride. I proceeded cautiously and was determined that this would be a positive and joyful experience for both of us. The planning of the wedding, which would last for one day, would not override the importance of the marriage, which was for the rest of their days.

Everything went fairly smoothly. We had set aside money in an account for this day so were not "caught unaware" of the financial demands. We knew the reception was going to be at our club, had a band selected, a friend do the invitations and the flowers and chose a photographer. The priest who had married us was willing to come to town to marry Betsy and Tim. They wanted a Mass in a Catholic Church. So far, so good.

It then came time to make a list of wedding attendees. What I had always known would be difficult proved to be excruciating. I have a huge family and my husband has a large extended family. The groom also has a large extended family and of course we all have a lot of friends. We were forced to assess all of our relationships. This was not easy.

We began by writing down the names of everyone we hoped to include, a number too extensive and beyond what the site could hold. Then we divided the list into old friends, new friends and friendships we were just now pursuing but hoped to still have in the future. This was an interesting exercise but didn't really help shorten the list.

We were trying to avoid the obligatory invites or the invites that happen just because people are connected to each other but not necessarily to you. This tends to arise when you socialize with groups of people but are not equally close to all of the members of a group. It became increasingly clear that some folks were going to be left out.

Many of our friends have children who are already married which made the list formation somewhat easier. If they had invited us to their children's weddings we, in turn, would invite them to ours. This sounds a little "tit for tat" but we were looking for anything to help simplify the process and this logic seemed fair and balanced. We discovered, however, that time changes relationships. Just because we felt close to someone a few years ago didn't mean we had the same level of intimacy now.

There had been weddings to which we were not invited that we hoped we might be, and were told by others, noting our omission, that we simply had to understand. The parents could not invite the whole world, we were told, and there were financial and spatial considerations and so forth. We were not to take this personally.

But, of course, it felt personal. It felt extremely personal. It hurt. When parents of the bride and groom host a wedding celebration for the children whom they love dearly, they must carefully select the people with whom they want to celebrate. They want those people, whom they also love dearly, to be there to honor the happy couple. Joy multiplies when shared with those you love. But you first have to determine who those people are. And it is supposed to be everyone.

At this point the concept of a "destination" wedding or even an elopement has a momentary appeal. You can avoid the whole "list" thing all together. But, you will also miss out on sharing one of the happiest days of your children's lives with family and friends. There is a feast in the making and you want it to be enjoyed by as many as possible. You decide to bring on the banquet.

Our list was eventually finalized and the wedding was beautiful. Our daughter and son-in-law are blissful newlyweds and we are now looking forward to our oldest son's wedding. We have a smaller role to play as parents of the groom and this list will be even less comprehensive than the last. It has gotten a little easier though. While we heard a few complaints about our choices and omissions, people generally did seem to understand. They sensed an absence of malice in the list's determination.

As I reflect on this list-making it occurs to me that I have been trying to make it onto lists my entire life. In elementary school it was birthday parties and the honor roll. In junior high it was pajama parties and team lists. In high school it was graduation parties and cast lists. In college it was a sorority rush list and the Dean's list. In the professional world it is "Top Docs," "Top Lawyers" and the "Who's Who" of everything. And, of course, there is always a wedding list.

I have finally realized that there is only one list that I should be concerned about making: God's list. I should be very concerned that my name is written in the Book of Life. I should be very concerned about being among those who are washed clean by the Blood of the Lamb. When the sheep and goats are separated I certainly hope to be among the sheep. I have been told what I need to do to insure that this happens. It is not a secret. It is called the "Good News."

There is going to be an amazing banquet in heaven with the finest wines and the juiciest meats. This is a banquet that I don't want to miss. As the old song tells me, "Oh, when the saints go marching in, oh, when the saints go marching in, Lord, I want to be in that number." I truly want to be in that number. I want to make that list.

Day 1.) Do you find list making troublesome or difficult? Have you ever experienced backlash from omitting someone from a list? Do you avoid planning social events because it requires including and excluding? Ask Jesus for an awareness of anyone you may have hurt knowingly or unknowingly and forgiveness for any pain this caused.

Day 2.) Have your feelings been hurt when you were not invited to something? Can you find it in your heart to forgive this omission? Do you think you may be overly sensitive to situations where someone is left out? Lay any past wounds before Jesus and ask for His help in healing the hurts.

Day 3.) Has it been a preoccupation in your life to be included on lists? If you look back can you see a pattern emerging which equates making a certain list with defining who you are? Have you ever made it your goal to be included in something only to find that once you "made the list" it wasn't worth it? Take a moment to reflect on some of your personal goals and how Jesus might perceive these goals.

Day 4.) Have you ever looked down your nose at someone who was omitted when you were included? Have you ever felt looked down upon for the same reason? Have you ever refused to attend something because a loved one was not included or someone you disliked was? Did you feel justified in doing so? Ask Jesus to help you to determine what He would have done in these situations and to provide clarity for future dilemmas.

Day 5.) Do you believe in a heavenly banquet to which we have all been invited? Is it important to you that all of your loved ones respond "yes" to this invitation? Do you see it as your responsibility to spread the word about this heavenly feast? Ask Jesus, the bridegroom, to give you the courage to tell others about this wedding feast He is preparing for us and what we need to do to be present.

Day 6.) Do you believe that we are all called to be saints? Does it embarrass you to admit that you want to be a saint? Do you believe in the communion of saints in heaven who are ready and willing to intercede for us? Reflect on anything in your life that may be preventing you from being counted amongst the multitude of saints.

Day 7.) Do you find yourself getting caught up in the planning of an event and missing the purpose? Do the settings, the clothes, the attendees, the decorations and accouterments distract you from the real meaning? Do the entertainment values sometimes mean more to you than the true values? Ask Jesus to give you a heart that goes deeper and looks past the superficial to get to the core.

I had fallen and I couldn't get up. It sounds like a joke from a bad TV ad until it is you lying on the ground hurting. I really stink at bowling (my average is 103) and I was determined that I was going to focus and improve my score during my second game at Couples Bowling League before the holidays. As I was trying to stay low and release the ball to the king pin (advice from a fellow bowler) I slid over the default line and ended up on my butt, with my legs up in the air, hitting the back of my head. My fall was not graceful or attractive.

Friends from the nearby alleys rushed over to see if I was okay. I really wasn't sure. They tried to help me up and then I knew that something was wrong because I couldn't put pressure on my left leg at all without feeling a lot of pain. I had suffered from a herniated disc in the past, and the pain down my leg suggested I might have done the same thing again. Not good.

Fortunately, my husband is an orthopedic surgeon and I have seen him go into his "Doctor" mode many times for many people. I had not, however, been the recipient of his look of concern and intensity. His "Doctor" face was interesting and scary at the same time. He had me lie down on the bench where I usually sit to wait to bowl and began to examine me. He was afraid I had broken my hip. After wiggling this and that (and lifting and stretching and tugging on me asking, *"Does this hurt?"*) he diagnosed a pulled hamstring. I tried to sit up at this point and was told I looked very pale and to lie back down. I began to shake and cry. I was in shock.

This was Friday December 18th exactly one week before Christmas. My thirtieth wedding anniversary was in 4 days on December 22nd. My extended family Christmas Eve celebration is held at my home every year which involves about 50 people. Every fourth year I host my husband's extended family on Christmas Day featuring a turkey dinner with all the fixings. This was the fourth year and the guest number was around 25. We were also having an engagement party for my son and his fiancé on December 29th for about 40 people. Following that we had plans to go cross-country skiing up north to celebrate the New Year. The timing was not good.

My husband and a friend led me out to the car the way trainers help injured football players off the field, one supporting each armpit. Once home I scooted up the stairs on my derriere and plopped into bed. We were supposed to go to a Christmas party that night after bowling. It didn't happen. We were supposed to go to another Christmas party the following night. That didn't happen either. My doctor, who also happened to be my husband, told me it would take 4 to 6 weeks to heal and that I had to lay low. And he meant it. Bummer!

Everything that I had to do to get ready for Christmas kept racing through my mind. Not only did I still have Christmas shopping to do but with the kids coming home I also had to shop for food. I like to have their favorites on hand when they come home to visit. It is one of the ways that I try to let them know how welcome they are and how much I love them. I had a new son-in-law coming this year as well as my son's fiancée. I wanted to fill their stockings and even out the gift "piles."

Well, what I wanted to do and what I was able to do were two very different things. Fortunately, the majority of my Christmas shopping was done and the presents were wrapped. It was going to have to do. I had bought a few stocking stuffers for each of the kids and it was going to have to be enough. Similarly, I had mailed most of my Christmas cards already and decided the rest would not be missed. My usual quandary of "Is this enough?" for each person was resolved. It had to be.

A friend expressing her concern and listening to my rambling of unfinished business put it all in perspective for me. She reminded me that Mary rode on a donkey in the cold while nine months pregnant and delivered her baby in a cave. That was how the first Christmas was celebrated. No decorations, no fancy wrapping, no stockings, no feasts. All of the stuff we think we need to do to make Christmas happen is superfluous and frivolous. The gift is the infant Jesus our Savior.

Reflecting on Mary's suffering and discomfort on the road to Bethlehem made my pain seem very small indeed. I did not break my hip or rupture a disc. I did not have a closed head injury. I did not need to go to the hospital, have surgery or wear a cast. I simply tore my hamstring and it was going to hurt for awhile. I was going to have to slow down.

This is when I received the most beautiful Christmas gift of all: I felt at peace. I stayed home and watched cheesy, made for TV movies with my husband on the Hallmark Channel. I finished knitting projects and read spiritual books. I made phone calls connecting with old friends. I taped the Christmas cards I received all over the house and savored the photos and the nativity scenes. I decided to have all of our Christmas parties catered without guilt. I was not supposed to be on my feet and had to let others do for me what I could not do for myself. My fall was turning out to be an incredible gift.

People that I did not even know cared about me called to see if I was okay. Others sent get well emails and snail mail cards. My future daughter-in-law's parents sent a flower arrangement. The outpouring of love and concern was truly touching. My youngest son did grocery shopping for me and ran needed errands. My daughter acted as a hostess at our gatherings. All pitched in to help and all of the family celebrations went smoothly. Everyone was extremely grateful for the time spent together. The quality of the food and the presents was not what mattered. Each person's presence mattered.

What I originally thought to be a misfortune turned out to be a blessing. Like Saint Paul on the road to Damascus, God literally has to knock us off of our horses sometimes to get our attention. Once we can no longer "do" we have plenty of time to reflect and just "be." It is in the quiet and the "being" that God can reveal His plans for us and remove the scales from our eyes. The pulled hamstring allowed me to feel God's pull toward Him and away from the busyness of the season. It may have been the best Christmas present I will ever receive.

Day 1.) Have you ever been "knocked off your horse" by a sudden ailment only to realize that the rest was exactly what you needed? Do you have a hard time slowing the pace of your life? Do you have difficulty accepting periods of non-productivity? Reflect on a time when you were disabled and consider the pros and cons of the experience.

Day 2.) Do you tend to over-schedule your life? Do you constantly make plans and then sometimes wish that you had no plans? When you set aside time to relax does this respite quickly become filled with inconsequential tasks? Reflect on the balance of activity and inactivity in your life.

Day 3.) How would you assess your handling of holidays? Do you set aside time to ponder the true meaning behind holy days? Do you insist on making your celebrations prayerful and meaningful? Consider the family traditions which bring you the most joy and peace and contemplate how you might improve your traditions.

Day 4.) Do you sense a need to simplify any arena of your life? Is your approach to decorating elaborate? Does your gift-giving tend to be over-the-top? When you entertain is it a labor of love or an overwhelming task? Ponder any area of your life which might benefit from simplification.

Day 5.) Have you ever received flowers, a note, gift, call or visit from someone that was totally unexpected? Is there someone in your life who might be in need of such a consideration? Take a few moments right now to send someone a quick note letting them know they are in your thoughts.

Day 6.) Think about a time when you have fallen. Reflect on your physical wounds as well as your wounded pride. Which took longer to heal? Who was there to help you up and help you heal? Have you been this person to someone else? Contemplate the falls of Christ as He carried his cross and Simon the Cyrenian enlisted to help Him. Place yourself in the scene.

Day 7.) A pulled hamstring hurts but a tug on your heartstring helps. Make a list of your most recent heartwarming moments. Think about those small gestures that brought a smile to your face or brightened the day of a loved one. Compose a prayer of gratitude to the Lord for all gifts great and small and ask for continued opportunities to bring the light of Christ to the world.

Growing up in a big family of modest means produced a group of siblings who love to play games. Board games were cheap entertainment as was card playing, charades, sing-a-longs, paint by numbers, car and airplane models and puzzles. We loved *Monopoly, Life, Stratego, Battleship, Sorry* and all of the popular games of the day. My father's birthday was New Year's Eve and we got together each year to celebrate him and have game marathons. The word-game people would play *Scrabble* or *Boggle*; the thespians enjoyed Charades or *Pictionary*; the brainiacs *Trivial Pursuit* and the card players *Shanghai Rummy, Hearts, Dollar Poker* or *Crazy Eights*.

People who married into the family would often comment on how competitive we all were. This always came as a surprise to me because I just assumed that all families were like this. You play to win. Even my mother, when playing cards or a board game with the little ones, would never let them win. They had to develop skills and be victorious on their own. Adults who said they didn't want to play and then floated in and out of the room shouting out answers were seriously chastised. Trying to turn a *Scrabble* tile over to make it look like a blank was not considered funny; it was cheating.

I attempted to pass on this love of games to my own children and found that it worked particularly well at our cottage. We just didn't seem to make the time to do this at home but when we were gathered up north, especially on cold or rainy days, the game playing was continuous. The older kids definitely had the advantage over my youngest son at most games and the lack of victories sometimes discouraged him. So he and I began to do jigsaw puzzles.

We started with easy ones, 100 or 200 pieces and then worked our way up to 500 and 1000 piece puzzles. Some of them were educational with pictures and names of Presidents and States and some were just landscapes and pretty pictures. We had a system of turning all of the pieces over, sorting by color, doing the edges first and then each working on a certain portion of the puzzle separately until we could attach them. The attachment part was really fun and usually an incentive to keep working until we could attach our separate portions again.

This past Christmas was a whirlwind of activity with lots of entertaining, guests coming and going and new family members being worked into the traditions. On New Year's Day, when I was taking down the tree and decorations, I noticed the family game I had purchased sitting unopened in the corner of the room. Oh well, I thought, we just didn't have the right moment for family game time this year. I went to put it on a shelf in the mud room and discovered a 1000 piece jigsaw puzzle still unopened my sister had given me for my fiftieth birthday. It was a scene from the year "1957" complete with greasers, poodle skirts, a drive-in and lots of cool cars.

Billy, my youngest, had a couple more days before he had to be back at college and I suddenly knew what I wanted to do. It had been several years since we had done a jigsaw puzzle together and I figured I could entice him if I did the initial turning and sorting. I dumped the pieces out on the kitchen table, much to my husband's dismay, and got to work. My husband, knowing that once I get started on something like this I become obsessed, just shook his head anticipating what the next few days would be like.

This together time turned out to be one of the highlights of my Christmas vacation. I did the edges and Billy started working on one of the Thunderbirds. We would occasionally help each other look for an odd piece that was eluding us, describing it in detail by color and shape and then jointly scouring the table until the mystery piece was found. Puzzle making is not competitive, but offers a certain sense of accomplishment to the one who finds the difficult piece first. Attentive to detail and with an eye for subtleties, Billy would generally beat me at locating those tough pieces.

My husband used to say, when we were teaching our kids to ski, that his favorite part was riding up the chair lift with each of them. Whoever got to the bottom first (which was never me!) would ride up with dad and have casual, easy conversation. I used to feel this way about picking the kids up from school or sports practice. Those rides in the car were great opportunities to just chat about whatever was on their minds. Once they started driving, those precious opportunities for conversation were lost. Doing the jigsaw puzzle with Billy brought back those good old days.

The conversation was easy, unforced and pleasant. Sometimes we would just quietly work side by side. Sometimes we would chat about his upcoming semester, his plans for next year, funny things that happened with his friends or things that concerned him. His phone would ring and I would smile when he would tell a buddy he was doing a puzzle with his mom. That he didn't seem to mind admitting this made me feel good.

It took us a couple of days to finish. I always used to let him put in the last piece so, in line with that tradition, I left a small number of the sky pieces for him to complete when he got up his last morning home. He tends to be a late sleeper so I had gone mall-walking and when

I came home it was finished. It was a thing of beauty smiling at us from the kitchen table and we both felt a silly sense of accomplishment for having completed it.

At one point near the end of the puzzle, there were two pieces that I could not find anywhere. It was obvious that they were not amongst the remaining pieces because they were a different color. There were two holes in the middle of my puzzle and it was bugging me. I suggested that maybe someone at the puzzle factory was having a bad day and decided to short us two pieces out of spite. My kids are always accusing me of turning everything into a "conspiracy theory" and Billy just shook his head and laughed at the sickness of this comment. He assured me they would turn up.

I got down on my hands and knees and looked for them. I had glanced at the floor previously and not found them but this time I was on all fours intently searching the rug. Sure enough, there they were. They had been right at my feet all along but it wasn't until I got down on my knees and searched with a sense of urgency that I had discovered them.

This is so much like life. Sometimes we can't find the very thing we are looking for until we get down on our knees with a sense of urgency and pray about it. Then, we will frequently discover that what we were seeking all along was right in front of us and we were simply missing it. The thing I had missed most during my Christmas vacation was quiet down-time with my kids. The jigsaw puzzle provided me with the opportunity to fill in that missing piece. It gave me one on one time with my son who had been right there all along.

Day 1.) Are you a game-playing family? Do you have any fond memories of game-playing from your youth? Do you recognize the opportunity to get to know family and friends through games played around a table? Consider adding a fun family activity to your next get-together and potential benefits to be derived from this.

Day 2.) Think about some of the best conversations you have had with a loved one. Was there a particular environment that seemed to spur these conversations? Is this an environment that you can recreate? Consider making quality conversation time a priority and how you can bring this about.

Day 3.) Is there a piece missing from the puzzle of your life? Have you been actively searching for this missing piece? Lay this concern before the Lord and trust in His promise to "seek and ye shall find."

Day 4.) Is there a person in your life whom you may be overlooking? Do you attempt to set aside one on one time for all of your loved ones? Reflect on the quality of your personal encounters lately and ask the Lord if there is any person in need of your attention.

Day 5.) Are you reluctant to ask for what you need in relationships? Is there someone with whom you wish to spend more time and have been hesitant to ask? Do you tend to protect yourself from possible rejection? Take this concern before the Lord and ask for guidance with respect to your desire for intimacy.

Day 6.) What kind of a participant are you? Do you consider yourself to be a good sport? How do you handle winning and losing? Is there someone with whom you avoid playing games because of antagonism? Grade your level of gamesmanship and how you might improve if necessary.

Day 7.) Reflect on yourself as a conversationalist. Are you more likely to do most of the talking or most of the listening? Are you able to remain focused on what the person speaking to you has to say? Are you comfortable with intermittent silence? Have a conversation with the Lord about anything weighing on your heart and be sure to allow time to listen.

Most of my life has been spent making plans and making lists. A common exclamation was "I need to have something to look forward to!" when my life got dull and quiet. I was always looking for a project, something to break the monotony of being a housewife and stay-at-home mom. I proceeded to do theatre, songwriting, recording, volunteer work, join groups and clubs, plan parties, direct, choreograph and generally make sure my calendar was full of activities. Stay busy, busy, busy was my mantra.

Even as a youngster my father referred to me as a "social butterfly." I was determined to be popular, hang out with the "cool" group, get invited to the right parties, go to everything there was to go to and avoid staying home—at all costs. I joined a sorority in college to ensure a plethora of social activities and once married, joined the local newcomers club to again be the recipient of a variety of social invitations. Eventually, we joined a country club and had access to the wide range of athletic and social offerings a club can provide.

Clearly, sitting still and being quiet were two concepts very foreign to me. Moving and shaking were literally what I did best. Once, when asked to participate in a "silent" weekend retreat at a local seminary, I went into panic mode. The thought of being quiet for an entire 48 hour period scared me and I really did not think that I could do it. It was undoubtedly exactly what I needed but, nonetheless, I declined at that time.

Turning 50, joining our parish Scripture Study and becoming an "empty nester" all kind of converged on me at once, inviting me into a time of reflection. Setting aside time throughout the week to study God's Word quieted me down and made me aware of the benefits of being still. My journaling and prayer time in the morning, a daily examination of conscience, checking in with God throughout the day and attending daily Mass whenever possible became activities to treasure rather than obligations to be checked off my list.

This is when the concept of learning how to knit began to call me. My mother has always crocheted and is constantly working on an afghan, baby blanket, hat or scarf for someone. She is a regular participant at the fiber ministry at our church. Mom gets tremendous satisfaction out of making things for others and great joy from still being productive and creative at ninety.

Similarly, many women that I know love to knit and are always working on one project or another taking great delight in their creations.

It had been suggested that I give it a try. My mom had tried to show me how to crochet years ago, but I was not ready at that time for the "sitting still" necessary to finish a project. Now, the timing was right, and the clicking of the knitting needles beckoned to me. I wanted to learn how to knit.

A friend of mine owns a knitting store in our town and had invited me to visit her shop many times. I felt like a kid in a candy store when I arrived for my first knitting lesson. The beautiful yarns on the shelves lining the walls, the tables of women working on their projects, the pattern books and sample garments hanging about gave the shop a warm, welcoming feeling. It was cozy and I just wanted to get a cup of tea and settle on in with the rest of these women clicking away.

"What would you like to make?" my teacher inquired. I figured I had better start with something simple so as not to get discouraged or overwhelmed by the size of the task.

"A scarf" I replied. As a singer I am always concerned with staying warm and protecting my throat and thought a cozy scarf would be perfect. Next came choosing the yarn. There were so many colors and types of yarn that I didn't know where to start. She led me to the sale bin, as this was my first excursion into knitting and not sure what my aptitude would be, probably wanted to minimize my cash investment. There was a slate blue and grey cashmere yarn on sale. Blue is my favorite color. That was it.

Months and many scarves later that first blue, cashmere effort is still my favorite. There are a few mistakes and inconsistencies in the pattern but that first attempt did help me to perfect the art of knitting and purling. I hardly recognize myself now sitting at the kitchen table trying to fit in a couple more rows on a project before heading to bed. Occasionally my husband and I will be invited somewhere, look at each other and shake our heads "no." We would rather spend a quiet evening at home. He loves to read and I love to knit and we are very content just being quiet, side by side, enjoying the peace.

My eldest son was a little concerned about this when he was home for Christmas recently and noticed how much time I spent sitting at the kitchen table knitting. I tried to explain to him that after years of feeling that my value was wrapped up in doing, accomplishing, succeeding and generally trying to make a name for myself in the community I have finally realized that I have value just by being a child of God. I showed him the chemo caps I had made for cancer patients and explained the need for baby blankets when infants are released from hospitals. I was knitting for a cause.

He said that sounded great but that I had always talked about going back to school and hoped that was still on the horizon. He is a pretty results-oriented person and was obviously not feeling that I was using my time or talents productively. I assured him that I was going to apply to a two-year program at the local Jesuit Retreat House in the fall to pursue spiritual direction. He seemed relieved to hear this and satisfied that I had some concrete plans. He just could not recognize this nesting mom inhabiting the body of the go, go, go mom who was once racing off from point A to point B.

Actually, I feel closer to God when knitting than when doing almost anything else. I think of Him as the knitter and each of us as the yarn, similar to the potter and the clay. He is fashioning us into beautiful garments if we but let Him create the pattern. Occasionally we get misdirected and there are flaws in the work but He can undo the flaws and help us begin anew. Some of them just get woven into the pattern as little scars that make it our own and are beautiful to Him.

I have been working on scarves for my daughter and son-in-law and have decided to pray for each of them as I knit and purl the rows. I sometimes pray the Rosary or Chaplet of Divine Mercy and love the rhythm of the prayers and stitches. I'm not sure how Jesus and Mary feel about this multi-tasking, combining prayer and knitting, but I somehow think that they don't mind. Mother Teresa instructed us not to worry about doing great things but to do small things with great love. This "social butterfly" has landed and the knitting needles have become her wings. Little stitches with great love.

Day 1.) Is there a particular craft that you enjoy? Do you see God at work in your bursts of creative energy? Do you derive a great feeling of satisfaction from completing your projects? Reflect on a recent "project well done" and any awareness of God working with you or through you.

Day 2.) How comfortable are you with sitting still? Has there been any recent change with respect to your desire for sedentary activities? Do you invite God into your sedentary time? Review the less hectic aspects of your life and consider inviting the Lord to share these with you.

Day 3.) Have you ever been described as a "social butterfly?" Do you tend to always be making plans? Do you consider having no plans a good thing or a bad thing? Think about your plans for today, this week, this month or this year and reflect on whether or not you have included God, or members of your faith family, in these plans.

Day 4.) Think about yourself as clay in the potter's hands. Do you allow God to do the molding as He sees fit? How comfortable are you with your "pot?" Place yourself on a shelf with other pots molded by the Lord and share your assessments.

Day 5.) Read Psalm 139 paying close attention to verse 13: "You formed my inmost being; you knit me in my mother's womb." Think about God knitting together your bones and your flesh and how wonderfully you were made. Write your own psalm of praise about being made in the image and likeness of God.

Day 6.) Has there been a particular age or birthday which was a real turning point in your life? Was there a particular incident which led you to a period of deeper reflection or introspection? Can you recognize God calling you into a more intimate relationship, spiritual renewal or true conversion?

Day 7.) Is there a project you have abandoned due to a lack of interest or total frustration? Is it possibly the right time to revisit this project? Does the fact that you have left projects unfinished nag at you or disturb you? Pray for direction and motivation with respect to abandoned projects and the enthusiasm and perseverance necessary to complete unpleasant tasks.

"Are you on the right road?" asks a billboard featuring a large picture of Jesus with imploring eyes on I-75 outside of Detroit. I have passed this sign many times and the question tends to haunt me. This inquiry came to me recently as I was reflecting on an accident I had several years ago and how it redirected my life.

The year was 1990. I had been married for eleven years and a stay at home mom for six of those years. Our three children were 7, 5 and 2&1/2. On a Sunday in May, I was driving them to a brunch at my brother's home to celebrate my parents' 50th wedding anniversary. This was before our family became religious about seat belt use. Billy, the youngest, was in the back seat dancing to music on the radio.

We were hit broadside by another car as it was switching lanes to get to an exit. The driver thought the exit was on the right, and then realized it was coming up immediately on his left. He told the officer later that he didn't see our car as we were in his "blind spot." I tend to think he didn't see us because he didn't look but, in any event, he totaled our car.

Billy went flying from the back seat to the front and ended up on the passenger floor on top of the 3 dozen bagels we were bringing to the brunch. This may have cushioned his fall but did not prevent him from breaking his femur on the dashboard while in flight. He went into shock and could not communicate to me that he was hurting when I asked if everyone was okay. He would not, however, let me put him down. Even the paramedic arriving on the scene missed the injury. My husband, an orthopedic surgeon, upon examining Billy, did not.

Billy spent a couple of weeks in the hospital and the remainder of the summer in a cast from the waist down. He was already a hefty toddler and the added pounds of his cast put him at about the maximum weight that I could carry. We owned an old red wagon which had been sitting unused in the garage collecting dust. We cleaned it up and this became our method of transportation for getting around town until his cast was removed. He eventually relearned how to walk while I reassessed the direction of my steps.

Up until the day of this accident I had been obsessed with theatre. After staying home with the kids all day I couldn't wait until my husband got home from work so that I could head off to a rehearsal. I wanted to sing, dance and act. There was an abundance of opportunities at that time for females my age and type. I was anxious to do as many roles as possible while the timing was right.

In addition to the rehearsing and performing there was a huge social element. The cast and crew tended to go out after rehearsals to socialize and unwind. Musical theatre is a very high energy endeavor and it is difficult to just go home and sleep after belting out songs or tap dancing all evening. After watching *Mr. Roger's Neighborhood* and *Sesame Street* all day, the adult conversation and interaction was a welcomed change.

I feel such sorrow reflecting on this now because it is so clear that my priorities were all messed up. My three precious children were such blessings, as was my amazing husband, and I should have been savoring all moments with them rather than heading for the door. I was very much a product of "you have to make time for yourself," "what about MY needs," "you can have it all" and all of the rest of the messages being blasted at me from the TV and women's magazines. I should have been asking myself the question from the billboard: "Are you on the right road?"

Fortunately for me, (though clearly unfortunately for Billy) the accident jolted me into a reassessment of my priorities. My family suddenly became the only thing I cared about. I realized how quickly you can lose a loved one and how all of my blessings had been in a sort of "blind spot." They were there but I wasn't seeing them. My own selfish desires were obstructing my view.

The rest of the summer was spent cherishing all of our family activities. It was a particularly hot few months in Michigan that year and little Billy, who loved the water, could not go swimming due to his cast. This required extra creativity on my part to keep him amused while the other kids were swimming, but I felt so grateful that he was alive and healing that I viewed all as a blessing.

I do not think that God caused this accident to get my attention. God has given us free will which results in bad choices and permissive evil. An extreme case of this would be terrorists flying planes into towers in New York City and killing thousands. A mild case would be a driver using bad judgment and harming one child. God is, however, with us through all of our pain and can use all things for good.

I went on to do theatre after this but not as frequently and not with as much attachment. My primary role was as a wife and mother. I needed to approach this role with as much enthusiasm as I did when taking center stage. The applause of the world is quite fleeting as opposed to the "out of this world" reward we will receive for investing in our children and our marriages. There may be no spotlights, fancy costumes or sets but God is the Director and He has cast me in this particular production. I must make sure I eliminate the "blind spots" and keep this show on the right road.

Day 1.) Has there been an accident in your past or in the past of a loved one that was life altering? Are you able to find anything good that resulted from this? Are there any "scars" either physical or emotional that still linger? Talk to Jesus about any healing which you seek for you or a loved one.

Day 2.) Are you on the right road? Do you feel yourself moving towards God or away? Do you take the time daily to reflect on your journey and ask God to direct your steps? Do you believe in a loving, personal God who truly cares about the day to day direction of your life? Speak to God about your desire for intimacy with Him and ask Him to guide your steps.

Day 3.) Are you aware of any "blind spots" in your life? Are there blessings which surround you that you are failing to see? If you are aware of the blinders are you willing to take the steps necessary to remove them? Ask Jesus to help you to see as He sees and to remove anything which may be obstructing your view.

Day 4.) Is there an activity or a passion in your life that is taking up too much time and attention? If this is a gift from God are you using it to give Him glory? How attached are you to this and is this attachment causing you to neglect any other responsibilities? Speak to God about your gifts and the use of these gifts and tell Him of your desire to balance passions and responsibilities.

Day 5.) Do you get bogged down by the day to day drudgeries of your life? Do you frequently feel that what you are doing seems unimportant and monotonous? Do you resent having to be a nurturer and the one who has to take care of everyone else? Talk to Jesus about your frustrations and resentments and ask Him to recharge and refresh you.

Day 6.) Do you feel bombarded by messages on TV, radio, print, billboards and the internet which contradict your values? Is the person they are telling you to be contrary to the person God is calling you to be? Are the things that the world seems to value different from your core Christian values? Take a moment to reflect on the role God is asking you to play and pray for the strength and willingness to accept that role.

Day 7.) What kind of a "billboard" are you to others? If you could write a message on your billboard to advertise to the world what would it be? Is there someone in your life who has acted as a type of "billboard" to you, a sign directing your steps? Is there someone who sends only negative messages? Think about how the living of your life can serve as a message to others and what you would like that message to be.

An "ah" moment is much smaller than an "Aha!" moment. It is like a quiet "oh...I see" moment. There is not a flash of lightning or a roar of thunder. It does not conjure up the same visions that an "Aha!" moment might like a burning bush or a heavenly creature appearing in the sky or the smell of roses. When people say they have had an "Aha!" moment it's almost as if you can see a light appearing over their head. An "ah" moment is much subtler than that. This is why one can frequently miss God in the "ah" moments if one does not look very closely.

We were taught in Catholic school that every soul has a guardian angel assigned to them to assist them in every moment of their life. The guardian angel prayer is still engrained in my memory: "Angel of God, my guardian dear, to whom God's love entrusts me here, ever this day be at my side to light, to guard, to rule and guide, Amen." I attribute most of my "ah" moments to my guardian angel sent by God to watch over me. Some people call these coincidences or intuition or gut instincts. My mom and I refer to these as our "angel" moments.

A while ago when I was hurriedly backing out of my driveway I heard something tell me to "stop!" I stepped on the brakes and turned around to see a car parked in front of the house across the street right where our driveway ends. I was centimeters away from hitting that car when something told me to stop. "Ah" I thought, that was my guardian angel looking out for me. I proceeded to say a heartfelt prayer of thanks.

Similarly, when walking across the parking lot in front of our CPA's office with tax returns in hand last winter, trying to make a deadline, I suddenly thought to myself "be alert!" I had been rushing to get there on time and was juggling my purse, my forms, my keys and the zipper on my coat when this thought flashed through my head and I looked up to see a big patch of black ice on the parking lot. I definitely would have slipped if not for this warning and once, again, I whispered "ah...thank you guardian angel!"

My mom told me recently of a time when my sister dropped her off at a medical building for a consultation with a specialist. My sister went to park the car and my mom had to navigate her way to the elevator and the correct office. She has problems with her vision and started to see flashing lights and could not make out which way to go. She was wandering down a long hallway when a woman appeared and said she looked like she needed help. The woman then escorted her to the elevator and delivered her to the correct floor and nurse's station. When my sister finally found my mom and realized how many steps she had to take to arrive at her destination she was truly amazed that she had made it. My mom attributed this to one of her "angels."

Another time when my mom and dad left a grocery store their car ran over a smashed grocery cart in the middle of the road and began dragging it along as they drove. They pulled off to the side of the road not sure what to do next. This was before they had a cell phone and neither one was capable of walking a great distance to get help. A truck pulled over with two men in it who proceeded to jack up the car, remove the cart and send them on their way. My mom files this amongst her "angel" moments.

My nephew got a nudge one day to stop in and see grandma. He had been involved in EMS training and had his medical supplies in his truck. It just happened that my mom had fallen earlier that day and had a bleeding wound on the back of her head of which she was unaware. My nephew noticed this immediately and bandaged up the wound and took her to get stitches.

Another sister was visiting mom one Sunday when mom started to say things that didn't make sense. Mom would search for a word but not find it and substitute another word that wasn't appropriate. She was going through the motions of preparing a meal but couldn't seem to remember how to do the simplest things. Fortunately, my sister was there and recognized this as a TIA, a mini-stroke, and got her to the hospital and necessary treatment.

Some people would consider each of these moments just a stroke of luck. The right person or thought just happened to appear at the right moment and provide the assistance or warning required. I prefer to see it all as Divine intervention and answers to prayer. My mother has many people storming heaven with requests for her safety and well being every day. Surely, the people who appear in her life, at just the right time, when she is in need, have been sent by heaven to assist this remarkable ninety year old woman who has spent her life nurturing others.

I was sitting at my kitchen table recently doing paperwork complaining to my husband of neck and shoulder pain. I had been to a body sculpting class the day before and had probably overdone it with the weight training. My husband was looking through the mail as we were discussing this and tossed me a "comfort gel pack," a sample, which had just come in the mail as a heat therapy application for pain. I had been thinking that I needed to find a massage therapist to relieve my symptoms but instead heated the gel pack up in the microwave and set in on my shoulders. I continued this throughout the evening and the following morning my pain was gone.

"Ah" I thought, my guardian angel has come through, once again, with just what I needed to remedy my situation. I could choose to see it as just a coincidence, but these coincidences have happened too many times, to both my mother and me, to be just random acts of kindness. I would have to be a very "stiff necked" person not to see God at work in all of these "ah" moments. They may not be as big as "Aha!" moments, but they certainly serve to remind me that God and His angels are "ever this day at my side, to light, to guard, to rule and guide." Amen.

Day 1.) Reflect on any "ah moments" you have had in your life recently. Do you file these amongst coincidences or God-incidences? Are these rare occurrences or something that happens frequently? Pray for ears to hear, eyes to see and a heart that is open to the many ways God is at work in your life.

Day 2.) Have you ever felt a prompting to assist another person in a particular way? Have you ever felt that God was using you to communicate a special message to another soul? Do you ask for opportunities to be used by God as He sees fit? Reflect on how Christ has no hands now but ours, no feet now but ours and no voice now but ours.

Day 3.) Have you ever ignored a recurrent nudge only to realize later that it was an opportunity sent by God? Have you ever refused to have your plans altered or your path rerouted due to stubbornness or rigidity? Consider a chapter in your life which had an unhappy ending and how the ending might have changed with an attitude readjustment.

Day 4.) Think about people in your life who have acted like angels towards you. Did you thank them sufficiently for the help or support offered? Reflect on the kindness shown and compose a letter of gratitude, however delinquent, to ensure that they are made aware of your appreciation.

Day 5.) Do you call on your guardian angel often or at all? Have you ever sent your guardian angel to assist another? Has anyone ever told you that they sent an angel to assist you? Pray the guardian angel prayer and a prayer of thanks to God for your heavenly companions.

Day 6.) Reflect on the quote attributed to St. Francis de Sales: "Make yourself familiar with the angels and behold them frequently in spirit; for without being seen, they are present with you." Faith requires belief in things which cannot be seen. Take a leap of faith and behold with the eyes of your heart.

Day 7.) The prayer of St. Michael the archangel describes him as one who defends us in battle. Are you aware of the spiritual battle going on around you? Do you ask for this protection against the evil spirits "who roam throughout the world seeking the ruin of souls?" Pray a fervent prayer of protection for yourself and your loved ones.

"Medium" seems to best describe me in so many ways. I am 5'5" tall and weigh 125 lbs. The panty hose package always places me in the "medium" bracket. At 52 years of age I am in, what is frequently described as, mid-life. I was not the oldest or the youngest in my family but in the lower middle. My intelligence level is medium and my athletic abilities are medium, as well. I am purposely choosing not to use the word "average" here because I like medium better. I even like my steaks medium.

Being a size "medium" and "medium" talented sits alright with me. It is being "medium" holy that concerns me. I am reading *The Life of Faustina Kowalska* written by Sister Sophia Michalenko right now and the holiness of Sister Faustina is truly inspiring. This humble Polish nun, with hardly two winters of schooling, left behind a spiritual diary which is counted among the outstanding works of mystical literature. Her extraordinary visions gave rise to *The Divine Mercy* devotion which is popular among many Catholics today.

I also just finished re-reading *Practicing God's Presence*, a book about Brother Lawrence for today's reader written by Robert Elmer. Brother Lawrence was a seventeenth century monk who wrote a little booklet entitled *The Practice of the Presence of God*. In it he describes his conversations with God while working in the back room of a monastery kitchen or behind a stack of broken sandals. This was a simple, uneducated monk who basically tried to turn everything that he did into a prayer. His goal was to pray always, every moment, no rules or systems, just keep conversing with God. He tried to remain aware of the presence of God always, whether peeling potatoes or kneeling at the altar.

One of the women who led me to Bible study years ago had a special something about her that always drew me in. I couldn't quite put into words what it was and even told her one time that I wanted this special something that she possessed. She smiled at me and told me that it was "Jesus." She had an air of holiness about her, a kind of a glow, and she emanated such joy that I simply wanted to order whatever she was having. She told me that she didn't always have it and that her husband actually refers to her in terms of before and after the "change." This was a spiritual conversion, a deepening of her faith and commitment to Christ, which she did not have to wear on her sleeve because it was written all over her face.

When you are in the presence of someone who is extremely spirit-filled you seem to know it. Similarly, when you are standing on sacred ground, you sense it. Jesus described himself as a shepherd and said His sheep know His voice. They recognize their Master. Conversely, when you are in a dark place, and the spirit within you senses an absence of Christ, you know that, too. I have had a bad feeling come over me at certain gatherings or establishments and thought that I needed to get out of there. Fast.

But there are also times when things do not seem so black and white. There are wolves in sheep's clothing. There are a lot of "spiritualities" floating around out there which insert Christian language into their teachings. They discuss the "goddess" within and each person's "divinity" and the "spirit guides" and we need to train ourselves to be attentive to this language. We are not to confuse the Divine who dwells in us with our own divinity. Without God we are nothing. Many claim to be spiritual seekers and, yes, we have been told "seek and ye shall find" but we must pay attention to who is guiding us and where we are looking.

So, to increase in holiness, to get beyond being "medium" holy, I must be very careful about who and what I choose to guide me. I must remember to "Seek ye first the kingdom of God" and that, above all else, God is love. Reading the lives of the Saints, studying Holy Scripture, deepening my prayer life are all good things, but if I have not love, of course they are nothing. If I fail to truly love God, and love my neighbor as myself, in the midst of my pursuit of holiness, then I will not even be medium holy. I would best be described as lukewarm. And Jesus said something about wanting to spit those lukewarm souls out of His mouth. They had no love and no passion within them.

I confided this to a Priest once and he told me that I seemed to be competitive about my holiness. He sensed from the concerns I had been expressing that I was in some sort of a "holiness game." It was as if I was moving along a holiness game board trying to check things off of my "to do" list before reaching the finish line. He reminded me that we cannot "earn" heaven, as we will always be undeserving, and that we are not to boast of our good works but if we must boast, boast in Jesus. He detected a "pride issue" (what a surprise!) and suggested I say a prayer called the "Litany of Humility."

He was right on, of course. He gave me a prayer card with this litany on it and I said it for awhile and then stopped for some reason. Most likely because it is one of the most difficult prayers I have ever tried to say. I found this prayer card recently and began saying it again. It begins "O Jesus, meek and humble of heart, Hear me. From the desire of being esteemed, deliver me, Jesus." This is followed by fifteen other desires from which to be delivered including the desire of being loved, honored, praised, preferred, approved and so on. The litany continues asking "That others may be loved more than I, Jesus, grant me the grace to desire it." This is followed by six other requests to elevate others and the grace to desire it.

I sometimes smile when praying this and interject, *"Jesus, you know I have issues with this...I can only do this with your help...please make this a sincere prayer!"* This seems to happen especially at the line that says "that others may be chosen and I set aside." After years of auditioning in the theatre and praying to be chosen, this request is really contrary to my prideful nature. But, I guess, that is why I need to say this litany with a sincere heart. It is a prayer for a conversion of my heart and its desires.

The last line says "that others may become holier than I, providing that I may become as holy as I should." Medium, less than or beyond, Jesus, grant me the grace to desire it.

Day 1.) Do the words "average," "medium" or "adequate" elicit any sort of reaction from you? Do you equate these words with "satisfactory" or "ordinary" as in ho-hum or so-so? Describe your experience with being average at a particular endeavor and your feelings about mediocrity in general.

Day 2.) Do you see yourself as striving for holiness? Is a quest for holiness on your list of plans and dreams? Does hearing someone described as holy have a positive or negative connotation for you? Reflect on 1 Corinthians 1:2 which says we are "called to be holy."

Day 3.) Are there any particular religious practices which you equate with holiness? Are there particular devotions or religious practices which you find disingenuous or showy? Are you drawn to tradition and ritual or do you have more of a tendency to blaze your own spiritual path? Reflect on those moments which you consider to be most sacred.

Day 4.) Consider those people in your life who best represent holiness to you. What qualities do these people possess? Do you see yourself as possessing these qualities? Pray that you might become holy as your Father in heaven is holy.

Day 5.) Compare being "holy" as in spiritually pure with being "holier-than-thou" as in being marked by an air of superior piety or morality. Society now seems to have a negative rather than positive view of those striving to achieve holiness. What is your view?

Day 6.) Is there a particular prayer you have difficulty praying? Are there particular phrases in Scripture or liturgy with which you struggle? Lay the difficult passages before the Lord and ask for a deeper understanding of His Word.

Day 7.) Reflect on the notion of "practicing the presence of God." Consider Brother Lawrence's attempts to be aware of the presence of God all day, every day, during every task, awake and asleep. Place yourself in the presence of God right now and be still.

I entered the pro-life movement kicking and screaming. Not because I was pro-choice, but just because I did not want to be one of "those people." "Those people" drove vans down Woodward during the dream cruise with pictures of dead babies on them. "Those people" stood in front of the abortion clinic on Southfield Road praying Rosaries and holding signs that said "Abortion is Murder." "Those people" seemed not to be able to talk about anything but abortion. I did not want to be one of those people.

I was in a Rosary group at the time with two friends who were very involved with the pro-life movement. They repeatedly suggested that I get involved in pro-life activities and I repeatedly smiled and said, *"Maybe...someday."* I had actually told God that I wanted to work for Him and use my talents to bring Him glory as long as it did not involve being one of those pro-life people. They say if you want to make God laugh, just tell Him your plans.

One of the two women in my Rosary group, who knew I had a background in theatre, told me she was in need of a program to present to the parish on January 22 of that year, the 30th anniversary of the Roe vs. Wade decision which legalized abortion in our country. She was the pro-life representative at our church and it was her responsibility to educate the parishioners on pro-life issues and attempt to keep alive a passionate debate on the subject. I had been hoping to find a way to combine my love of God and His Church with my love of theatre and performing and this seemed to be the perfect opportunity. I said yes.

This "yes" resulted in a lot of homework. Before I could put a program together I first had to educate myself on the pro-life movement. I began to read everything I could get my hands on pertaining to the pro-life issue and what I read amazed me. My first discovery was that Margaret Sanger, the founder of Planned Parenthood (the largest abortion provider in the world) was a proponent of eugenics. Her mottos were "more children from the fit and less from the unfit" and that birth control and abortion were to be "a light in our racial darkness." She was not as concerned about a woman's choice as she was in preventing Catholic, Hispanic and African American women from reproducing.

I then read Norma McCorvey's testimony, the "Roe" in "Roe vs. Wade," and discovered that she never had the abortion on which her case was based. She gave the baby up for adoption instead. She also had lied about being gang-raped and about not knowing who the father of her baby was. She is now 100% pro-life and wants the truth of her story to be told. She works tirelessly to have the "Roe vs. Wade" decision reversed.

Sandra Bolton is the "Doe" of "Doe vs. Bolton"—the companion case to "Roe vs. Wade"—which legalized abortion for all nine months of pregnancy for any reason. Sandra Bolton's testimony clearly states that she had no desire to have an abortion. She actually had to flee her state to avoid having the abortion her lawyer scheduled for her. She signed paperwork presented to her by her attorney because she thought it would return her children to her from foster care. Instead, this paperwork was used by her attorney to build a case for women to procure an abortion at any point in their pregnancy for any reason.

I kept reading and it seemed the entire abortion industry was based on lies. Dr. Bernard Nathanson, a former abortionist and founder of NARAL (National Abortion Rights Action League) tells in his pro-life testimony that the league simply made up their statistics and then fed them to the American people. Knowing that most people like to be on the side of the majority they simply fabricated polls that said that most Americans supported abortion rights. They also fabricated the number of "back alley" abortions allegedly taking place in our country to stir up a fervor for "safe and legal" procedures.

Carol Everett, who worked for Planned Parenthood before becoming a pro-life activist, admitted that the first thing they were told to do when speaking to high school students was to get them to make fun of their parents. Planned Parenthood didn't want the students going to their parents, when confronted with a pregnancy. They wanted the students to come to their clinics. They knew by their own statistics, as well as outside statistics, that after visiting a school the number of pregnancies increased. The abortion industry is a business, and the more unwanted pregnancies, the greater the profits.

Story after story revealed deceit and cover-ups. I visited the *Priests for Life* website and found testimonies of abortion survivors. Most people don't know that this group of individuals exists. These are people whose parents attempted to abort them but due to botched abortion techniques the "fetuses" actually survived. These "contents of the uterus" are alive and well and telling their stories today.

There are also numerous testimonies of people who are "products of rape" whose mothers chose not to have abortions. One of these "products of rape" is Rebecca Kiessling, a mother, lawyer and pro-life activist, who travels the country speaking out on her right to life as well as the right to life for all. She refers to herself not as a "product of rape" but as a child of God.

I compiled several of these testimonies, as well as those which dealt with post abortion grief and regret, and recruited volunteers to perform them in a reader's theatre format. Not able to find appropriate music to weave the testimonies together, I decided to try and write some songs myself. The program was entitled *Life Stories* and debuted on January 22, 2003 at Holy Name Parish in Birmingham, Michigan.

I am now one of "those people." I am willing to enter into a dialogue about abortion with anyone at any time. I have been seen standing next to a van with a picture of a fetus on it that says "Pray to End Abortion" with a Rosary in my hand. The *Priests for Life* website states that "America will not reject abortion until America sees abortion." I finally get it. The unborn have no voice. We have to do the kicking and screaming.

Day 1.) Is there an organization for which you have a particular disdain? Do you tend to lump all members of this organization together? Have you ever had direct contact with a member of this organization which served to either change or solidify your position? Explain your aversion to any particular group and examine your conscience to determine the fairness of your opinions.

Day 2.) Compare and contrast the "pro-life" and "pro-choice" labels. Reflect on whether or not you consider these titles to be an accurate description of each group's agenda and membership.

Day 3.) Are you familiar with Norma McCorvey, Sandra Bolton, Bernard Nathanson, Carol Everett or Rebecca Kiessling? Have you ever visited the "Priests for Life" website or heard testimonies of abortion survivors? Pray for the courage to approach the issue of abortion with an open mind and heart and study the history of Roe vs. Wade and its effect on our society.

Day 4.) Consider the role adoption has played within your family or the family of a loved one. Try to list the many lives touched by a single choice of adoption versus abortion. Write a prayer of thanks for the many blessings realized by the gift of this one precious life.

Day 5.) There have been roughly 50 million lives lost to abortion in the U.S. since January 22, 1973, when Roe vs. Wade made abortion the law of the land. The "walking wounded," those hurt physically and emotionally from the after-effects of abortion, are too numerous to count. Ask the Lord if there is a person you are in a special position to assist who may be suffering from these wounds.

Day 6.) Our society tends to view fertility as a disease to be treated rather than as a gift to be celebrated. Reflect on being made in the image and likeness of your creator and on the privilege of being able to bring another life into the world. Consider the uniqueness of each member of your family, fashioned by God, the author and creator of all life and give thanks.

Day 7.) Is there a particular organization or cause you have been resisting the call to join? Considering your talents and gifts do you feel you could be an asset to this group? Prayerfully approach the Lord requesting a discerning spirit with respect to this issue.

To witness or not to witness, that was the question. Last fall one of my sisters invited me to try an interfaith book club which met one evening a month at a local library. My sister knows that I love to read spiritual books and am always looking for opportunities for faith-sharing. September is a time when I frequently search out new involvements for the cold weather months. This was an opportunity to spend time with my sister and intensify my faith journey. I decided to give it a try.

The first matter of business initiated by the facilitator was to invite each of us to say a little something about ourselves. She began with the person on her left and asked each woman to share something about her background and what prompted her to attend the meeting that evening. This sharing of backgrounds caused the first "warning siren" to go off in my head. The comments were disturbing to me.

The first woman explained that she had been raised Catholic but had issues with any religion that considers itself "the one, true faith." This got a hearty laugh from the crowd. She is now a Buddhist who dabbles in the spiritual practices of many different faiths. The second woman was a Muslim who had issues with any religion which "tries to convert people." She talked about past experiences with missionaries who tried to shove their "Christ" in her face. This also received knowing smiles and nods from everyone. The third woman practiced a religion I had never heard of before, Baha'i, and also spoke of blending aspects of many faiths.

A few other women introduced themselves. It seemed that almost everyone had been raised in a particular faith, left that faith to try other faiths and now practiced a spiritual "combo platter" of religious offerings. It was then my turn to speak. I said something about basically being "all Catholic, all the time." There was a detectable look of concern on nearly everyone's face so I felt the need to add something. I stammered that it was probably time for me to bust out of my Catholic box and gain exposure to other religions. This minimized the reaction I had sensed but still wasn't endearing me to the crowd.

My sister was next. She explained that she had Catholic roots but was married to a Jewish man. They had chosen to raise their two daughters in the Jewish faith. She still considers herself a Catholic though she does not participate in any particular parish. She commented on not really feeing a sense of belonging with either the Catholic or

Jewish faith. She tends to feel like an outsider and continues to look for a spiritual home.

This elicited more knowing nods and responses from other women present. They could relate to this. Some were Jewish but had grandchildren who were Christian or relatives who had married people of other faiths. Most could definitely relate to the effects of blending religious traditions and not being clearly able to describe what faith they practiced. They joked about the difficulty of having to check a box on a typical form which asked you to specify your religion. "Unknown" seemed to be the best answer.

The last person to describe herself was the facilitator. She said that she is a Minister at a local Presbyterian Church but stressed that her church welcomes all. She thinks of it more as a non-denominational church and encouraged all to come and walk an "interfaith labyrinth" unique to their property. She acknowledged that there are many paths to God and does not try to convert anyone to Christianity.

I felt the need to question her on this. I had never heard of a Presbyterian Minister who did not preach the message of Christianity. I said something about being surprised that she did not feel it was her responsibility to draw all in her congregation to Christ. Did she not feel compelled to share the Good News and "go out and make disciples of all nations" as part of her ministry? (This is called the "Great Commission" for a reason, not the "Great Suggestion!") No, she replied. She did not.

This stirred up many negative comments about organized religion and its emphasis on conversion. Organized religion was purported to be responsible for all of the wars in the history of the world. The scandals of various churches were brought up as well as general hypocrisy witnessed by the women present. Since I had identified myself as a Catholic, there was an attempt by others to avoid mentioning the Catholic Church by name when presenting these criticisms. It was clear, however, that Christianity was the primary culprit and more specifically, Catholic Christianity.

I began to get a very unsettled feeling. It was becoming clear to me what these women were "against" but not really what they were "for." Well, except for being general "spiritual" seekers and desiring world peace. This became apparent when they began to discuss what we were going to read and how and if we were going to pray. It was going to be difficult to find material or prayers that appealed to everyone. Some mentioned being offended when prayers include the name of God and Jesus. We ended the meeting with a silent prayer time allowing everyone to pray to whomever they wished.

The following Wednesday I was discussing this experience with the other Catholic Scripture Study leaders and explaining why, I had decided, this was not a fit for me. One of them, after listening attentively, challenged me about my decision. She was concerned that there would be no one to represent the Catholic viewpoint if I withdrew. She was clearly disappointed that I did not feel up to this challenge. I told her I would take the matter under advisement.

I then ran into another CSS leader in the hall. This was the woman who had first led me to bible study years ago. I greatly respect her opinion. I explained the interfaith book club and how religions that attempt to "convert" were looked down upon. She said that if someone had the cure for cancer they would want to share it with others. They would yell it from the rooftops. She added that we have something greater than that. We have victory over death, the Good News of the Gospel of Jesus Christ which leads to eternal life. How could I not share it? Why would I choose to belong to any group that made it clear they did not want me to share it?

I now had two conflicting pieces of advice: one suggesting that I return and attempt to be a Catholic witness and another suggesting that I not return to a group where it had been made clear that witnessing was not welcomed. I decided to seek out my friend Mary. Mary is a mentor in the faith and my sort of go-to person on issues of faith and morals.

Mary's initial response was that my spirit seemed disrupted. She reminded me that the fruits of the Spirit are love, joy, peace, patience, kindness, goodness, faithfulness, gentleness and self control. She commented on the joy and peace I always experienced when I attended Scripture Study or cantored the weekend masses. These fruits seemed to be absent at this book club meeting. She called to mind our studies of Ignatian Spirituality and the importance of discerning spirits and taking everything to prayer. She asked if I had prayed before making my decision to go to the interfaith book club.

My response was "no, I had not." I had bounded off to the meeting without a lot of forethought as to what I would find there. I envisioned myself as a Catholic action figure named "Witness" who would be able to represent and calmly explain the Catholic viewpoint and draw all to Christ. Even though I had the best of intentions about how I was going to work for the Lord I forgot to first ask Him if my plans were in line with His plans. The unsettled and almost agitated feeling I had from the moment I set foot in the meeting seemed to reveal that this was not in line with the Spirit's plans for me.

History has never been my best subject and I clearly was not prepared for discussions about Church actions during the Crusades, Pope Pius XII and the Holocaust, witch hunts, the pedophilia crisis and other hot button issues being raised. I know that many things have been written to explain the church's handling of these various crises but I had not studied them in enough detail to provide responses to the women's accusations. I was not qualified or prepared to handle the job of spokesperson for the faith.

It was also clear that many in the group had been victims of overzealous attempts to witness in the past. I had to be very careful with my words and my tone. Not witnessing in this case may have been better than bad witnessing. Since my leg was shaking and jaw was tightening and I did not want to speak in anger I had chosen not to speak. An annoyed, defensive voice may have done more harm than good.

I decided that rather than returning to the interfaith book club I would purchase and read books to educate myself on my own faith. My faith journey would benefit more from reading *Rome, Sweet Home* by Scott Hahn than it would from reading *Eat, Pray, Love* by Elizabeth Gilbert. Maybe after educating myself a little on church history I could revisit the group, be better equipped for lively debate and make more of an impact.

I recently asked my sister if she had continued to participate with the book club. She said that she had gone back only once and felt that the group was not a good fit for her either. The last she heard the group had disbanded. Possibly in trying to be all things to all people they ended up really satisfying none. The group had dissolved and my quandary was solved but an opportunity to witness was lost as well. Myself, I cannot absolve.

Day 1.) Have you recently had an opportunity for interfaith sharing? Do you seek out opportunities to learn about other faiths? Are you able to stay calm and be respectful when opinions are expressed which are contrary to your own? Reflect on what went well or turned sour during any faith sharing opportunities you have had.

Day 2.) How well do you know your own faith? Do you feel adequately prepared to defend your faith when it is under attack? Do you know where to go for answers to questions you may have about your faith? Reflect on your preparedness for religious debate.

Day 3.) Do you believe that God is the author and creator of all life? Do you agree with the statement that "God doesn't make junk?" Are you able to see the face of God in every person, even those with different sets of beliefs and those who oppose you? Pray for the ability to see as God sees and loves as He loves.

Day 4.) Are there people of different faiths within your own extended family? How does this affect the family dynamic? Reflect on the positive and negative aspects of blending faith traditions.

Day 5.) Reflect on Matthew 28:19 "Go, therefore, and make disciples of all nations." Do you have a personal desire to share the gospel message with others? Do you consider this your responsibility? Do you resent it when others want to share their religious beliefs with you? Contemplate the word "conversion" and what it means to you.

Day 6.) Consider your behavior and life choices and rate yourself as an advertisement for your faith. If your faith was a product you were selling would anyone want to buy it? What opinion would people have about your God from their observations of you? Review your "product" in terms of packaging, ingredients, shelf life and usefulness.

Day 7.) Do you currently belong to any particular group which is not a good fit for you? Do you continually feel like you are trying to fit a round peg into a square hole? Have you continued your membership in a group because you cannot find a gracious way to withdraw? Prayerfully reflect on your current memberships and ask for help in discerning whether or not these memberships are moving you toward God or away.

"Protect us from all anxiety as we wait in joyful hope for the coming of our Savior, Jesus Christ." These words, spoken as part of the Eucharistic Prayer at Catholic Mass, always speak directly to me. I am a worrier. I don't want to be a worrier but I just am. Knowing that worrying is a sign of weak faith, I worry about being a worrier. I pray that God will forgive my worrying and lift it from me. I long to be protected "from all anxiety" like the Eucharistic prayer states.

Sometimes, the Priest inserts the word "needless" in front of "anxiety" in this prayer. This makes the matter even worse for me. I want to be protected from ALL anxiety, not just needless anxiety. How do I know which of my anxieties are needless and which are not! I don't want to start categorizing my worries into needless and valid during the Eucharistic Prayer at Mass. Since, I am a traditionalist I like it when the words of the Mass are always the same, especially when those words speak directly to my heart.

I can't really remember a time when I wasn't a worrier. I used to have a hard time getting to sleep when I was little because I thought a bad guy was going to come and get me. I still sometimes have night-terrors and wake up screaming and climbing out of my bed because I dream that someone is coming at me. My husband does not find this amusing.

Watching Alfred Hitchcock movies and *The Twilight Zone* were definitely not good choices for me. I can still vividly recall one episode when someone was buried alive. I was also very disturbed by *The Birds, What Ever Happened to Baby Jane, Hush, Hush, Sweet Charlotte* and later *Jurassic Park, Jaws* and *The Exorcist.* Movies about plane crashes, abductions and serial killers haunted me for months. I don't see anything like that anymore but the pictures from my younger days still flash into my mind occasionally.

Bringing three children into the world greatly increased the number of things I had to worry about. Reports of Sudden Infant Death Syndrome, accidental drowning, choking, strangulation by the string of a hooded sweatshirt, kidnapping and a host of other tragedies cried out to me from the television set. It seemed that no matter how hard you tried, you just couldn't protect your children from danger. It was a jungle out there and there was really no way to keep my children from entering that jungle.

There is a painting that I love of two little children crossing a bridge and a beautiful angel with wings outstretched walking beside them protecting them from harm. It is so consoling to me, as a parent, to know that heaven is watching out for my children and to know that God loves them more than I do. I attempt to cover my children with prayer everyday and place them in the Lord's hands and ask His blessings upon them. Even so, there have certainly been a lot of "close calls," brushes with danger, as into every life some rain must fall.

My daughter Betsy rode down the basement stairs in her walker once when she was an infant. My mother-in-law had stopped by to visit and I began to prepare lunch for her and forgot that the gate to the basement was open. One moment of distraction caused a near fatality. Fortunately, she landed wheels down without a scratch.

This same daughter was once pulling twigs out of a drain at the pool with her "swimmies" on and ended up with the top half of her body stuck under water somehow. I looked up just in time to grab her and she coughed the water out of her lungs and was fine...so many close calls.

My oldest son took some friends out on our boat at the lake when he was in high school and one of them cut his legs on the prop when climbing back into the boat. My son thought he had the engine in neutral but it was, in fact, still spinning slightly. A trip to the local ER determined that his friend suffered only from flesh wounds but there was a lot of blood. Having to explain to another child's parents how he got injured when entrusted to your care is even worse than dealing with your own child's injuries.

As a young teenager, I once had to confess to the parent of a child for whom I was babysitting that he had fallen off of the changing table. I had turned around to reach for something and in an instant he flipped onto the floor. He happened to be fine but this truly haunts me to this day. Again, one moment of distraction or bad judgment can have devastating consequences.

So, now, I worry. All of the close calls leave a little imprint on my brain that says there is hidden danger everywhere. When the kids start driving, you remember every accident and near miss that has happened on the road and tell them over and over again to be careful. We hit some black ice on I-75 one winter and had a rollover accident resulting in ski poles just missing my youngest son's head.

When I think about finding God in the worrying I realize that I cannot. He is not in the worrying and the anxiety. All of those nagging doubts and fears and "what ifs?" come from the evil one. The evil one wants us to live in fear and have no peace.

What I can do is turn to God in the midst of my worrying and hand it over to Him. I can lay all of my anxiety at the foot of the cross. I can say, "*Jesus, I trust in You.*" All is a gift. Our children are gifts from God on loan to us until He calls them back to Himself. I must ask myself if I truly believe that we are to know, love and serve God in this world, so that we may be with Him for all of eternity in the next.

Yes, I truly believe this. So, there is really nothing to worry about.

Day 1.) Are you a worrier? Is worrying problematic for you? Do you frequently receive instructions from friends not to worry? Lay your worries before the Lord and trust in His ability to lovingly handle all of your concerns for you.

Day 2.) Consider the Scripture passage: "Can any of you by worrying add a single moment to your life-span?" (Matthew 6:27) The Lord tells us not to worry about tomorrow, what we are to eat, drink or wear. We are to surrender control of our lives to God. Hand it all over to the Lord and believe in His promise to provide.

Day 3.) Can you think of a time when worrying ruined an otherwise positive experience for you? Revisit the experience and consider how enjoyable it would have been if you were worry free. Rewrite the day looking through confident, joyful eyes. Pray for forgiveness for anyone's spirit you may have dampened with your anxiety.

Day 4.) Worry, like joy, can be contagious. Reflect on a family member who may have been the recipient of your worry gene. Make a conscious effort to eliminate the shadow of worry from your family tree. Pray that all doubts and darkness be lifted from you.

Day 5.) Pray the serenity prayer: "God grant me the serenity to accept the things I cannot change, the courage to change the things I can and the wisdom to know the difference." Separate your present concerns into things you cannot change and things you can. Pray for serenity and courage, respectively.

Day 6.) Think of a person you know who seems to obsessively worry about things. Now call to mind someone who always seems to be at peace. Compare the quality of time spent with both people. Reflect on the lessons to be learned from the variety of personalities in your life and pray "make me a channel of your peace."

Day 7.) Consider St. Peter walking on water to meet Jesus until he was overcome with fear and began to sink. Put yourself in Peter's place as Jesus extended His hands to lift Peter out of the sea. Reach your hands out to Jesus now and ask Him to deliver you from whatever fears may be pulling you down and engulfing you.

There is a mean voice that lives inside of me that somehow emerges at sporting events. This is especially the case when one of my children is on the playing field. My general attempts to see the face of God in every person and to be loving and forgiving seem to go on a leave of absence when I sense that someone is harming my child.

I rode a kid once pretty hard who was playing my son in soccer. The moms had determined that this individual was a dirty player and every shove and elbow I witnessed elicited a scolding from me on the sidelines. The player, who obviously could hear all of my reprimands, finally decided he had heard enough and flipped me off. Well, I was livid!

This young man's mother got wind of this and arranged a meeting for him to apologize to me. When I saw how nervous this adolescent was and how difficult it was for him to cough out the words it was I who felt shame and sorrow. I apologized to him for goading him. I was the adult, after all, and should have known better than to push his buttons and incite his anger. I think I learned more from his apology than he did.

I should have remembered this incident when I was getting angry in the stands at another father for chastising my son. My youngest was playing grade school football and was supposed to block for this other man's son. The father kept yelling out, *"Block, #42!" "That was your man, #42!" "Hit somebody, #42!"* Well, the mother of #42—me—did not like having her son chastised and brought forth her mean voice to tell that father a thing or two.

And we wonder why we cannot achieve world peace. We cannot even maintain peace between families on the same sports teams in the same stands. Avid fans will say that you should stay away from the water if you don't want to get wet. Yelling from the stands is part of the game and if you can't handle it don't get involved in sports. But isn't there something to be said for the motto "Good Sports Welcome Here?"

In addition to playing both offense and defense in football, one of my sons was a kicker and one was a long snapper. Fortunately, they were not on the same teams at the same time. That might have been stress overload for me. They both generally performed their tasks successfully but, of course, the successful completion of tasks is not what is remembered.

My eldest son once missed an extra point in a critical game against the team's fiercest rival. The snap was good and the hold was good but my son just missed it left. We lost the game and the comments in the stands were not kind.

My youngest son got called up to varsity his sophomore year to replace an injured long snapper. I don't think my son had ever given much thought to the technique of long snapping prior to this game. He had been playing football since he was eight years old and this motion had come pretty naturally to him. The first snap was over the punter's head and his next attempt was a grounder. We lost that game, also, as a result of turnovers and the comments in the stands were equally unkind.

People love to rally around a hero but when you are the goat you find yourself remarkably alone. This is why I specifically remember two people who rallied around my sons after their unforced errors.

The first was an alumnus of the school, a former high school and college football player, who called my eldest son on the phone the day after the game. This alumnus, who is a prominent local attorney, emphasized all of the positive things my son had done throughout the game as a linebacker and fullback. He also reminded my son of all the extra points and field goals he had made in his high school career and told him not to focus on this one negative moment.

The second was my husband's father. Grandpa attended all of our kids' games and was a fixture in the stands despite rain, snow or distance from home. After my youngest son's miserable debut on varsity as a long snapper, Grandpa stayed up talking with him late into the evening. I don't know exactly what was discussed but heard it had to do with picking yourself up when you have fallen, continuing to try your best and learning from your mistakes. Both sons went on to play many more games and always with a lot of heart.

Heartless would best describe much of what I have heard in the stands over the years. I have been guilty of this myself and can only attribute it to a "mob" mentality. One voice joins with other voices in the throng of fans and we no longer feel accountable for one shout amongst many. This is simply a convenient excuse, however, as we are certainly to be held accountable for our own shouts.

What we seem to forget is that there is a person underneath that uniform, a living, breathing child of God. The individual sitting across from you in the stands is also a child of God and possibly a player's parent or the wife of the coach. (I have also been the wife of the coach in the stands and have heard some pretty nasty things about my husband's choices!)

In the Prayer of Saint Francis, a favorite of mine, are the words "Make me a channel of your peace, when there is hatred let me bring your love, where there is darkness, only light and where there's sadness ever joy." The prayer continues "O Master grant that I may never seek, so much to be consoled as to console."

I will always be grateful for the consolation offered to my sons after some of their lowest moments on the playing field. It is a reminder to me to get rid of the mean voice and to channel peace rather than shouts. In the end, I will be alone in the stands before my God watching the replays of my life. I hope He will keep the penalty flag in His pocket.

Day 1.) Have you ever felt you were in need of "anger management?" Do you have issues with verbal outbursts? Reflect on a time when you said things in anger which you later regretted. Ask God to forgive you for this offense and ask this of the persons involved if possible.

Day 2.) Do you see a pattern of uncivilized behavior emerging when you are placed in certain situations? Have you ever considered avoiding these situations until you could properly control your emotions? Make an honest assessment of environments that are troublesome for you and pray for the strength to overcome this problem.

Day 3.) Are you overly sensitive to things that happen to your children or loved ones? Is it difficult for you to accept that failure and disappointments are a part of life? Consider the expression "that which does not kill us makes us stronger." Place your loved ones in God's hands asking Him to lead and guide them where He wants them to go.

Day 4.) Reflect on the phrase "grant that I may not so much seek to be consoled as to console" from the Prayer of St. Francis. Is there someone in your life in need of consolation right now? Ask the Lord to reveal to you anyone who might be in need of consolation and how you can be of service.

Day 5.) Recall a time when someone offered you or a loved one consolation after a major disappointment. Can you see God at work in the kindness offered and the healing which resulted? Reflect on the directive from St. Paul in Romans 12:15: "Rejoice with those who rejoice and weep with those who weep." Consider how much of a difference this kind of support can make.

Day 6.) Think about some of the lessons learned on the playing fields of your life both in victory and defeat. Compare and contrast your athletic struggles with your faith journey. Do you recognize God's presence in all the arenas of your life?

Day 7.) Ponder the request "make me a channel of your peace." Consider how you can become a peace-maker rather than a conflict-maker. Watch a recent replay of a scene from your life and determine how you could have avoided being assessed a penalty. Review the film, make adjustments where necessary and then stick to your game plan.

A Burt Bacharach song called *Knowing When to Leave* has been playing in my head lately. The opening lyric to the song tells me to "*Go while the going is good, knowing when to leave may be the smartest thing that anyone can learn...Go!*" I suppose this lyric has been floating in my head because I have been involved in a lot of breakups lately.

The recurrent theme of the breakups is that I just don't seem to fit in. I have a longing for intimacy and connection but often feel I am on the outside looking in, even with those to whom I am supposed to feel close. As the lyrics to the song mentioned above suggest, I begin to feel that it is time for me to leave and then attempt to do so graciously.

The first breakup involved a group of women with whom I had gotten together to share birthdays. This tradition went on for several years and the group dynamic was simply not working for me. Most of the people in the group had more in common with each other than they did with me. I always felt that there was an inner circle and an outer circle. I could not seem to break through the barriers guarding the inner circle and discuss those things weighing on my heart.

The second breakup concerned a couples' dinner group and was a little more complicated because men were involved. It was not just my comfort level at stake here but my husband's as well. Most of the people in this group went "way back." We were trying to insert ourselves into friendships that had a long history. I found that loneliness can be experienced in the midst of a group as easily as it can when you are truly alone.

The third breakup was between me and a woman who was my spiritual director. It is not uncommon for these relationships to end when your journey along side each other brings you to a fork in the road. You may each simply decide to take a different path. But this particular journey ended prematurely due to an almost constant butting of heads on moral, theological and doctrinal issues. We were both Catholic, but on opposite ends of the liberal and conservative spectrum.

My phone doesn't ring as often these days. This is the price you pay for choosing to walk away from certain circles. It seems to fall into the "can't live with them, can't live without them" category of experiences. No man is an island. I can't live without relationships and still have a longing for intimacy. But I do try to assess if each relationship is moving me towards God or away and then act upon that determination.

Maybe that is what God wanted me to learn. "Our hearts are restless until they rest in You" comes to mind. I was attempting to satisfy my longing for intimacy and connection with God's creatures instead of going directly to the Creator. He has put a void in each one of us that only He can fill. Resting in Him is the only way to end our restlessness.

I have also learned that I am more of a one-on-one person than a group person. Group conversations often tend to revolve around subjects in which I have no interest. They move in a direction I do not wish to go. I find myself smiling and nodding, thinking that there are things being discussed that might be better left unsaid. I either do not have an opinion or do not feel inclined to share my opinion.

There is also something that occurs that I have labeled "group think." This is when the group decides that they don't like a particular person, place or thing. It becomes important to the group that they are all in agreement about the matter and equally uncomfortable when you voice an opposing viewpoint.

There were several individuals, in each of the groups to which I belonged, that I wanted very much to befriend outside of these groups. I tried very hard to let each of them know how much I valued their friendship and how I hoped we could pursue a relationship in the months to come. As we had many things in common I did not sense that this would be a problem.

I was naïve. It has become clear that a few of these women associate my lack of loyalty to their group with a lack of loyalty to them. It is either all or nothing. I am either one of them or I am not. Fortunately, this was not the case for all and I did manage to salvage a few quality relationships. These women told me that they greatly value my friendship and would not let me go. This was truly music to my ears.

The song that has been playing in my head also advises one to "Sail when the wind starts to blow" and "Fly while you still have your wings." These phrases sound poetic and flowery and painless. But, in actuality, "bowing out" of a relationship and "knowing when to leave" causes pain no matter how you do it or say it. I have hurt others and I have been hurt.

But there has been gain from the pain. I was afraid to bow out of these relationships for a long time because I didn't want to be on the outside looking in. I thought I needed that sense of belonging, even if, much of the time it was a pretend belonging. But, of course, I was already on the outside looking in; I just didn't want to acknowledge it. There is a gain in making an honest assessment of my relationships.

There is also a gain in turning to God to fill the void within me and the longing for intimacy that no one else can satisfy. Scripture tells me that He will raise me up on eagle's wings and that if I fly to the sunrise or sail beyond the sea, He is there. With Him I never have to worry about knowing when to leave or breakup. My relationship with God is a permanent, as in eternal, relationship. Now that is a song worth singing.

Day 1.) Have you been involved in a particularly painful "breakup?" Did you initiate the breakup or did someone else breakup with you? Do you feel a sense of relief about this relationship coming to an end or do you have lingering doubts about the rightness of the termination? Lay the wounds of all involved before the Lord and pray for healing and closure.

Day 2.) Do you think of yourself as more of a group person or a one-on-one person? In which situation do you find it easiest to be your authentic self? Do you recognize the need for both types of socializing in your life? Invite the Lord into your friendships and ask Him to lead you to those persons who are most open to Him.

Day 3.) Do you welcome God into your conversations? Would your conversations change with the awareness that God is always present? Examine your conversations from the last 24 hours and search out anything you might not have said in front of a heavenly audience.

Day 4.) Do you consider yourself more of a leader or a follower? In conversations do you tend to do most of the talking or most of the listening? Are you as comfortable in groups where you play a dominant role as you are in groups where your contributions are minimal? Consider how you can have more of a positive impact on any of the groups to which you belong. Try to see yourself as Jesus sees you.

Day 5.) Ponder the observation made by Saint Augustine "Our hearts are restless until they rest in you." Is there a restlessness with which you have been grappling? Quiet your mind and heart and place yourself in the presence of the Lord. Rest in Him.

Day 6.) Do you have a longing for intimacy that can never quite be satisfied? Do you often feel that you are more of an observer of other people's intimacy than a participant? Do you have a greater desire for closeness with others than they seem to want to reciprocate? Take your desire for intimacy before the Lord where there are no limits to His outpouring of love, grace and mercy.

Day 7.) Reflect on the concept of unconditional love. This is something that most of us seek but are incapable of giving. Place yourself before the Lord and ponder Romans 8:39 where it is written that nothing "...will be able to separate us from the love of God in Christ Jesus our Lord."

A woman from my core group at Bible study last year gave me a gift on the last day of class. It is a daily reflections book entitled *Praying with Saint Paul* published by Magnificat, a Catholic Publishing House. She thought it would be appropriate and timely since we are studying Saint Paul's *Letter to the Romans* this year. Appropriate it is since I use it every day as part of my morning prayer and journaling time, and it has greatly enhanced my understanding of Saint Paul's words. It was a perfect gift.

I think of the woman who gave it to me every time I use it. I'm sure she has no idea how much it has meant to me. A book that cost $12.95, given to her facilitator as a thank-you for a good year, may have seemed like a small, easily forgettable gesture. But it has touched me more than many other gifts I have received, with much higher price tags, because it was given out of love and gratitude.

This thoughtful gesture crossed my mind when I was doing my examination of conscience this morning. This Examen is broken into five sections: Gratitude, Petition, Review, Forgiveness and Renewal. The Gratitude section, which is first, can sometimes go on for a very long time. I have so much for which to be thankful. I began today thanking God for Saint Paul's words in my daily reflections book which really spoke to me. Then I thanked Him for the woman who had given me the book, and her generous and grateful heart.

I was off and running. I had finally gotten a good night's sleep after several evenings of insomnia and I was grateful for that. I was grateful for another day of life, for the very air that I breathe. I was grateful for the sunshine coming through the kitchen window, for the coffee in my cup, my cozy room, my health, my husband, my family, my faith community and my country. Once I begin praising and thanking God for things it is difficult to stop. It is all a gift and I am truly grateful.

This reflection caused me to consider the whole matter of gift giving and how we can distort it. For years on Christmas and birthdays in our large family we tried to purchase something for everyone. This effort became overwhelming and eventually we drew names. This alternative was not necessarily meaningful either because sometimes you would draw the name of someone you did not know very well. You would head out to buy something having no idea if it was going to please the person, and sometimes not be there when it was opened.

There were always members of the family who would buy a little something for everyone in addition to the drawing gift. The children certainly enjoyed these extra surprises but, sometimes as an adult, it was uncomfortable receiving a gift when you had nothing to offer in return. This discomfort prompted the "emergency" gift stash of generic things which might be appropriate for anyone, in case there was someone at the gathering you felt to be in need of a gift. There was not a lot of thought behind some of these gifts.

Our consumerist society thrives on these gift-giving customs. Retailers want us to keep buying, using that purchasing power to keep the dollars flowing. In our family, in addition to Christmas, Easter and birthdays, there is often a new baby, Baptism, First Communion, Confirmation, graduation, wedding, anniversary, house warming or the like which calls for the purchase of a gift. We like to acknowledge and remember each other, but, at some point, the obligatory gift giving starts to feel a little empty.

This realization has caused my extended family to begin to support a family in need at Christmas time instead of buying gifts for each other, a step in the right direction. At a recent family bridal shower, instead of a party favor for each person, the hostesses donated money to Haiti to help the earthquake victims. This gesture seemed like a great alternative to the goody bag concept. Little by little we are catching on to the idea that buying things for people who don't really need anything, when there is so much need in the world, makes no sense.

My one niece was way ahead of the game on this one. For years, she has given me a handwritten note at Christmas, explaining that in lieu of a gift, she was supporting a child in need. What a feel good gift! One brother followed by contributing to Smile Train and Operation Smile, organizations that repair cleft palates in children overseas, in lieu of gifts. This gesture truly warmed my heart.

What we are finally realizing is that the best gifts that we give and receive do not have a dollar value. They are gifts of the heart. They are gifts that say I love you, am thinking of you and celebrating you. They can be a handwritten note, a smile, an embrace, a photo, a song, a prayer, your time or just a thought. These are generally our most memorable gifts and the ones for which we are most grateful.

This brings me back to gratitude. One of the Gospel stories that always left the biggest impression on me was when Jesus cured the lepers and only one returned to thank Him. That question of "Where are the other nine?" haunts me. The Forgiveness section of my Examen frequently includes my need of forgiveness for forgetting to be grateful. Praise and thanksgiving should be jumping off of my lips all day long for all that the Lord has done for me. I regret to admit that it frequently does not.

I have begun to work hard at being aware of all of the gifts that surround me and that I encounter every day. Some of these are tangible. I have a scarf that I love that a friend of mine made for me. My sister made me a bracelet of black and silver that compliments most of my wardrobe and I wear it often. Another sister gave me a book on rhyming that I refer to when I am songwriting. My mom has crocheted numerous afghans, rugs and pot holders that are all over our home. I have received many books from friends that have truly been life-altering.

But the most precious gifts I have received are those less tangible. Faith, hope and love are at the top of that list. I need to express profound gratitude to my God for those gifts. Then I need to start giving those gifts away. A line from a song in *Godspell* comes to mind: *"All good gifts around us are sent from heaven above, so thank the Lord, oh thank the Lord, for all His love, I really want to thank you, Lord."* Give gifts with love, receive gifts with love and be grateful. 'Tis a gift to be simple and it is really quite simple.

Day 1.) Think about the gifts you have received that have meant the most to you and why. Is there a special gift you are still waiting to receive or a special gift you are longing to give?

Day 2.) Do you tend to give as many gifts as you receive or would you say that you tend to give more or less than you receive? Which gives you more joy and why?

Day 3.) Do you have difficulty accepting gifts? Do you tend to compare the value of gifts given with the value of gifts received? Does it bother you when the monetary values of gifts given and received are not equal? Pray for a spirit of generosity and the ability to appreciate the thought behind gifts more than their cost.

Day 4.) Reflect on having an attitude of gratitude. Recall a time when you may not have been as grateful for a gift given as you should have been. Does Jesus asking the question "Where are the other nine?" call to mind a particular circumstance when you did not express gratitude? Tell Jesus of your gratitude now.

Day 5.) Consider doing an examination of conscience. Divide your examen into 5 sections: gratitude, petition, review, forgiveness and renewal. Is there a particular section which proves difficult for you? Lay any difficulties before the Lord and ask Him to reveal why you find a particular section problematic.

Day 6.) Think about the gift-giving traditions within your family. Do you feel the traditions need to be changed in any way? Would you feel comfortable being the person to initiate change if you feel it is required? Consider whether or not love is the motivating force behind the giving and receiving of gifts in your family.

Day 7.) Consider the gift of Jesus laying down His life for His friends. Consider the gifts of salvation and eternal life. Place yourself at the foot of the cross and meditate on Christ's love for you and your love of Him.

Part 2

God Calling...
please pick up!

When I was about halfway through writing these essays, my husband and I took a trip to Florida to escape a fierce Michigan winter. I was still referring to my stories as "my writing project," having not yet settled on a title. I would sit at the computer working and hear voices taunting me. *"What makes you think you can write?"* the voice would ask. *"Who do you think is ever going to read this?"* it would persist. *"You really have nothing worthwhile to say and no one cares what you think anyway."* *"You are going to embarrass yourself!"* *"Admit that you are way out of your league here!"*

I headed to Florida full of doubts and not really sure I should continue with the project. This same doubting had happened earlier in the process and I had been encouraged to continue by two friends who had read a sampling of my work and wanted to read more. Now that I was halfway through my task, and had told several people that I was working on something, it would have seemed like a greater failure to throw in the towel. I was looking for a sign to tell me that the project had value and that I should persist through the doubts.

We nestled into our pew at Saint William's Church in Naples to hear the homily for the Second Sunday of Lent. The Gospel Reading was the story of the Transfiguration, when Jesus took Peter, John and James up the mountain to pray and was transfigured before them. His clothes became dazzling white and they saw Him in His glory. Moses and Elijah also appeared and began conversing with Him. The story ends with the voice of God speaking from a cloud saying, *"This is my chosen Son; listen to Him."*

During the entire homily the priest's words seemed to speak directly to me. His opening line drew me right in. *"Let's face it,"* he said, *"most of us are never going to have Jesus appear to us in His glory, chat with Moses and Elijah on a mountaintop or have the Lord God speak to us from a cloud. But, God is trying to speak with us every single day, in so many ways, and we are simply not answering. We are just not picking up."*

I turned to my husband at this point and said, *"'God calling, please pick up!' That would be a great title for my writing project."* He nodded his head and said yes, he liked that. I had suggested many other titles previously and he had not been crazy about any of them. This was a good sign.

The priest went on to discuss a study that found the average American spends nine hours a day interacting with media. We are attached to our communication devices whether it is our cell phones, blackberries, I-pods, CDs, DVDs, televisions, computers, the internet or something else. The only thing we do more than this is breathe. Yet, most of us set aside little time for communicating with God. He is there; we are simply not checking in.

I again turned to my husband, with wide eyes, and said something like, *"this is exactly what I've been trying to say in my essays! God is with us every moment but we simply aren't tuned in."* He patted my hand and gave me a "yes, dear" nod and then indicated that he was trying to listen to the priest also and that I needed to stop talking. Alright, okay, I would listen but I was really excited.

This enthusiastic priest then told numerous stories that most people would consider coincidences but that he interpreted as examples of God communicating with us. His parents once got two, separate, flat tires on the way to close on a new home. After the second tire blew, his mother turned to his father and emphatically stated that they were not going to buy that house. Another time his elderly father's car broke down but fortunately it happened right across the street from his auto mechanic. Yet, another time, his friend yelled out to the heavens for help with a faulty auto part and the part immediately became functional.

Just before leaving for Naples, I had completed an essay on "angel moments" that spoke of many God-incidences that have occurred to my mother and me. Now I was suddenly listening with complete attention to this priest's sharing of similar moments in his life experience. His sermon was becoming the sign I had been looking for to encourage me to continue with my writing project. This was one timely call from God, at a moment when I really needed it, and I was definitely picking up.

My husband got an earful on the way out of church. *"It was like the priest was writing a chapter of my book for me! I felt like he was speaking directly to me, telling me to persevere. If we found his stories interesting, maybe someone out there will find my stories interesting also,"* I exclaimed. We were both pumped up and smiling from our good fortune. After randomly choosing this parish and this Saturday Mass in Naples, at a time when we were both unsure about a rookie's chance for success in the world of writing, we were touched by how encouraging the priest's words were to both of us.

Our plan after Mass was to head to the local bookstore and purchase some reading material. I had made every effort to pack lightly so as not to have to check a bag, and had not brought anything to read. I headed to the "Religion/Inspiration" section to check out the selections. One title jumped out at me and as I browsed the introduction I received one more sign telling me that I was on the right path.

As this book was beginning to take shape, in the cold months back in Michigan, I had decided that it would be best used as a journaling companion. The idea to write fifty-two essays, one for each week of the year, followed by questions to prompt journal entries, had just been solidified. I felt that the fifty-two chapter, week-by-week approach, might fill a niche with non-daily journalers. It could also serve as a supplement for daily devotional users who occasionally wanted to read something with a little more substance.

Almost near the end of the introduction to the book I had selected, the author said he had produced many reflections during the past year but here were "fifty two" he had decided to publish. That number jolted me. Fifty two was the very number I had decided upon. It worked for him and it was going to work for me. *God calling, please pick up!* was going to be fifty-two chapters long and it was going to be completed. God had my complete attention. The doubts were gone and this author was inspired.

A friend of mine recently gave me a jar of exfoliating cream as a hostess gift. This made me chuckle since I don't really have much of a beauty regimen. I frequently fall into bed at night without doing much to myself at all. The woman who gave it to me is an absolutely lovely lady with porcelain skin who always seems perfectly coiffed. I, on the other hand, am not—which probably prompted her gift. She knew I needed it.

I have never been much of a girly-girl. I buy my cosmetics at the grocery store and wait until my nail polish is almost completely chipped off before applying new, sometimes on top of the old. I do not have pierced ears and only recently began plucking my eyebrows at my hair stylist's insistence. I have been known to wear clothes more than once without washing them and have been busted for having visible stains on an item or two. I also confess to occasionally doing my errands in modified pajamas.

The morning I tried the body exfoliating cream in the shower I was in need of a lift. I was scrubbing away the dead skin cells with a product that told me I was about to "discover a refreshing experience for the whole body."

The label also claimed: "Stimulates...Refines...Invigorating granules take even rough, hardened skin to glowing smoothness." I had not been having a good week. I began to wish there was an exfoliating cream for my bad behavior.

A few days prior I had sworn at the bridge table. I trumped my partner's trick playing a little too quickly and directed an expletive at myself. There was an audible gasp in the room. I was extremely embarrassed and apologized profusely but I could not undo it. I realize that I should not even have that word in my repertoire or floating in my stream of consciousness but, alas, cursing and I go way back. I would like to exfoliate that.

I was driving my mom to twelve o'clock Mass at a neighboring parish that same week. On the way there I was becoming annoyed because she did not like the route I had chosen and kept telling me so. Mom likes to go a certain way to get to most places and always feels her way is best. It took us a long time to get out of church because she likes to speak with everyone she knows and she moves very slowly. We were then late for a luncheon date I had planned with my daughter. I should have allowed extra time, but I did not. I was nudging her along, speaking loudly and clearly and repeating myself because mom is hard of hearing.

No crime in any of this, of course. Mom is ninety years old and amazing at that. I was simply becoming impatient and crabby because I was hungry. It was a Friday in Lent and I was fasting. I then proceeded to complain about how I hate fasting and talk about the things I had given up for Lent. The worst thing that you can do when you are attempting to sacrifice for the Lord is look miserable and begin to cry, *"Woe is me, look at how I am suffering!"* I would like to exfoliate that.

During a phone call to reorder checks from my bank I snapped at the customer service representative. This was a 1-800 call which first required me to put in my account number. Then another prompt asked me for my social security number. There was then a request for my account number again along with a routing number. All of this followed a series of prompts asking if I spoke English or Spanish and offering an entire list of things I could accomplish with an automated teller. There were pauses between each of these steps where I listened to jazzy music. The last step referred me to an actual person who then asked all of these same questions again. I wasn't particularly kind to her. I would like to exfoliate that conversation.

March in Michigan can be a very long month. Christmas seems long ago and spring is still far away. The days are short, cold and grey. I tend to get a case of the "blahs." The "blahs" is a little pity-party I throw for myself. I start to imagine that everyone else is having a wonderful life except me. I envision gatherings of friends laughing at dinner parties, while they clink their wine glasses and have a marvelous time. I enlarge the pity-party by weighing myself or examining my face in a mirror. A pity-party is all about me.

The surest way to get over the "blahs" and end the pity-party is to get over oneself by being "other" oriented rather than "self" oriented. I would need to stop focusing on my wants and needs and think about what I might be able to do for someone else. Maybe someone else would like to receive an unexpected gift, a simple gesture of kindness, and I could help them overcome the "blahs," the same kind of transformation I needed most.

But instead, I turned to exfoliation in the shower. The body exfoliating cream did a wonderful job of removing the dead skin cells and scrubbing my rough, hardened skin to a glowing smoothness. I was working on the outer me and seeing the results of that transformation. But what was I going to do about the inner me. What about my crabby, selfish, sinful self? How was I going to bring about that transformation?

Fortunately, there is an exfoliation for the soul. It is called God's incredible mercy and forgiveness. It is expressed in the song "amazing grace, how sweet the sound, that saved a wretch like me." I have access to the Sacrament of Reconciliation and a loving, compassionate God. I can present all of my ugliness, impatience, profanity, selfishness, unkindness, failings and shortcomings to the Lord, express my remorse and ask for forgiveness. The next thing that happens is the most amazing of all. I am washed clean.

Now that's an exfoliation treatment I can believe in. And it is also a gift.

Day 1.) Consider any behaviors you would like to "exfoliate." Submit yourself to the exfoliation treatment of God's incredible mercy and love. Repeat as necessary.

Day 2.) Have you recently thrown a pity party for yourself? Take your concerns before the God who loves you and lay all of your anxiety at His feet. Converse with the Lord as you would a friend; lay it all out and let it all go.

Day 3.) Are your moods seasonal? Are there certain times of the year when you fight feeling blue? Consider turning to the Lord with greater frequency when you are burdened, increasing your prayer time rather than your pleasure time. Make this the first day of your retreat with the Lord.

Day 4.) Equate the sloughing of dead skin cells with sloughing the dead weight of sin. Consider the refreshed, invigorating feeling of being scrubbed clean and experiencing a glow. Ask the Lord to lift anything from you which may be preventing His light from shining through you.

Day 5.) Think of the many hostess gifts you have received. Guests bring a gift to thank you for inviting them to your gathering and make sure you are aware of their appreciation. We are all invited to a banquet in heaven. Is there anything you would like to offer your host?

Day 6.) One of the most difficult passages in Scripture is when Jesus instructs us to throw a party and invite the marginalized, those who cannot return our invitation. Think about those in your life who are the most difficult to love. Pray that God will provide you with the opportunity and the courage to reach out to one of those most estranged persons.

Day 7.) We know that something must be emptied before it can be filled; old skin must be shed before new skin can thrive. Think about becoming a new creation in Christ Jesus and what it means to put on Christ. Review the shedding of the old and all that must be placed in the discard pile.

There was a period of time in the middle portion of my life when I began to drift away from the church. It wasn't like I made a conscious decision to do so. I just started drifting. Many people that I knew were describing themselves as "New Age" and finding fault with organized religion of any kind. Their attitude had an impact on me as well as general laziness with respect to spiritual pursuits. I was getting out of my faith exactly what I was putting in at the time: very little.

A line from a daily reflection book I've been reading entitled *Praying with Saint Paul* reminded me of this recently. In his reflection on conversion and grace, Anthony Esolen admits: "I too turned a corner of the road, and met a Christian gentleman whom God used to return me to the light. Were it not for that man, that instrument of grace, I would not be writing this now." God sent me just such a person.

My friend Mary and I have been pals since first grade at a Catholic grade school in Detroit. We used to crown the Blessed Mother in her backyard in May singing *Immaculate Mary*. We went to the same all-girl Catholic high school and were roommates our freshman year in college at the University of Michigan. I sang at her wedding and we started our families at about the same time. Shortly thereafter, her husband's job required them to move out of state. We had a long distance relationship for several years.

Eventually she moved back to Michigan and we attempted to pick up our friendship where we had left off. The only problem was that she was a very devout, practicing Catholic and I was merely going through the motions of my faith. By this I mean that we were attending church on Sundays and our children were enrolled in the Catechism program after school on Mondays. But I was not really engaged or passionate about my faith in any way.

Very slowly, over many cups of coffee and tuna fish sandwiches, Mary relit the flame that I had almost let go out. I would tell her that I had a problem belonging to a patriarchal church that didn't care about women. I would complain about annulment just being Catholic divorce. I would ask where it says in the bible that homosexual behavior is sinful and question the church's teaching on birth control and the male priesthood. I basically conjured up each of my hot button issues and challenged her to give me an explanation that I could accept.

And she did. She very patiently responded to each of my questions and doubts with Catholic answers and sound apologetics. She defended the faith and led me to all of the resources I needed to explain and understand the church's positions. I did not even know that there was a book entitled *The Catechism of the Catholic Church*. Unbelievable, but true. I had never read *Humanae Vitae* or any of the other encyclicals. I didn't even know how to say the Rosary alone and hadn't participated in the Sacrament of Reconciliation in years. She had a lot of work to do.

I have always been an avid reader and with her guidance I simply read my way back to Christianity and more specifically Catholic Christianity. Instead of reading Oprah's picks or Danielle Steele I was now devouring C. S. Lewis, Scott Hahn, Peter Kreeft, The Lives of the Saints and anything published by Magnificat, Loyola Press, St. Ignatius Press and other Catholic and Christian Publishing Houses. The more I learned the more I realized how little I knew and how far I had to go. I continue to enjoy every step of the process.

Mary and I still meet for coffee and bagels or tuna fish sandwiches and iced tea. She is my mentor in the faith and a companion on the journey. I still consult her when a scripture story doesn't make sense to me or I am asked a question about the faith that I can't answer, but there is a difference in my approach. I am not fighting her anymore. I no longer try to be confrontational or put her on the defensive but desire to jointly seek truth and walk the walk of faith together.

Our friendship and collaboration has resulted in the making of several Christian CDs. After encouraging me to get involved in the pro-life movement, Mary and I performed locally in a pro-life program which we dubbed *Life Stories*. Mary also invited me to co-host a program on Michigan Catholic Radio a few years back called *Booklights and Footlights* allowing me to review Catholic books and entertainment venues. We continue to brainstorm about ways of sharing our faith and spreading the Gospel message.

It scares me to think how far I would have drifted if God had not placed Mary back in my life. I just did not have many faith friends at the time and was very caught up in the culture of the "me" generation. The themes were "If it feels good do it;" "If you can't be with the one you love, honey, love the one you're with;" "I am woman, hear me roar" and things must be done "My way." There was not a lot of room for God in the "me, myself and I" agenda of the day.

The opposite of drifting is walking with determination towards a goal. In Hebrews we are told to "Run with perseverance the race that is set before us." I am now completely convinced of my goal and the race that is set before me. I thank God that when I was drifting away He sent Mary to steer me back on course. Like the author of the reflection cited above, I, too, turned a corner of the road and met a Christian woman whom God used to return me to the light. Were it not for that woman, that instrument of grace, I would not be writing this now. The Lord truly has done wondrous things for me and holy is His name.

Day 1.) Are you now or have you ever found yourself drifting away from your faith? Was there a particular person or event which halted the drifting and redirected your path? Reflect on what may have caused your drifting and be alert to any warning signs which may indicate the pattern is re-emerging.

Day 2.) Do you believe that God places people in our lives for specific reasons? Is there a person in your life who has acted as a catalyst for your faith pursuits? Is there a person you have been resisting or ignoring because you aren't comfortable with the message they are conveying? Pray that God will direct you to quality relationships and companions on the journey.

Day 3.) Have you ever tried to reconnect with an old friend only to realize that you have both changed too much to continue the friendship? How do you respond to another's assertion that you have changed? Make an honest assessment and evaluation of ways in which your priorities have changed and try and determine whether you are moving towards God or away.

Day 4.) Is there someone in your life you can use as a sounding board concerning issues of faith and morals? Are you willing to seek out a more knowledgeable person than yourself and ask the unsettling questions? Pray that God will lead you to a mentor in the faith.

Day 5.) How well do you understand the tenets of your faith? Do you feel adequately prepared to defend your faith when it is under attack? Do you seek out reading material which explains or clarifies complex issues? Ask God to give you a longing for spiritual reading which will help you to grow in knowledge of Him and His church.

Day 6.) Is there anyone in your life whom you consider to be a bad influence on you? Do you find yourself in situations leading to a "near occasion of sin" with certain individuals? Are you strong enough to say no to invitations which may cause you to stumble and fall? Reflect on any of the "weeds" in your life which may be preventing the good seed of faith to grow.

Day 7.) Reflect on the passage from Hebrews 12:1-2 "...let us rid ourselves of every burden and sin that clings to us and persevere in running the race that lies before us while keeping our eyes fixed on Jesus, the leader and perfecter of faith." How is your race going? What are the burdens that cling to you? Are your eyes fixed on Jesus? Contemplate your goal and the training necessary to achieve that goal.

My mom wrote a poem once about all of her children. Well, she wrote it about the twelve she had at the time, and then added a line about the thirteenth after she was born. The line attributed to her eleventh child, me, says "Teach little Patty to share her toys with Bobby our precious baby boy." This line turned out to be very providential as little Patty, now fifty-two-year-old Patty, does not really like to share.

My friends actually know this about me and have stopped asking me if I want to split an entrée or salad when we go out to dinner. They also know that I am not big on ordering a community dessert and then passing it around so that everyone can take bites with their spoon. When I order something it generally means that I plan to consume it and do not look favorably upon someone reaching in for a share of my portion.

This tendency of mine goes back to Girl Scout Cookies. Girl Scout Cookies were a hot commodity in our home. When we were old enough to have fifty cents we could purchase our own box. Thin Mints were my favorite. I would write my name on my box of cookies and then hide them on the back shelf of the fridge. I distinctly remember counting how many I had left in the box after each tasting. I also remember a few times when some were missing. I guess this would be called forced sharing. I didn't like it.

Obviously sharing was a "big family" issue. Growing up in a large family required a lot of it. I shared a room, a bed, a dresser, a closet, clothes and bath water amongst other things. This reality would lead one to believe that I should be an accomplished sharer. If practice makes perfect then I should be pretty good at it by now. But even though most of my siblings are quite comfortable with sharing, I am not.

Relationship sharing is particularly difficult for me. Intellectually I know that there is plenty of love to go around and that love actually multiplies when shared. It increases rather than diminishes. But sometimes I just wanted to have my mom and dad to myself. Sometimes I just wanted to have a sibling to myself. Sometimes I still want to have a walking buddy, golfing buddy, bridge buddy, special friend or child to myself. And I definitely like having my husband all to myself.

There is also the issue of space. I like to have my own space. Maybe I should call it "turf." When I first began to do local theatre I staked out a few groups near my home and became sort of a regular at these venues. I did not like it at all when my younger sister began to audition, and get cast, at these same theatre groups. "Mine!" I kept thinking, not a whole lot differently than when I was four and didn't want to share my toys. The toys had simply morphed into other less tangible things.

Of course I know that this is contrary to the spirit of Christianity. If someone asks you for your cloak you are to give them that and more. If someone asks you to walk a mile with them you are to walk two. In *The Acts of the Apostles* we are told that the early Christians shared everything they had. Wow. Impressive. I have been known to share clothing or books or information but everything that I have goes way beyond toys.

This sharing issue came to mind when I read the first line of the Mass Reading today. Genesis 37:3 says "Israel loved Joseph best of all his sons, for he was the child of his old age; and he had made him a long tunic." Unfair, I thought! Favoritism! He loved Joseph best of all and made him a special coat! How was that supposed to make the others feel?! Well, clearly, not too pleased since they proceeded to try to kill him. Fortunately, a last minute change of plans resulted in Joseph being sold into slavery instead.

Joseph's brothers did not want to share their father's love, affection or admiration with him. They became consumed with jealousy resulting in a gravely immoral act. They sold their brother into slavery for twenty pieces of silver. Stories that begin with sibling rivalry, selfishness and pride usually do not have happy endings. This one actually does, however, due to God's intervention and ability to use all for good. But today's reading only took me so far over coffee at my kitchen table.

Coincidentally, my eyes scanned a theatre program on the table next to my journal just after reading this. My two nieces, who are siblings, performed a Broadway revue at a Senior Activity Center the previous evening that I happened to attend. They are both fine vocalists and talented performers in their own right. But it is when they harmonize and sing together that they are truly at their best. They have a unique blend and wonderful chemistry during their duets that had me riveted. The talent and joy seemed to multiply when they were performing together.

They were sharing the stage. They were sharing their voices. They were sharing the applause and the accolades, the love and hugs coming from their parents, relatives and friends who were present. This was sibling revelry, not rivalry, and it was a beautiful thing to behold.

This is God's design. God is love and all who live in love, live in God. There are no boundaries. It is unquantifiable. The circle of love will just keep expanding and growing. But we must first open our hearts and extend a hand to either draw others, or be drawn, into the circle. We have to share. Little Patty is continuing to learn this lesson.

Day 1.) How would you grade yourself as a sharer? Is there a particular thing you find it most difficult to share? Has your willingness to share increased or decreased as you have aged? Reflect on Acts 2:44 "…all who believed were together and had all things in common."

Day 2.) Have you ever had a particular moment of stinginess which has come back to haunt you? If you had to do it over again would you have shared rather than hoarded? Has someone refused to share something desirable with you? Consider the repercussions of a single act lacking in generosity.

Day 3.) Call to mind a person in your life who has been exemplary in the area of sharing. Say a prayer of gratitude for this person and the lessons learned from their example. Ask the Lord to give you a generous heart and a greater awareness of the needs around you.

Day 4.) A closed fist will prevent you from letting go of an object but will also prevent anything else from entering your hand. Do you have a tight grasp on something which is preventing you from receiving something else? Contemplate opening and extending your hand to Jesus and be ready to receive what He longs to give you.

Day 5.) Have you ever been a reluctant sharer or the recipient of something given reluctantly? How did the reluctance color the sharing experience? Reflect on 1 Corinthians 13:3 "I may give away everything I have, and even give up my body to be burned-but if I have no love this does me no good."

Day 6.) Have you ever made a sincere effort to share something with another and found them too uncomfortable to accept your offering? Have you ever similarly refused to accept another's offering due to pride? Consider the role of a humble and contrite spirit with respect to giving and receiving.

Day 7.) Is there something that Jesus has been asking you to share that you feel you simply can't give up? Consider your talents and possessions and determine how great your sense of attachment is to each. Converse with Jesus about anything He may want you to share and pray that your desires match His desires.

We are told as Christians that we are to be "in" the world but not "of" the world. We are to keep our eyes on heaven, on things above. There are earthly desires and heavenly desires and we are to focus on the latter. We are not to concern ourselves with matters of the "flesh" but matters of the "spirit." This is, of course, easier said than done.

It has been over a year since I was involved in my last theatrical production. Like a recurrent itch that needs to be scratched, after a year of not performing I get a strong desire to be on stage. A friend of mine recently told me about a new local theatre that was auditioning people for a musical. I went to their website to check it out.

The show seemed very clever and depicted two people writing a musical in front of the audience. The cast was comprised of two men and two women who almost never left the stage, performing a wide range of musical numbers. I have performed in this type of small, ensemble show many times and this one seemed like a good fit for me.

I checked the dates of the show and the rehearsal schedule. There was one small conflict with an out-of-town trip my husband and I had scheduled. I decided I could persuade him to rearrange our schedule if I was cast. He wouldn't like it but it would be worth it. This was rationalization number one.

My weekend was full of commitments and there was only one possible time I could audition during the two day casting call. I had to get the first appointment on Saturday morning or this was not going to work out for me. The director honored my request which took care of obstacle number two.

Youtube.com carries musical clips of most shows. I decided to investigate the vocal ranges and types of actresses who had performed in this production in the past. I found them to be quite young. Concerned about my age-appropriateness I consulted a theatrical director whose opinions I respect. He said to go for it. Poof! My third concern had vanished.

The lyrics to the show were available on line and I scanned them for obscenities. There were quite a few expletives but nothing that appeared sacrilegious. I don't really have a problem with off-color humor as long as it does not attack my faith or my God. My rationalizations were going strong.

Amazon.com carried the CD and I had one delivered overnight so I could familiarize myself with the music before my audition that Saturday. After a careful examination of the text I discovered that one female character removes her shirt to reveal a lacy bra and both females participate in a lesbian kiss. I could not rationalize my way past this.

I canceled my audition. I had been justifying my decision to audition despite many alarms going off in my head but the last alarm was a voice yelling *"You can't do this!"* Yes, I had a strong desire to perform in a show. Yes, the production was to be held in a hip, old suburb with many new theatrical venues. Yes, the timing seemed right and I really liked the type of play being produced. But the answer this time had to be no.

My husband was relieved. He is really not crazy about me doing a show. He knows that it requires several nights a week of rehearsal and several weekends of performing. During that time he would come home to an empty house, eat his dinner alone and spend his evenings alone. He has never told me not to audition for a show but definitely prefers our evenings spent together. Theatrical commitments can be hard on a marriage.

Reflecting on the nice rhythm of our lives these past few months makes me glad that I did not find a show to do. We have enjoyed quiet, simple evenings together and a nice closeness that I know would have been sacrificed if I was at a theatre several nights a week. I sing at our church weekly and have other singing engagements occasionally. That will have to do.

But, this is a dilemma that I face over and over again: I want to perform but do not want to cause scandal. I want to be "in" the world and not "of" the world but the stage continues to call me. I know I am not supposed to bury my talents in the ground or put my light under a bushel basket. But I also don't want to promote vice over virtue. This thespian needs to know the answer to "What would Jesus do?"

Answering this question gets a little tricky. Jesus did dine with prostitutes, tax collectors and the dregs of society. He avoided the Pharisees. He said those who were well did not need a physician but those who were sick did. He came not to call the righteous but the sinners. He was definitely out amongst the people. I do not think this means I am to sit in my suburban bubble and only see likeminded women in my Catholic Scripture Study.

But how far outside of my bubble do I dare to go? How much do I rock the boat? One of my favorite songs from the musical *Guys and Dolls* is *Sit Down You're Rockin' the Boat*. Shortly before that song in the play, Sarah, the "mission doll," is lamenting to her Grandfather about Broadway. She says she just wants *"to get away from this whole place. To go somewhere...where..."* *"Where the sinners are all respectable and well behaved?"* her Grandfather asks.

There is no such place. Sinners are not "respectable and well behaved" and that describes all of us. All of us have a tendency towards sin. We are required to fight that tendency however. Before I venture outside of my bubble, and confront the spiritual battle in the world, I need to put on the armor of God. I also need to make sure that nothing I do will cause any of Jesus' little ones to be led astray. I must avoid that "near occasion of sin" and I know what this includes for me. Seedy theatre heads the list.

Sarah also tells the Broadway folks in *Guys and Dolls* to "*Resist the devil and he will flee from you.*" Sometimes this means not scratching my theatrical itch. At least, it was clear that I was not to scratch it this time. I thank the Lord for making His voice loud and clear when I was trying so hard to drown it out. I will enjoy a winter in the world of my home and not the world of theatre. End of dilemma. End of drama...for now.

Day 1.) Are there certain dilemmas you find yourself facing over and over again? Do you ask the Holy Spirit for wisdom and counsel with respect to these challenges? Pray the words from Psalm 119: "From every evil way I withhold my feet, that I may keep your words. Through your precepts I gain discernment."

Day 2.) Are you comfortable with the instructions to put on the armor of God and to put on Christ? Do the words from Colossians 3:12 "clothe yourselves with compassion, kindness, humility, gentleness and patience" inspire you? Reflect on the components of God's armor and Christ's clothing in which you must immerse yourself.

Day 3.) How often do you venture outside of your bubble? Are you willing to put yourself in situations where you are exposed to people of different socio-economic backgrounds, faith traditions or value systems? Are you able to remain grounded in your faith when confronted with diversity? Ask Jesus to give you a steadfast spirit and a heart which recognizes the face of God in every person.

Day 4.) Name some of the "near occasions of sin" for you. Consider situations which seem to encourage inappropriate behavior and persons who tend to lead you into temptation. Say the Lord's Prayer slowly pausing at "lead us not into temptation, but deliver us from evil." Lay all concerns about problematic situations before the Lord.

Day 5.) Search your conscience for times when you may have been an agent of temptation to another. Review Luke 17:1 where Jesus said to his disciples, "Things that make people fall into sin are bound to happen, but how terrible for the one who makes them happen." Reflect on when you may have caused one of these little ones to fall.

Day 6.) Have you recently found yourself muting your conscience? Are there activities which you would not pursue if you knew it was almost time to meet your maker? Review your pastimes and consider which ones you would keep and which ones you would discard if you knew you had very little time left on this earth.

Day 7.) How often do you rock the boat at home? How important is harmony in your household to you? Do you take into account the effects of your actions on others before committing to outside activities? Do others in your household consider the effects of their actions on you and other members of the family? Pray for peace in your family and ask for help in prioritizing the desires of your heart.

A consistent theme in some recurrent dreams of mine is not being prepared. The dreams have different settings and plots but the end results are the same. I wake up in a panic, quite relieved that I was only dreaming.

The first dream finds me back at college walking the University of Michigan campus in Ann Arbor. I know I am too old to be there and really don't belong but somehow I end up in a classroom and am supposed to take a test. Everyone is expecting me to know the material and I realize that I bought the text book but have never opened it. Sometimes I find that I have missed an entire semester of a class because I didn't check my schedule carefully enough. I am totally unprepared for whatever is going on around me.

The second dream finds me trying on clothes in my closet in an attempt to get ready to go to a party. I keep putting clothes on and taking them off and can't put anything together. I can't find the pieces that go together and keep searching through disorganized clutter. Eventually I realize that I have missed the whole affair because I could not find appropriate clothing. I did not make adequate plans for my attire.

The third dream is actually referred to as "The Actor's Nightmare" by people in the profession. I am on stage in a role that I did many years ago and am expected to know my lines and blocking but I have no idea what I am doing. The other actors are going through the staging of the play and feeding me cue lines and I have no idea how to respond. I attempt to sing lines of songs and remember choreography but it is a jumbled mess. I am disappointing everyone with my lack of preparation.

Another dream along these lines takes me back to my days as a waitress. My entire station is filled with customers, sometimes the entire restaurant, and I have neglected to wait on them in the order of their arrival. I am moving as fast as I can to service them all at once but am inefficient and clumsy. The task is simply overwhelming me and I cannot deliver the goods and meet everyone's expectations.

These dreams call to mind periods in my life when I used to procrastinate. I was one of those students who tried to pull "all nighters" in college and frequently felt inadequately prepared for exams. I've also been late for functions because I did not plan out what I was going to wear in advance or allow enough time to get ready. Memorizing my lines in theatre did not come easily to me and I tended to wait until the last minute to do this undesirable task. The waitress anxiety morphed into stress when hosting dinner parties at my home and not being sufficiently prepared when guests arrived.

Fortunately, I am no longer a procrastinator. I now do the least desirable things on my list first and cannot stand to have anything hanging over my head. I no longer stand in line at the post office on April 15th waiting to mail my income tax returns or buy last minute Christmas gifts on December 24th. I now allow plenty of time to drive to a desired destination and serve meals to guests that I can make ahead of time. I generally arrive early for flights at the airport.

The definition of procrastinate in my *New American Webster Dictionary* says "delay action." What it should say right after that is "causes stress." The reason I decided to stop procrastinating was because I could no longer handle the stress. I was racing to get from point A to point B and frequently ready to pull my hair out when I arrived. This resulted in a lot of speeding tickets and substandard performance.

I also became the mother of three children and had to be organized and anticipate their needs. One of them happened to be quite a procrastinator himself. His procrastination added to my procrastination equaled household chaos. For the sake of survival in our family at least one of us had to reform. I figured since I was the adult it should be me.

As a reformed procrastinator, I now tend to be early for just about everything. My husband and I have been known to take scenic tours of neighborhoods when we are heading to a party because we don't want to arrive prior to the starting time. Like a former smoker having little tolerance for smokers, I now have very little tolerance for tardiness and disorganization. Why can't those folks just get their acts together?!

This intolerance is something I have to learn to overcome. People do march to the beat of different drummers and some of those rhythms are simply slower than others. After repeatedly becoming annoyed because a particular friend kept me waiting at restaurants I discovered that she had a health issue which made it difficult for her to move quickly. She had a legitimate reason for her tardiness and I needed to be understanding.

One of my most embarrassing moments occurred as a result of my lack of understanding. My husband and I decided to play golf one afternoon and I was to meet him on the first tee after he went to the locker room to change his shoes. The course was wide open at first, but, as I continued to kill time on the putting green, several golfers showed up and teed off. We were now going to be behind several groups instead of being able to sail around as I had initially hoped. I envisioned him up in the men's locker room shooting the breeze with his buddies and enjoying some laughs. I was not amused by this delay.

Eventually he sauntered out to the tee looking freshly showered and wearing a different set of clothes. I was no longer feeling fresh at all and was wearing my angry face. I began to blast him with questions about his delay of action and apparent lack of consideration. He wondered how I could not have heard the sirens approaching and stopping in front of the club. He had spent the last forty five minutes saving a man's life he had found ashen on the floor of the men's locker room.

Oh, I mumbled, suddenly becoming quiet. I was worried about teeing off ahead of the crowd and he was upstairs administering CPR to a fellow club member. He kept a man alive doing mouth to mouth resuscitation until an ambulance arrived with the proper equipment. I had assumed that this delay was due to dallying with his friends. It was actually the opposite of procrastination. It was prioritization.

I have been a procrastinator and have kept people waiting. I have been unprepared and disorganized. I was one of those bridesmaids who did not have oil in her lamp when the Bridegroom was coming. Now, after attempting to correct most of these behaviors, I need to be tolerant of other procrastinators. It may well be that they just have a different set of priorities. Most importantly, I need to be extremely grateful that while I was still a procrastinator God loved me. May I not procrastinate in returning that love to Him.

Day 1.) Are you now or have you ever been a procrastinator? Was there a turning point that you can recall that caused you to change your behavior? Is there someone in your life who has a tendency to procrastinate? How do you respond to this tendency? Ask Jesus for a compassionate heart towards those less organized and punctual than yourself.

Day 2.) Do you have any recurrent dreams? Do they represent any aspect of your life that needs attention? Are their certain people that tend to appear often in your dreams? Have you ever felt that God was speaking to you through dreams? Ask God to open your mind and heart to anything that your dreams may be able to teach you.

Day 3.) Do you make "to do" lists? Do you generally do the least desirable or most desirable things first? Is spending time with God something that makes it to your "to do" list? Do you consider prayer time a desirable or undesirable task? Do you ever ask God how you can serve Him or what He would like you "to do" for Him? Try to quiet your mind and let God lead you to how you might serve Him today.

Day 4.) How tolerant of a person are you? Is there someone in your household or close to you whose behavior pushes your buttons? Why do you think this particular behavior bothers you so much? Is it possible that you have a tendency towards this behavior also? Pray about becoming a more tolerant and loving person.

Day 5.) Can you think of a time when you jumped to false conclusions before giving another person a chance to explain? Is it easy or difficult for you to give a person the benefit of the doubt? Is it easy or difficult for you to apologize when you are wrong? Has someone been quick to judge you before you were given a chance to explain? Ask Jesus to give you eyes to see, ears to hear and lips to speak truth.

Day 6.) How are your time-management skills? Do you consider yourself to be an organized person? Do you generally feel that your priorities are in order? Have you ever been burned as a result of lack of preparedness? Have you ever missed an important deadline resulting in a missed opportunity? Since time is a gift from God ask Him to help you to make your best use of it in ways that give Him glory.

Day 7.) When you hear the parable of the ten virgins who took their lamps and went out to meet the bridegroom, how do you react? Do you align yourself with the five who brought oil for their lamps or the five who did not? When the bridegroom comes and welcomes those who were ready into the wedding feast with Him on what side of the locked door do you find yourself? Reflect on the final line of this parable "Therefore, stay awake, for you know neither the day nor the hour."

Fred Rogers used to sing a song in his happy neighborhood about waiting. It went something like this: "Let's think of something to do while we're waiting, while we're waiting, think of something to do." I haven't watched *Mister Roger's Neighborhood* in over a dozen years but I frequently find myself humming this little ditty. I have trouble with waiting.

About midway through my life I overcame a procrastination and tardiness issue and now I am almost always early. I am talking about being almost embarrassingly early. I frequently wait in my car until the appropriate arrival time not wanting to interfere with a hostess who is still making preparations for her guests. I have such a reputation for being early that if I am 3 to 5 minutes late people will call my cell phone to make sure that everything is okay. I just don't like to keep people waiting because I don't like to wait.

The problem with being early is that when things don't run on time you have doubled the amount of time you will spend waiting. Recently I was on an airplane that was delayed over an hour due to some paperwork issue. I was crammed in a middle seat surrounded by loud talkers, feeling slightly claustrophobic, and annoyed that the pilot kept thanking me for my patience. Like I had a choice! I had already been at the airport for three and a half hours and we hadn't even been de-iced yet.

I generally don't mind waiting my turn for service as long as the line is clearly established and the person providing the service is working to the best of their abilities. I do mind a salesperson enjoying a personal phone call or having a long, not work related conversation with someone while I am waiting. I also definitely mind people taking cuts, or salespeople helping the first person who gets their attention rather than the person who has been waiting the longest.

My children know that these things annoy me and strongly encourage me not to say anything. They will watch me get agitated and knowing that I am about to say, *"Excuse me, I believe I was next!"* whisper, *"Mom, don't say anything!"* Sometimes I will listen to them and sometimes my desire to speak overrides their non-confrontational natures.

I am very understanding when waitpersons are busy and can't get to me right away. It is easy to deduce in a crowded restaurant that one of the waitpersons hustling back and forth is probably assigned to me. But, I do appreciate it when they at least introduce themselves and say they will be with me shortly. It is the "no eye contact I'm going to ignore you until I'm ready" that really bugs me. It is nice to be acknowledged and at least know help is on the way.

Since I don't work outside of the home, I have the benefit of being able to choose the best hours to run errands and make appointments to minimize the amount of time I have to spend waiting. I choose these carefully. I also choose business professionals based on reputations for being prompt and running on time. Some people are known for making you wait and I definitely avoid interaction with those people when possible.

Waiting at the doctor's office seems to be on most people's list of least favorite things to do. My husband, an orthopedic surgeon, knows this and makes every effort to run his office on time. Occasionally, due to extra people being worked in or a complaint of leg pain which turns out to be a tumor, he gets behind schedule. He has actually walked out to the waiting room and apologized for the delays and invited anyone unable to wait to reschedule. Like me in a busy restaurant just wanting to be acknowledged by my waiter, most patients appreciate this courtesy. They want their time to be respected.

Despite an aversion to waiting and all efforts to avoid it, most of us will spend large chunks of our days in line for something. We wait at the Secretary of State office. We wait at the bank and the grocery store. We wait in traffic. We wait for correspondence and get put on hold. We wait for answers, for good news and bad news. I had an uncle in a nursing home a few years back who was literally waiting to die. He could not understand why God would not just come and take him. He waited for several years before God decided his time had come.

The Gospel Reading for the Fourth Sunday of Lent got me thinking about waiting recently. It was the story of the prodigal son which of course, I had heard many times before. But this time there was a phrase that jumped out at me. "While he was still a long way off, his father caught sight of him, and was filled with compassion. He ran to his son, embraced him and kissed him." The father catching sight of him "while he was still a long way off" implied to me that he was looking for him, that he was waiting for his return. Since the father in this story is synonymous with God, our heavenly father, it reminded me that my God is waiting and watching for me.

Lenten hymns are full of the theme of returning to God. A song called "Hosea" tells us "Long have I waited for your coming home to me and living deeply our new life." What is even better than hearing that the father was looking and waiting for the son is the fact that when he caught sight of him he ran to the son. He had waited a long time for his return and now that he saw him in the distance he was not going to wait any longer. The longing was over. It was time for the embrace and the kiss.

When my God is so patient with me, my tendency towards impatience is embarrassing to say the least. He has waited through my party girl phase, my rebellious phase, my "if I want it I'm going to have it" self indulgent phase and many other prodigal like phases. I have squandered goods and been a pleasure seeker much like the prodigal in the story. The words "Come back to me with all your heart, don't let fear keep us apart" in the Hosea song are truly a balm for a repentant heart.

I now have an answer for the "Let's think of something to do while we're waiting" song. How about pray. How about get my life in order. How about make myself a channel of God's peace when the tension, agitation and conflicts rear their ugly heads. I think that would work well in Mr. Roger's Neighborhood. I think it would work in mine as well.

Day 1.) How patient of a person do you consider yourself to be? Do you have issues with waiting? Do you try to anticipate when you will be waiting and plan "something to do while you're waiting?" What is your least favorite place to have to wait? Reflect on the times you have been patient versus impatient and how God might have been at work in your attitude and reactions.

Day 2.) Can you think of a time when someone has been incredibly patient with you? Do you feel like you deserved this kindness? Did you let the person know that you were appreciative? Did it inspire you to want to return the kindness to this person or to another person? Ask the Lord to help you always to "wait in joyful hope" and to show gratitude to those who are waiting on you.

Day 3.) What is your typical reaction to the prodigal son story? Do you see yourself as the prodigal, the elder brother or the father? Do you find the action in the story fair? Can you envision God as the loving father who, while you were a long way off, sees you and runs to embrace you? Place yourself in the embrace of the father and consider what you would say to Him and Him to you.

Day 4.) "Come back to me with all your heart, don't let fear keep us apart. Long have I waited for your coming home to me and living deeply our new life." Do these words from the song Hosea speak to you in any particular way? Do the general themes of returning to God in the Lenten Hymns call you? Can you easily believe in a loving, personal God who has a longing for you? Reflect on ways you have been holding yourself back from God and ask for help in removing these barriers.

Day 5.) Do you consider yourself to be a confrontational person? How do you feel about someone taking cuts in front of you in line or someone making you wait unnecessarily? Have you ever chastised someone for these behaviors? How did you feel after you did so? Pray for the wisdom to know when to speak and when to remain silent.

Day 6.) Is there someone in your life who always makes you wait? Can you accept this about this person? Are you this person to someone else? Do you consider yourself respectful of other people's time? Thank God for the gift of time and another day of life and ask Him how to use your time more wisely.

Day 7.) Reflect on how you have used your time and talents thus far in your life. Have you squandered them or developed them? Considering that you are a work in progress what kind of grade would you give yourself? If God decided to call you home today would you feel ready or like you needed more time? God is waiting and anticipating your return to Him. Search your heart for what you need to do while you await His call.

One of our more enthusiastic leaders at Bible Study recently suggested we use a God Box as a conversation starter. A God Box is filled with objects from everyday life. It parallels how Jesus often spoke in parables to explain the Kingdom of Heaven. Jesus would say that the Kingdom of Heaven is like yeast or the Kingdom of Heaven is like a sower of seeds. A God Box is a way of creating a modern parable. The Bible Study facilitators each filled a box with different household items. They then asked members of their group to select an item and tell everyone how God is like that object.

The exercise was very interesting. One person chose an eraser and then explained that God is like an eraser, erasing all of our mistakes. A pair of eyeglasses prompted the response that God is like this pair of glasses helping us to see things. An ace bandage elicited a comment about God wrapping up our wounds and helping us to heal. As I was looking through my junk drawer at home I found an old cell phone and threw that in the mix. One woman reached for the phone enthusiastically saying that she has felt like God has been calling her this entire year into a deepening of her faith.

One smart student commented on how God is not like the box at all because you can't put God in a box. Clever! God is infinite and unquantifiable and all-encompassing. But I would take that one step further and assert that the entire world is a God Box because He made everything in it. He is the uncaused cause, the alpha and the omega. He is the author and creator of all life and everything present in the world. It should, therefore, be very easy to find God in all things if we but take the time to look.

Herein lies the problem. Many of us aren't looking. Those that are looking must constantly contend with a society that wants to take God out of the equation. Not only do they not want to acknowledge that God is our creator but they really don't want His name mentioned at all. No prayer in schools, no "In God We Trust," no "Ten Commandments" in public buildings, no "one nation under God" in the Pledge of Allegiance, no Judeo-Christian references at all. God made the box but there is to be no mention of God within the box.

The readings at Mass these past few weeks have primarily been from the Acts of the Apostles. These scripture stories are truly inspiring. Saint Peter, Saint Paul, Saint John and other disciples of Jesus are filled with the Holy Spirit and boldly preaching the Good News of the life, death and resurrection of Christ. They are grateful for the opportunity to suffer for the sake of Christ. They point all healings and miraculous events occurring in their midst back to God who is deserving of all praise and glory. All is being done in His Holy Name and all else is rubbish compared to the love, grace and mercy of God.

These readings should serve as a call for all believers to be bolder. Our country was founded on Judeo-Christian principles and we should not stand by and let our voices be silenced. We are supposed to have freedom to practice religion not freedom from religion. The separation of church and state proponents keep using their platform to squelch our religious freedoms. A quick review of history would reveal a different intent. We need to make conscious efforts to put God back in the equation.

In the Mass reading for today the leaders, elders and scribes warned Saint Peter and Saint John to never again speak to anyone in Jesus' name. Acts 4:13 first tells us "Observing the boldness of Peter and John and perceiving them to be uneducated, ordinary men, the leaders, elders and scribes were amazed" as these simple men had just healed a man crippled from birth. They were threatened by these remarkable signs and ordered them not to speak or teach at all in the name of Jesus. Peter and John responded that "It is impossible for us not to speak about what we have seen and heard." (Acts 4:20)

This response to the attempt to silence them inspires me. In a culture that now refers to the Easter Bunny as "Spring Bunny" and encourages "Happy Holidays" instead of Merry Christmas I see a need to reinsert God into His world. If I can't find a nativity scene in the public square then I definitely need to have one on my front stoop. If I can't hear Christmas Carols in the mall or on public streets then I definitely need to be singing them with my family and friends at private gatherings. My response to a society that tells me it prefers that religion not be discussed in public is to ignore that advice.

A friend of mine recently told me that she had prayed for me that morning. My name came to her as she was asking the Lord who was in need of prayer that day. I was touched by this. I, too, am not afraid to tell someone "I said a prayer for you today." I am also not afraid to say "God bless you" or "Aren't we blessed!" or "How good is God!" I love it when I am dining out with friends and they suggest that we say a blessing over our food. Yes, even in public we will bow our heads and thank God for the food we are about to eat and the hands that prepared it. It is a small and quick opportunity to witness, but it is an opportunity nonetheless.

The God Box project got me thinking about all of this. Once you start looking for God in all things and pondering how God is reflected in everything it is hard to stop. This morning when my alarm went off I considered how God is like that alarm nudging me to wake up, be alert and get going. Then when I had my coffee and roll I thought about how God is our spiritual food and drink. The salt and pepper shakers on the table and the light above my head reminded me how God is the salt of the earth and the light of the world. This is a great spiritual exercise and God is like exercise working our spiritual muscles. Okay I'll stop. But I encourage you to try the God Box project. And try not to be silent about it.

Day 1.) Do you make a conscious effort to find God in all things? Take a few moments to reflect on your surroundings and pray for an awareness of the many ways God is making His presence known to you.

Day 2.) Do you hesitate to mention God or discuss God in public? Do you ever pray with a friend over an issue of mutual concern? Are you embarrassed or put off by those who are not afraid to worship publicly? Discuss your concerns with the Lord and ask for a courageous faith.

Day 3.) The definitions of "bold" include "daring, brave and courageous" as well as "overstepping usual bounds, forward and impudent." When scripture tells of the apostles boldly proclaiming the good news it is to serve as a positive example for us. Consider an area of your life where you could stand to be bolder.

Day 4.) Pictures of your loved ones around your home serve to remind you of them and encourage you to pray for them. Similarly prayer cards, a crucifix or religious icons can serve to remind us of the Lord's presence and invite us into communion with Him. Do you have reminders of the Lord within view?

Day 5.) Atheism, agnosticism and secularism seem to be on the rise in our country as well as strong anti-religious sentiments. Have you personally felt pressure to be silent about your religious beliefs and practices? Reflect on a time you may have succumbed to peer pressure to play down your love of God and His church.

Day 6.) Have you ever had someone ask to pray over you or a loved one? Is praying over another something you are comfortable doing? Reflect on the passage from Matthew 18: 19-20 "whenever two of you on earth agree about anything you pray for, it will be done for you by my father in heaven. For where two or three come together in my name, I am there with them."

Day 7.) Consider putting together a "God Box" gift for a friend. Include a spiritual book, CD, prayer card, Rosary, cross, medal, pin or bread and wine. Choose items which you think will serve as a catalyst for your friend's faith journey. Pray that God will send you companions for the journey and ask Him to bless your friendships.

"Collage Catholics" is a nickname for those of us who were coming of age in the faith during the late 1960s and early 1970s. In 1967 when I was ten, a typical religion class homework assignment was to go through magazines and cut out pictures that showed "love" or "service" or "family." We were to paste these images onto a poster board and then discuss the relevance of our selections in front of the class. A favorite collage topic was "peace."

We made a lot of collages but learned almost nothing about the fundamentals of our faith. Folk Masses were very popular at this time with lots of guitars and songs like *Get Together*. The nuns' habits went from covering everything to revealing that they in fact had hair upon their heads and legs beneath their skirts. One of the nuns at our parish left the convent and eventually married one of the priests at our parish who had also left the priesthood. The times, they were definitely "a changing."

I remember lots of disagreements between my brothers and my dad about the length of their hair. Similarly, my mother and I would go round and round about the length of my skirts and the amount of blue eye shadow I was attempting to wear. Motown was encouraging "Dancing in the Streets" as an alternative to the riots taking place and John Lennon was chanting "Give Peace a Chance." It was a time of "free love" and the priorities were sex, drugs and rock and roll. It was also a time when an entire generation of adolescents was not properly catechized.

Recently at the Easter Vigil, held the Saturday before Easter Sunday, new Catholics were welcomed into the faith. My son-in-law was among those making his profession of faith and being received into the Catholic Church. After months of preparation, the candidates were receiving the Sacraments of Baptism, Eucharist and Confirmation. I proudly heard his "I do" when asked if he believed in the teachings of the church and was ready to enter the fold.

Just the day before, on Good Friday, I had read a scathing article in a local paper about scandals in the church. It was written by a journalist who admitted to being a Catholic in name only, and who had been "church shopping" in the hopes of finding a more acceptable church. She had not found one as of the writing of her article. She confessed to rarely attending Mass and having her own "personal, deeply felt system of beliefs" rooted in her upbringing and strengthened by her own "faith quest." (Whatever that means!) Yet, she somehow felt justified calling herself an insider and spewing negativity about most of the church's teachings with respect to faith and morals.

This reporter's photo in the paper suggests that she is approximately my age. She is one of the "collage Catholics" who probably had grape juice and crackers at outdoor Masses in modified swim attire singing "Let It Be." There were many new things being tried in those days. But neither the core tenets of the faith or sound apologetics were being taught. Homilists avoided hot button issues in an attempt not to offend anyone. Thus, we have a generation of Catholics with little or no faith formation. Many of them now have soapboxes such as our local newspaper from which to preach their messages of anti-Catholicism.

This all made my son-in-law's entrance into the church even more meaningful for me. In an age where anti-Catholicism is the last acceptable bias, he chose to study the church's teachings and respond, "Yes, I believe." At our parish in Birmingham, Michigan, twenty two adults chose to enter the Catholic Church this Easter. Culture may encourage an "anything goes" mentality but the people joining the church are seeking something else. They are familiar with the Catechism of the Catholic Church and agree with its content and message.

Most "collage Catholics" could benefit from the Rite of Catholic Initiation for Adults offered to those wishing to join the church. Instead, most of them lean toward the "Imagine" philosophy spelled out in the John Lennon song. The song tells them to imagine no heaven, no hell, no religion, no countries, nothing to kill or die for, everyone living for today. Oh, there are also no possessions, no greed or hunger and a brotherhood of man. This is basically the theme song of the no rules and no doctrine crowd who blame religion for all of the wars in the world. There is no mention of God in this song.

One of my favorite websites, Spiritdaily.com, recently led me to an article written by Sam Miller, a prominent Cleveland Jewish businessman, entitled Be Proud to be a Catholic. Mr. Miller explains that the Catholic Church educates 2.6 million students everyday at the cost to the church of 10 billion dollars, and a savings to the American taxpayer of 18 billion dollars. He further instructs that the Church has 230 colleges and universities in the U.S. and 637 hospitals. He points out the high percentages of inappropriate sexual behavior among clergymen and women outside of the Catholic Church versus the 1.7% of Catholic clergy who have been found guilty of pedophilia.

The "free love" society of a few decades ago produced many sinful behaviors which continue to leave their mark on the walking wounded of today. The pedophilia crisis is just one of these. Abortion is another. Interestingly, the path to avoiding these behaviors is clearly spelled out in the teachings of the Catholic Church. But, too many choose to ignore this path and carve out their own system of beliefs rooted in their own upbringings and established by their own faith quests. Spiritual and moral chaos is often the result.

As I watched my son-in-law being welcomed into the Catholic Church I was reminded of his adoption as an infant. He was conceived by his birth parents before they were ready for the responsibilities of parenthood. Rather than opting for abortion, they chose to bring him into the world and put him up for adoption. Another couple, who could not have children of their own, anxiously awaited the birth of this child and welcomed him lovingly into their family. They raised this fine young man who eventually met and married our daughter and has now become a member of the Catholic Church.

The answer to a lot of questions along this journey was "yes" and "I believe." Someday, I hope to hold a little grandchild in my arms after he or she has been baptized into the faith. That leaves this "collage Catholic" truly feelin' groovy.

Day 1.) How satisfied are you with the faith formation of your youth? If there are gaps in your knowledge are you inclined to educate yourself in areas where your knowledge is lacking? Make a list of issues or concerns you have with church teachings and commit to seeking out a mentor in the faith who can address any concerns.

Day 2.) Have you ever encouraged a friend to attend your church services or join your congregation? Is faith fellowship important to you? Do you have an adequate supply of peers whom you consider to be companions on the journey? Ask the Lord to lead you to quality friendships and fellow believers.

Day 3.) Does the John Lennon "Imagine" song elicit any particular reaction from you? Do you pay attention to the lyrics of songs that have pleasing melodies but questionable messages? Are there any other popular songs which you find disturbing because the messages contradict your faith? Pray for the backbone required to resist and not financially support products contrary to your values.

Day 4.) Have you ever written a letter to an editor or politician expressing outrage over their views or agenda? Conversely, have you ever praised a high profile person who chooses to take the higher ground? Reflect on the passage from Ecclesiastes 3:7 instructing that there is "a time to be silent and a time to speak."

Day 5.) Do you have an interest in studying other faith traditions? Have you ever attended a worship service or religious celebration of another faith? Were you able to see the beauty and recognize the sacred in the other traditions? Ask the Lord to help you to see the commonalities rather than the differences of our brothers and sisters in other faiths and to be an agent of peace rather than division.

Day 6.) Are you a person associated with "bad-mouthing?" How frequently do you criticize your spouse, your family, your faith community or your country? Review your conversations from the past 24 hours and ask Jesus to enlighten you about antagonistic or negative comments. Ponder the passage from the Eucharistic Prayer: "In the midst of conflict and division, we know it is you who turn our minds to thoughts of peace."

Day 7.) Have you or a loved one personally experienced any negative effects from the decades of "sex, drugs and rock and roll?" Are there any lingering scars or wounds which still require healing? Place yourself with all your brokenness before Jesus, the Divine Physician, and tell Him of your need for healing and desire to be made whole.

A friend of mine made a sign for my wall in her finest calligraphy which reads "Golf Equals Theatre." She did this at my request during a phase in my marriage that I have dubbed the fun contest. The fun contest is based on the premise that a marriage doesn't work well if one person in the marriage is having more fun than the other. At least, it was clear, that the marriage of this writer was not working well when the fun did not seem to be in balance.

We moved to Birmingham, Michigan after my husband finished his residency and went into private practice as an orthopedic surgeon. I quit my job at this time to stay home with our children. I did this willingly and happily and have always felt lucky that I did not have to work outside of the home. Running the household and raising the children was my job and working hard to provide for our family was my husband's job. We were both very content with our roles and the "work" aspect of our relationship was in balance.

Conflicts seemed to arise over what each of us considered to be fun. When my husband had free time he always chose, weather permitting, to head to the golf course. I, on the other hand, preferred to head to the theatre and do a show. There was resentment from both sides about how much time the other person was spending on their fun. The intensity of the time commitment in the evenings, when I was rehearsing a show, seemed to my husband to be excessive. I would argue that it just appeared excessive because it was a concentrated commitment.

There seemed to be only one way to prove my point. For an entire year I kept track of all of my husband's golf games, golf trips, golf lessons and range time. I then compared this to my last theatrical endeavor in terms of hours spent away from the home. He was actually surprised when I presented the numbers to him and he saw how many more hours of golf fun he had enjoyed over my theatre fun. He then asserted that he works hard enough to deserve all of these hours of relaxation. I, of course, countered with the "I work hard also and don't have a starting or quitting time" argument.

Thus, the motto "Golf Equals Theatre" was born. He agreed to be supportive of one show a year which didn't conflict too much with golf season or family priorities. I agreed not to complain about his time spent on the course. Eventually, we both came to the realization that each of us looking for fun outside of our marriage was not a very good idea at all. We began to play more golf together and as a family. The shine was also beginning to wear off of the theatrical apple. My passion for theatre was about to be replaced with a passion for my faith.

There is noticeably no mention of God in the above description of the fun contest. That is because up to this point in my life, if "Golf Equals Theatre" described the fun quest, then "Holy Equals Boring" best described my thoughts on the faith quest. I truly had this fear that if I surrendered my life to God I would become boring. I had this vision of becoming a "jumper lady," the name my young son innocently gave to the ladies who worked at the Catholic bookstore because they always wore jumpers sporting different pins for every season. I was a pleasure seeker involved in a fun contest and the "jumper lady" prospect was not appealing to me.

Fortunately, a woman I knew from church invited me to attend an information session on Community Bible Study. This woman had a special something about her that had always drawn me to her. The other women that I met at the information session were also very dynamic and compelling. They were excited about their faith journeys and eager to share glowing reports about the effect of Community Bible Study on their lives. Their enthusiasm enticed me to make the commitment.

The first two studies introduced me to the books of Peter and Daniel. My enjoyment of the Peter study was not too surprising as I was somewhat familiar with the language and stories of the New Testament. But my fascination with the study of Daniel really took me by surprise. It was the opposite of boring. It was exciting! There was dream interpretation. There was Shadrach, Meshach and Abednego's survival in the fiery furnace. There was Daniel's survival in the lion's den and the story of the handwriting on the wall. It was an action packed adventure of the "God of Daniel" who was to be reverenced "For he is the living God, enduring forever; his kingdom shall not be destroyed, and his dominion shall be without end." (Daniel 6:27)

The material was not dull and the people were not boring. As a matter of fact they were on fire for the Lord and the fire was spreading to me. I found myself wanting to discuss my Scripture Study and the things I was learning with everyone I encountered which made my husband a little uneasy. He mentioned to me, more than once, that I do not have to talk about Bible Study everywhere I go. He had similar preconceived notions about the "jumper ladies" in our community. The wife involved in the fun contest was someone with whom he was very familiar. The wife on the faith quest was someone very new to him. He doubted there was going to be any fun to be had at all.

There was, in fact, plenty of fun to be had; it was simply a new kind of fun. It was the fun and excitement of getting to know God through His Word, the Holy Scriptures, which are His personal love letter to us. After a few years of Community Bible Study I switched to Catholic Scripture Study which was being offered at my parish. I took to it like a fish to water. The studies of John, Exodus, Revelation, Genesis and now Romans each spoke directly to me and caused a stirring in my soul. I was eventually asked to be a facilitator and now consider Wednesday morning Scripture Study one of the highlights of my week.

Story after story in the Bible reveals people falling to their knees when they are in the presence of the Almighty God. They literally hit the ground in awe. Story after story of the lives of the saints tells of their being in ecstasy in the presence of God. They praise God in all things, even for the opportunity to suffer in His name, and consider all else rubbish. There is nothing boring about this. It is the greatest story ever told and we are participants in the latest chapter. The Divine Author even promises the opportunity for all to win a prize. The crown of righteousness awaits "all who have longed for his appearance." (2 Timothy 4:8) It doesn't get any better, more fun or exciting than this.

Day 1) Have the amount or quality of extracurricular activities in your home ever caused a problem for your marriage or family? How was this issue addressed or does it still need to be? Take your concern before the Lord and ask Him to enlighten you on whether or not personal concessions are in order.

Day 2) Have you made an effort to enjoy the same types of activities which other people in your family enjoy? Do you realize the importance of common ground, common experiences and common interests for building intimacy? Consider the give and take required to live harmoniously with your loved ones.

Day 3) Do you have any particular notions about Scripture Study? Is this something which calls or repels you? Have you had a positive or negative past experience which has influenced your current impressions? Ask the Lord if He is calling you to deeper intimacy with Him by studying His Word and if so to provide you with the desire and opportunity.

Day 4) Have you ever felt left out because of a passion a loved one has for something which does not include you? Have your passions ever been pursued at the exclusion of your loved ones? Imagine your heavenly father waiting for you to spend time with Him as you jump from one passion to the next. Pause now and be passionate about Him.

Day 5) Consider the passage from Mark 10:9 "Therefore what God has joined together, no human being must separate." Is there any person, place or thing which you have allowed to come between you and your spouse? Ask the Lord to help you to do an honest assessment of your priorities and to keep God and family first in your life.

Day 6) Have you ever resisted a change only to find out that the change was the very thing you needed the most? Have you ever let preconceived notions about an activity prevent you from trying something which in retrospect may have been beneficial? Speak to the Lord about something you may be resisting now and ask Him to lead you where He wants you to go.

Day 7) Do you tend to view most things in life as a contest? Do there have to be clear winners and losers in many of the endeavors to which you are drawn? Is your concept of heaven big enough to include "all who long for his appearance?" Pray for the ability to see all as made in the image and likeness of God, running in the same race on the same team for a share of the same prize.

I have coffee with God every morning at the kitchen table. My day begins with God, Starbuck's French Roast, my devotionals and a yellow legal pad. After reading the daily Scriptures and various reflections, I quiet my mind and begin to converse with the Lord about my day. My journaling session typically ends with a section called "Renewal," when I offer my day, my prayers, works, joys and sorrows to the Lord and specifically mention what I plan to work on and in what ways I hope to improve.

Mornings with the Lord are great and I always feel enthused, recharged and ready to tackle whatever comes my way afterward. It is in trying to hang on to that "just out of the shower" feeling where the difficulties arise. It might best be described as the afternoon slump. I must remind myself that God is not just my breakfast partner and is, in fact, a 24/7 companion. If He dwells in me in the morning then He is certainly still there in the afternoon and evening. I just forget to check-in and keep my appointments.

God probably gave us children so that we would know what it feels like as a parent when our children neglect to check-in. Yes, we get the nice, mushy cards for our birthdays and Mother's Day and Father's Day and we know our children love us. But frequently many days pass without an inquiry or update. Their tendency is to call mom and dad when they need something. It is an incredibly nice surprise when one of the kids call just to say hello and that they are thinking of you. Occasionally they even call and ask if you need anything. This is the parent-child relationship at its best.

Sometimes, during my journaling time, I remember to ask my heavenly father how I can be of service to Him. I ask who might be in need of my help and who might need to hear from me on a given day. I make a promise to contact a particular person or do a particular thing. I am enthusiastic and committed in the morning and ready to make this happen. But, then, halfway through my day I often realize that I cannot see the plan through. It gets put on the back burner. I consider this breaking a date with God, being a "no show" and it always makes me feel disingenuous and like a naughty child.

Similarly, I frequently promise to be careful with my speech and avoid gossip or criticisms. I vow to remain positive throughout the day and refrain from negative thoughts or words. Then at some point in the afternoon when I am conversing with someone the negativity spews forth. Once again I am a promise-breaker and failing to avoid that near occasion of sin. Saint Paul seemed to understand this when he wrote, "What I do, I do not understand. For I do not do what I want, but I do what I hate." (Romans 7:15)

It gives me some consolation to know that the Saints encountered these same difficulties. Peter promised Jesus: *"Though all may have their faith in you shaken, mine will never be."* (Matthew 26:33) Jesus told him that before the cock crowed he would deny Him three times. Peter responded, *"Even though I should have to die with you, I will not deny you."* (Matthew 26:35) We all know how this chapter played out. Peter did in fact deny knowing Jesus and when the cock crowed he wept bitterly.

I have no doubt that Peter was sincere when making his promises to Jesus at the last supper just as I am sincere when making my promises at the kitchen table. We truly want to love and serve the Lord and keep all promises all day and night long. We want to be dutiful children. But it is, of course, more difficult to keep these promises once we leave the table. We need to constantly check-in and draw on the strength and grace of Christ, who dwells in us, to keep these promises. Any attempts to rely on our own strength will fall short. Saint Paul reminds us of the source of our strength: "I have the strength for everything through him who empowers me." (Philippians 4:13)

The promises I made at the breakfast table came to mind recently when I was describing my favorite moment at my son's wedding to a friend. It was being able to witness their vows from a seat in the second row right off of the aisle. I could practically reach out and touch them. They were both overcome with emotion, hand in hand, looking deeply into each other's eyes and promising love and fidelity until death do they part. I have complete confidence that they meant every word they said as they promised to love, honor and cherish each other in good times and bad, for richer for poorer and in sickness and health. It was an extremely powerful, holy and sacramental moment.

Once they left the table of the Lord the reception began, followed by a honeymoon and the beginning of their respective careers in medicine. This period might be compared to the "breakfast" chapter of their marriage. They are filled with joy, love and enthusiasm and ready to take on whatever the journey has in store for them. They have the support, prayers and good wishes of their family and friends and the ceremony has placed God at the center of their union. Their stomachs and their hearts are full and their cups are truly running over. They have every intention of keeping all of their promises.

But there will be an afternoon slump. There will be obstacles and challenges and times when they don't want to keep their promises.

Sometimes they will be just too tired, busy or distracted to care. This is the human condition. The spirit is willing but the flesh is weak. Thankfully, God was present at the breakfast table of their marriage and God will still be present during lunch, the afternoon slump and into the evening meal. They only need to check-in and draw on that strength. Revelation 3:20 says "Behold, I stand at the door and knock. If anyone hears my voice and opens the door, I will enter his house and dine with him, and he with me." They have invited Him in and the dining will continue through breakfast, lunch, dinner and beyond.

I am reminded to dine with the Lord throughout the day. I am reminded to break the fast and sit at table with the Lord, at least in my mind and heart, as I go through the motions of my day. Like a dutiful daughter I need to check-in with my heavenly father and ask if I can be of service to Him. I can ask Him to continue to guide my steps, thoughts, words and deeds. And above all I can praise and thank Him throughout the day for His constant companionship and presence. He is definitely not just for breakfast anymore. I am opening the door and inviting Him to dine with me in a movable and ongoing feast.

Day 1) Consider your morning rituals. Is spending time with God a part of your morning routine? In addition to prayers of petition do you remember to ask God how you can be of service to Him? Make a pledge to allow a certain portion of your morning to be spent quietly with the Lord.

Day 2) Do you remember to check in with God throughout the day? As often as you eat or drink, brush your teeth or hair, head to appointments or make calls do you also call upon the Lord and invite Him to join you? Place reminders on your calendar, cell phone, dashboard or pocketbook to prompt you to converse with the Lord freely and often.

Day 3) Reflect on the passage from Romans 7:15 "What I do, I do not understand. For I do not do what I want, but I do what I hate." What are some of the things that you tend to do that you would like to stop doing? Ask for God's help in this particular struggle.

Day 4) Ponder Peter weeping bitterly after denying Jesus three times. Then consider that Jesus told Peter he was the rock upon which Jesus would build His church. Is there something you have done which still causes you to weep and for which you desire forgiveness? Turn to the Lord for forgiveness and then work on forgiving yourself.

Day 5) Envision Jesus standing at the door of your heart and knocking. All you have to do is hear His voice and open the door and He will enter your house and dine with you. Open the door. Savor your dining experience with the Lord. What does He say to you and you to Him?

Day 6) Have you been to a wedding lately? Did you get a clear sense of the couple inviting the Lord into their union? If you are married reflect on your own ceremony and how sincerely you invited God into the center of your marriage. Invite God into your union now and ask Him for an increase in the love you have for each other and for Him.

Day 7) Is an afternoon slump something you encounter frequently? What is your least productive time of day? Is there a time of day when you seem to fight the most temptation? Are you experiencing a slump with respect to a particular project or commitment? Meditate on Philippians 4:13 "I have the strength for everything through him who empowers me."

On Easter Sunday at a gathering at my sister's home I discovered that my niece's children do not like vinaigrette dressing. It was my job to bring the salads and I had prepared two: one doused with red wine vinegar and oil and another with apple cider vinegar and oil. I noticed that the little kids passed on the salads and asked if there was a particular ingredient that the children disliked. Their mom explained that the dressing reminded them of "sassy spray."

I had never heard of sassy spray and, of course, had to inquire about this mysterious liquid. My niece informed me that it is a mixture of vinegar and water combined in a spray bottle. Her pediatrician had suggested she spray it in her children's mouths in response to "potty talk." Her one daughter went through a phase of spouting off all of the bad words she knew in rapid succession. Her mouth had been washed out with soap so many times that her parents were actually concerned about the amount of soap she had ingested. Thus, sassy spray was introduced in lieu of the soap.

Having suffered from "foot in mouth" disease myself, I began to think I could benefit from carrying around some sassy spray. Even better would be a pre-sassy spray or "think spray" to remind me to think before I speak. I once asked the daughter of a friend of mine, who is confined to a wheel chair, if she had "walked" at graduation. She responded that she had "wheeled." I told the son of another friend of mine, who is also confined to a wheel chair, that he would make a great stand-up comedian. He responded "yes" to the comedian but "no" to the stand-up part. I don't know if a spray exists that can help me.

The lesson in the sassy spray story for me was about associations. The kids no longer like vinegar because they associate it with something bad. My husband got ill from pizza once as a child and has had a hard time being around pizza for years. I did the same thing with an alcoholic drink called a "7 & 7." No more of those for me. Many of us have had to rethink associations of good and bad with particular persons, places or things based on our childhood experiences. What was once bad may now be good and vice versa. We have to reassess with an adult mind and decide if our associations still apply.

During a recent homily at our parish the priest admitted to refraining from wearing his Roman collar in public. He used to put it on without hesitation when traveling around town but now avoids wearing it when possible. He said this is in response to the public perception that the roman collar of a Catholic priest is now associated with pedophilia.

What was once an indication of a good and holy man, Christ personified, has now been reduced to the accessory of a child molester. This prejudice does such a disservice to the many men who have dedicated their lives to serving God and His people. But, like the association of vinegar with sassy spray, it will take a long time to undo the connection.

I used to associate country club with snob, Birmingham, Michigan with snooty, holy with boring, knitting and bridge with old and bowling with cigarettes. Over time all of these associations have changed for various reasons. As soon as we think we have something figured out is usually when we discover the exceptions and realize we can no longer label. Some think black is good and white is bad and some think black is bad and white is good. The same goes for Gentile and Jew, woman and man, servant or free. Saint Paul offers a whole dissertation on circumcised versus uncircumcised and what kind of animals a person can eat in his letter to the Romans. We may look upon this as trivial now but at the time, one was clearly associated with holiness and being within the law, and the other was not.

When we hear the word "Christian" today many think "right wing zealot." What is supposed to come to mind is love. More specifically, as the song tells us, "They will know we are Christians by our love." Apparently, most of us who are Christians have not been doing enough to reinforce the love aspect of this association. Without love we are but a banging gong or a clanging symbol. We are making a lot of noise but it is not a loving noise.

I happen to love it when people surprise me. By this I mean that when I have someone labeled as one thing in my mind (which of course I am not supposed to do!) and upon further investigation discover that they are something completely different than I had suspected. I encountered a woman at a tennis party, several years in a row, who totally intimidated me. The tennis party was supposed to be "just for fun" meaning noncompetitive, social tennis. Several times I was across the court from this woman who proceeded to smash balls at me. She was quiet, serious and didn't laugh much when I begged for mercy. She was advanced and I was a beginner who had no business being on the same court with her.

Eventually, we got to know each other off the tennis court and discovered that we have a lot in common. We grew up in neighboring parishes in Detroit and knew many of the same people from the old neighborhood. We both play golf and bridge and take our faith journeys very seriously. She had me pegged for a giggly, silver-spooned country clubber in a tennis skirt and I had her slotted as one of those tough as nails, win at all costs, competitive, athletic women. What was really her shyness I saw as unfriendliness and what was my defensive laughter she labeled as ditsy. Now, when the other person's name comes to mind we each tend to think of kindness.

There is a Litany of the Most Holy Name of Jesus in my Catholic Prayer Book similar to the Jesus Prayer. The power of the invocation lies in the holy name itself—Jesus. The name is the prayer. But there are also phrases from the litany of the holy name which serve to deepen our understanding of the power and presence of God's Son. Jesus is described as light, patient, obedient, humble, joy, justice, purity, refuge, our shepherd and dozens of other nouns, adjectives and verbs. This is the ultimate association game. At the name of Jesus every head shall bow and knee shall bend.

As Christians, whose eyes are to be on Christ at all times and whose goal is to emulate Him, we should hope that the mention of our names conjure up positive associations. My mother always told me that you get more bees with honey than you do with vinegar. I will strive for an association with the sweet rather than the sour and, hopefully, never again need sassy spray. I am also bringing potatoes next year.

Day 1) Think of both a negative and positive association from your youth which has now changed. Can you recall when and why the association changed? Is there an association which you are making presently deserving of a second look? Ask the Lord to enlighten you about any engrained biases which need to be removed or reassessed.

Day 2) How careful are you with your speech? Do you frequently find yourself speaking without thinking and regretting comments you have made? Meditate on Proverbs 21:23 "He who guards his mouth and his tongue keeps himself from trouble."

Day 3) Has someone ever told you they had you pegged as one thing or another? If you did not think the label was fair did this annoy you? Have you ever been proven wrong when attempting to label another? Reflect on the harm that labeling can do and seek forgiveness for those instances when you have been the perpetrator.

Day 4) When you observe a person with a religious vocation dressed in their appropriate garb does it elicit any particular reaction from you? What would you like your clothing to say about you? Does the passage from 1 Thessolians 5:8 which encourages "putting on the breastplate of faith and love and the helmet that is hope for salvation" speak to you in any way?

Day 5) Play the association game with words like faith-filled, loving, compassionate, humble, blessed, kind and holy. What individuals come to mind? Now play the same game with words like hateful, mean-spirited, selfish, antagonistic, bitter, deceitful and rude. Which game was easier? Consider the adjectives you would hope others would choose in association with you.

Day 6) It has been said that when we cross over to the next life we will know the effect of every thought, word and deed while we were on earth. Mark 4:22 explains "there is nothing hidden except to be made visible; nothing is secret except to come to light." Does this passage serve as an inspiration for you to change thoughts, words and deeds?

Day 7) Just as children need to learn that actions have consequences adults also must understand that we reap what we sow. What kinds of seeds have you been planting and how does your crop look? Are there weeds which need to be removed? Ask the Lord to give you rich soil and deep roots so that nothing can choke the word and destroy the fruit.

My youngest son got a job offer this week. After months of praying for this news it almost seems surreal now that it has come to fruition. My oldest son got married this past weekend. After months of preparation and anticipation it feels equally strange that this event is now in the past. My daughter and her husband will be celebrating their first wedding anniversary this summer. My husband and I now have two children married and our "baby" has graduated from college and is gainfully employed.

These milestones are difficult for me to grasp. "Sunrise, sunset swiftly flow the days." The writer of that song expressed the passage of time so well. "Seedlings turn overnight to sunflowers blossoming even as we gaze," sang the parents at their child's wedding in the musical *Fiddler on the Roof*. It is now the end of May and the stores are advertising for Father's Day and soon it will be the Fourth of July. Then we will be closing up our cottage for the summer. Zoom! Occasionally, I have the desire to stop time. I just want to hang onto a particular moment or phase and make it last just a little longer.

But, alas, I cannot. Time is a gift from God. I can try to use it wisely but certainly cannot control it. I can try to make every moment count. This is an awareness that comes with age. Life is precious. Time is fleeting. Don't put things off. Savor the moments. At both my son and my daughter's weddings I tried to memorize moments that I could store in my heart forever. At my daughter's wedding it was my husband walking her down the aisle and the look on the groom's face when he caught sight of her. At my son's wedding it was the look on the bride and groom's faces during their exchange of vows.

These were looks of love and moments of joy. I have also saved the message my youngest son left on our voicemail to tell us that he got the job. He sounds so incredibly happy. I want to be able to replay it and relive that joyful moment. The day my daughter's wedding video came I stopped what I was doing, plopped onto the sofa and watched her wedding again from start to finish. What a gift to be able to relive the joy of that day. I was able to see and hear things that I had missed the first time around. As hard as you try to be fully present and aware of your surroundings there is often sensory overload and too much to absorb. You have to choose where to direct your focus.

The passage of time came to the forefront of my thoughts at a funeral service I attended this morning as I focused on the first reading. It was from Ecclesiastes 3:1-8. "There is an appointed time for everything, and a time for every affair under heaven." It explains that there is a time to be born and a time to die, a time to weep and a time to laugh, a time to mourn and a time to dance. Verse 11, not part of this morning's reading asserts "He has made everything appropriate to its time." Our family had been celebrating weddings, graduations and employment offers while this family had been planning a funeral. All, however, are celebrations of different aspects and seasons of life, in God's perfect timing.

All are memorials. Things we want to commemorate. Times we never want to forget. I learned a lot about the woman who had passed away from the stories her children told at the service. She was adventurous. She was fun-loving. She enjoyed wine, music, golf and bridge. I smiled at this. I had only known the deceased in the past dozen years when she was already suffering from Alzheimer's disease. I was not familiar with her former self or the precious memories her children shared. Her husband chose the song "The Nearness of You" to be sung before the eulogies. This was a celebration of their love story. Their loving memorial inspired me to be a better wife and mother and to make the moments count.

The moments keep ticking away. For a brief instant this week I began to think that maybe all of the best moments have passed. God has been so good to me and my family that maybe we have used up our allotment of blessings. Maybe it wouldn't be right to even hope or ask for more blessings. As soon as this negative thought entered my head I was reminded of the prayer of Jabez, a little prayer in 1 Chronicles 4:10: "Jabez prayed to the God of Israel:'Oh, that you may truly bless me and extend my boundaries! Help me and make me free of misfortune, without pain!' And God granted his prayer."

In his book *The Prayer of Jabez*, the author Bruce Wilkinson explains how we have watered down the concept of blessing to something we say when someone sneezes. Instead, we need to understand that to bless in the biblical sense means to ask for or to impart supernatural favor. He says that when we ask for God's blessing "we're crying out for the wonderful, unlimited goodness that only God has the power to know about or give to us." He shares a story about a warehouse in heaven filled with packages tied with red ribbons. In these boxes are all of the blessings that God wanted to give to us while we walked the earth. But we never asked.

The little book *The Prayer of Jabez* has been sitting on the coffee table in my living room for some time now. The copyright on the inside cover indicates that it was published in the year 2000. I remember reading it several years ago and then placing it on the top of a stack of books that I like to refer to often. That I noticed it on a day when I was feeling overwhelmed by the goodness of God and the abundance of His blessings is not a coincidence. In response to a thought that said "my cup is so full; I probably shouldn't ask for anything else!" came the inspiration to ask God to bless me indeed and enlarge my territories, spurred by the little tan book on the table by the sofa.

So I proceed to ask God to bless our children. I pray that in His perfect timing He will bless them with children. I pray that He will enlarge our territories so that we can continue to serve Him and that His hand will be upon us as we attempt to walk the walk of faith. I cannot ask for more time than the twenty four hours in a day, but I can ask for help in making better use of the time that I have. I can ask for help in staying in the present moment, not looking back with regret and not looking forward with worry, but in making the most of this very moment. This very moment, the here and now, the gift of time is one of God's greatest blessings. There is a time to speak and a time to be silent. "He has made everything appropriate to its time." I think it is time for an appropriate silence. And I will savor it.

Day 1) If you divided your life into four seasons would you say you are in the spring, summer, fall or winter? What are some of the blessings you are enjoying that are unique to this season of your life? Do you feel that you are where God wants you to be on your journey towards Him? Ask Him to lead you and guide you.

Day 2) Do you feel as if time is passing too quickly and you cannot keep up with the pace of your life? Do you have trouble staying in the here and now and savoring the present moment? Stop all thoughts racing through your mind and place yourself in the presence of God. Be still and enjoy His loving embrace.

Day 3) The Lord gave us the Sabbath, a day of rest from the demands and responsibilities of the other days of the week. Do you honor the Sabbath and allow yourself time to recharge, refresh and renew?

Day 4) Does the warehouse in heaven of never asked for gifts encourage you to make your desires known to the Lord? Is there something for which you have refrained from asking because you feel it is too much or undeserved? Consider James 4:2 which tells us "You do not possess because you do not ask." Take your needs before the Lord.

Day 5) Do you consider time a gift from God and believe you are to use it wisely? Assess your time-management skills and ask God to enlighten you in any areas where you need improvement.

Day 6) Is time spent with God a priority for you? Have you seen the benefits of beginning your day with the Lord and asking His assistance in completing the tasks on your "to do" list? Lay your concerns before the Lord and ask Him to orchestrate the events of your day so that those things most important to Him get accomplished.

Day 7) Say the prayer of Jabez: *"Oh, that You would bless me indeed, and enlarge my territory, that Your hand would be with me and that You would keep me from evil, that I may not cause pain!"* Consider how your territories and your life can be enlarged so you can make a greater impact for the Lord.

Walking at the mall alone this week and trying to pray, I was bombarded with messages. Advertisements assaulted me from every store window. Some were spelled out in words and others were just visual. I am usually too engrossed in my conversation with my walking buddy to notice them. But this week, my buddy was out of town and I was attempting to converse with the heavens as I walked along. It was difficult.

My eyes first landed upon *Sex and the City-2* in a jewelry store window. I'm not sure what buying jewelry has to do with this upcoming movie but the owners certainly wanted the connection made. The window of Armani Exchange sported a picture of a man and woman on top of each other in the sand wearing very little. The Guess store window displayed a picture of a man between two women. He was kissing one while the other looked on jealously implying that a man could get not one, but two women, or even more, if he purchased clothing from that store.

There was a sign in front of Starbucks showing a woman in absolute ecstasy over her frappuccino. I mean her head is tossed back and she is clasping her hands together in front of her chest like she has never known such joy. I must confess that I have never personally seen someone this happy over their coffee. These new flavors must really be something.

Even the pictures from Destination Maternity show sexy mamas to be. Heidi Klum is featured in the front window in a little tank top and skinny jeans revealing about a seventh-month tummy and looking confident and beautiful. The models in the maternity shop window are frequently wearing spiky heels and sequins as if ready for a night on the town. The messages consistently shout that your sex life will be great, and you will have it all, if you will simply buy and use the products they are selling.

I was about to stand in line to purchase my $1.80 bottle of Ethos water before deciding that tap water from home would be fine. The buying bug just gets under your skin at the mall and you feel like you have to leave with something, even if it is simply a roll and a drink. Undoubtedly, carrying my Visa and ATM card is my first mistake since it keeps the purchasing options open.

Less than half a mile from this high end mall is a little Catholic Church where I frequently attend Mass. I met a friend for noon Mass there this week after having walked the fancy mall earlier in the day.

What a study in contrasts. The interior of this church is simple and worn. The carpeting is old, the adornments are nonexistent and the attendees are not at all concerned about fashion. On Fridays a van of elderly people from a nearby assisted living residence are wheeled and escorted into the church. They come not to buy anything but to receive.

Coincidentally, the sermon given on Sunday had a theme of contrasts. The Priest told of a time when he encountered a youth shot in the head as a result of a drug deal gone awry, juxtaposed to a resort he visited in the Dominican Republic where drug lords vacation. Both were involved in the buying and selling of goods but with very different outcomes. He told this story as a call to live out our faith in response to sin in the world. It was Pentecost Sunday which is when we celebrate the gift of the Holy Spirit. He reflected that receiving the Holy Spirit should compel one to go forth and make disciples of all nations. It is a moving Spirit, an active Spirit and a compassionate Spirit that we receive.

We sang the Psalm *"Lord, send out your spirit and renew the face of the earth."* The message in this Psalm is about renewal. It is about the gift of the Holy Spirit and everything becoming a new creation. It exclaims, *"How manifold are your works, O Lord! The earth is full of your creatures."* He made the world and everything in it and when He sends forth His Spirit they are created and He renews the face of the earth. This is a gift freely given and truly life altering. It is a very contrasting message to the goods being offered in the public square.

This past December a high end magazine did a feature on the homeless in Detroit. This happened to be their holiday issue so in the pages following the pictures of slumped figures in the corners of buildings was a holiday gift guide of luxurious gifts you could buy for the high-end recipient. There was a Cartier Balloon Bleu Automatic Watch selling for $30,100, a Brioni Custom Vanquish Men's Suit for $43,000 and a necklace of oval pink tourmaline stones and brilliant cut diamonds for $47,000. Even more frightening was a Gold Sequined Louis Vuitton Purse with a price available upon request. They did not even dare to list the price.

The advertisements promote the typical array of plastic surgery options, teeth whitening and cosmetic dentistry options, spa specials and medical weight loss centers. I always find it particularly incongruous when an ad for plastic surgery is placed across from an ad for Operation Smile or Smile Train, charities which fund surgeries for children born with cleft palates. Surgery for cleft palate repair overseas is supposed to cost approximately $250 making me wonder how many of these poor children's faces could be surgically repaired with what we spend on facelifts in our community. I also wonder how many of our homeless could be fed with the price of a watch, bracelet or designer purse.

We choose which messages will capture our attention and to which we will respond- those from the shiny mall or those from the well worn church. One of these is asking us to buy and one is inviting us to receive. I think there has been a message left on my answering machine. God left it for me when I was out walking this morning and I was unable to pick up. It says to meet Him at the little church across from the mall. There is a give-away going on there that is beyond belief. The price for all goods has already been paid. The gift is freely given and all I have to do is show up and get to know the man at the top. Then I am called to share the gift with others. What an invitation! What a message! I am definitely all in. And there is no Visa or ATM card required. This is one message I will not be deleting.

Day 1) How aware are you of the messages assaulting you from every form of media on a daily basis? Have you ever found yourself pondering the purchase of something you really don't need as the result of a clever advertisement that got stuck in your head? Have you suffered from buyer's remorse after giving in to an urge you should have suppressed? Pray for the gifts of discernment and self control.

Day 2) Do you tend to tune out messages from scripture because you have heard them too many times and don't feel that they are speaking to you? Do you have difficulty applying words written thousands of years ago to your present life? Ask the Lord for a receptive heart and fresh ears to hear the gospel message.

Day 3) What kind of message does your appearance and behavior send to others? Are you aware of the unspoken messages your choices send? What is the message you would like to communicate and what product, if any, would you like to sell?

Day 4) Do you believe that the gift of the Holy Spirit celebrated on Pentecost Sunday and received in the sacraments is an active and moving Spirit? Do you accept the great commission to go into the whole world and proclaim the gospel to every creature? Pray for the courage to activate the Holy Spirit in your life.

Day 5) Scripture is full of examples of angels being used as messengers by God to communicate important information. Can you think of a person in your life who has acted as a heavenly messenger to you? Have you been this sort of messenger to another? Tell the Lord of your willingness to be used as a messenger for Him and trust that He will provide you with the necessary words in His perfect timing.

Day 6) The messages of the world seem to revolve around perfecting our outer self and reversing the aging process. Yet, Scripture tells us to "be perfect, just as your heavenly Father is perfect." (Matthew 5:48) Plan a spiritual makeover to cleanse and perfect the soul and bring about a mature faith.

Day 7) Think of someone you know who tends to send mixed messages. Maybe their mouth speaks welcome but their body language says keep your distance. Maybe they go through the motions of religiosity but their hearts and minds seem far from the Lord. Reflect on any mixed messages you may be sending. Ask God to remove all deceit from you so that your yes means yes and your no means no.

A magazine was delivered to our home this week which ran a feature on the best of Detroit. There were 251 favorites and thousands of voters. You were told where to find the best restaurants, shops, burgers, desserts and wineries amongst other things. This made me think about my lack of concern for what others deem to be best. It also made me think about my experiences with house chardonnay.

I have always been content drinking cheap wine. I am happy with Two Buck Chuck and like to buy Sutter Home minis at the bowling alley. I have been out with people who consider themselves wine connoisseurs and who have actually instructed the wait staff to bring me a better glass of wine. They are well intentioned, but, truthfully, I prefer the house. These sophisticates really cringe when I plop the ice in my glass.

There are also women in my circle of friends who are connoisseurs of fine chocolate. They proclaim certain chocolates to be "exquisite, to die for, simply the best!" Those, they have presented to me for tasting, are truly delicious. But I secretly opt for M & M Peanuts, Snickers or a Kit Kat Bar when I crave chocolate. I do not deny that others have refined, delicate palates but am merely admitting that I do not.

What I do deny is that just because a majority of people say that something is so, actually makes it so. After this issue circulates the cries of "we must go to such and such a restaurant or shop because I have heard it is the best!" will begin. We have been invited to try many a gourmet restaurant and returned home hungry after being offered a weed salad and a sprig of this or that. We paid more and got less for these tastes of the "best."

Another magazine, a weekly golf publication running a special edition "for stylish women golfers" was recently delivered to our door. The cover displayed a female golfer swinging a golf club in a sequins evening dress with chandelier drop earrings. It was not until page 68 out of 80 that you stumbled upon "For Your Game: Instruction."

There were pages of articles and pictures dealing with the best of golf fashion and toys. You were urged to fill your "toy box" with colorful bags, groovy shoes, accessories with "serious bling" and even handmade golf jewelry. There were also hair and makeup tips and a section entitled "From the course to cocktails" featuring a bright animal print, peep toe shoe with four inch heels. A quote in bold print declared

"As a model and a golfer, what you wear is the most important decision you can make."

And all this time I thought it was about how you played the game! It's not about skill, class, inner peace or even the hokey-pokey. It's about what you wear and what's in your toy box! Pardon the sarcasm but I found this "for her" issue of this magazine really annoying. Somehow I can't see these same writers taking us behind the scenes with world famous male golfers getting a facial, highlights or mani-pedi.

My husband is an excellent golfer and has played with the same putter for over 30 years. He also plays in a hickory stick golf outing every year and tends to score well with his collection of wooden shafted golf clubs. He got a hole in one at this outing a few years back playing with a wooden shafted club borrowed from a friend of his. It is not so much about having or wearing the latest and greatest but who is swinging the club.

Marketing experts are constantly trying to convince us what is best for us. Their products and services hold the keys to happiness for us, and, if we would just listen to them, we would be able to choose what is best. After suffering from buyer's remorse one too many times, I am now completely convinced that the sellers do not at all know what is best for me. I now avoid the magazines and catalogues that come in the mail and rely on a higher authority. That authority can be found in the world's best seller, Holy Scripture.

Since "all Scripture is divinely inspired and has its use for teaching the truth and refuting error, for reformation of manners and discipline in right living, so that the man who belongs to God may be efficient and equipped for good work of every kind" (2 Timothy 3:16-17) it is difficult to do a "best of" with respect to the Bible. But one of my personal favorites is the story of Martha and Mary.

Martha and Mary were sisters and they welcomed their friend Jesus into their home. Martha bustled around tending to the serving and Mary sat beside the Lord at His feet listening to Him speak. Martha complained to Jesus that her sister had left her by herself to do the serving. The Lord said to her in reply, *"Martha, Martha, you are anxious and worried about many things. There is need of only one thing. Mary has chosen the better part and it will not be taken from her."* (Luke 11:41-42)

Mary chose the better part sitting at Jesus' feet listening attentively. She kept her eyes and ears on Jesus. He was her teacher and received her focus. This was the one thing needed and the most important decision I can make each day. I need to focus on Christ. I need to put on Christ. This is choosing the better part.

Another gospel story dealing with better, best and wine comes to mind concerning Jesus' first miracle at the wedding feast at Cana. When the wine ran short the mother of Jesus said to him, *"They have no wine."* (John 2:3) She then told the servers, *"Do whatever he tells you."* (John 2:5) Jesus proceeded to change the water, from six stone jars each holding twenty to thirty gallons, into wine. The headwaiter commented on how the inferior wine had been served first. The host was now bringing out the good stuff.

This story reiterates that the most important decision you and I have to make each day is to "do whatever he tells you." His direction is the one thing needed and we receive this from a most high authority, the mother of God. It appears that there will be excellent conversation and very good wine involved. It is also clear that in at least one instance, the house wine was made by Jesus himself and deemed the best. This confirms what I already knew about house chardonnay. God said it, I believe it and that settles it.

Day 1) How influenced are you by what others deem to be best? How influenced are you by packaging, labeling and brand name goods? Have you ever courageously announced that something reputed to be the best was not very good at all? Pray for the honesty and judgment to recognize quality and authenticity.

Day 2) Do you see yourself as more of a Martha or a Mary or both? Do you find yourself resenting the fact that Mary is seated at the feet of Jesus while Martha does all the work or do you resent Martha's criticism of Mary's choice? Place yourself at the feet of Jesus and listen to what He has to tell you about the one thing necessary.

Day 3) Place yourself in the scene at the wedding at Cana. Imagine you are one of the servers being told by Mary to do whatever He tells you. You have just witnessed Jesus changing water into wine. Do you now believe in miracles? Are you open to the miraculous in your life? Reflect on a time when Jesus in fact turned nothing into something in your life.

Day 4) Have you received a publication in the mail lately with an article that particularly annoyed you? What was it about the article that pushed your buttons? Would you consider canceling your subscription and writing a letter to the editor describing your displeasure? Ask Jesus how and when you should use your voice to bring Him glory.

Day 5) Does the magazine quote "what you wear is the most important decision you can make" elicit any particular reaction from you? Have you ever wanted to shout that the emperor is naked like the child in the story of "The Emperor's New Clothes?" Contrast how much time you spend worrying about how you look on the outside with how you look on the inside. The world sees one and God sees the other. Whom shall you please?

Day 6) Do you agree with 2 Timothy 3:16-17: "All Scripture is inspired by God and is useful for teaching, for refutation, for correction, and for training in righteousness, so that one who belongs to God may be competent, equipped for every good work?" If this is in fact our rulebook should we not all become as familiar as we can with its content and message? Can you commit to reading a passage from Scripture every day?

Day 7) Consider the passage from Ecclesiastes 1:9 "Nothing is new under the sun." How many times have you tried something that said "New and improved!" or "Now better than ever!" only to discover that the original was still the best? People change jobs, neighborhoods, schools, churches, spouses, hair color and the like to satisfy a craving for something new and better. Reflect on a time you went back to what was tried and true after experimenting with what was billed as "new and improved."

A baby shower invitation I received recently requested that each attendee purchase a favorite children's book, in lieu of a card, to accompany their gift. This directive resulted in my spending a most pleasant afternoon perusing the children's section of a local book store. Trying to determine which story was my favorite proved most difficult and I ended up buying several. The ones that brought back the warmest memories seemed to revolve around the word "little."

It was interesting to me how the lessons contained in these simple children's stories are still so applicable today. *The Little Engine That Could* by Watty Piper encourages a positive attitude, perseverance and helpfulness. "I think I can! I think I can!" has become the mantra for children of all ages when faced with a seemingly insurmountable obstacle. It instructs us to dig deep and not shrink from opposition or difficulty.

The Little Red Caboose by Marian Potter is another story about a train. It reminds us to bloom where we are planted. Even though the little caboose always came last and felt unimportant and ignored, he eventually had the opportunity to save the day. He slammed on his brakes and held tight to the tracks when his train was starting to slip back down the long, tall mountain. He never again wished to be anyone but himself.

The Three Little Pigs by Paul Galdone has always been a favorite of mine. The pigs could choose to build their houses out of straw, sticks or bricks. Only the house made of bricks could withstand the huffing and puffing of the big bad wolf. What a fabulous lesson in making sure there is a solid foundation under what we plan to build. When the storms and wolves come, what we value will be protected.

The lesson in the story of *Chicken Little*, who kept claiming that the sky was falling, is not to believe everything that one hears and to be courageous. The story of "The Little Red Hen" tells us to be industrious. He planted the grain of wheat, reaped it, carried it to the mill, made the flour into dough and baked the bread. None of his friends wanted to help with any of the work. But, they were all very willing to help eat the bread when it came out of the oven. Unfortunately, they had to learn that one reaps what one sows.

Lessons in honesty are prevalent in many children's stories. Aesop's Fable *The Boy Who Cried Wolf* teaches us to be honest in our speech. Hans Christian Anderson's *The Emperor's New Clothes* teaches us to be honest in our assessments. It took a little child in this story to make the observation that the emperor was not wearing anything at all. It is this honesty and simplicity that Jesus refers to in answer to the disciples' question of who would be greatest in the kingdom of heaven. *"He called a child over, placed it in their midst, and said, Amen, I say to you, unless you turn and become like children, you will not enter the kingdom of heaven."* (Matthew 18:2-3)

Several years ago I read the book entitled *All I Need to Know I Learned in Kindergarten* by Robert Fulghum. The title came from the first essay in the book listing lessons normally learned in American kindergarten classrooms. The author explained how the world would improve if adults simply followed the same rules as children, such as sharing, being kind and cleaning up after themselves. Interestingly, Fulghum's essays, especially this title piece, have been criticized for being trite and saccharine. (Wikipedia)

This criticism reflects a world that has become too cynical, hardened and sophisticated. There were similar criticisms of the musical *The Sound of Music* when it made its debut, a movie that happens to be a household favorite. Its enormous success would indicate that many other households enjoy themes considered to be trite and saccharine. Themes of good overcoming evil, standing up for one's principles and placing one's trust in God will hopefully always be welcome in this world. It would certainly help the world to improve if we would just remember to look at it through the eyes of a child.

The song *What a Wonderful World*, sung by Louis Armstrong, was my choice for the mother and groom dance at my son's wedding. The lyrics about trees of green, red roses, friends shaking hands and saying "I love you" provided the perfect backdrop for that precious moment. These are little things and simple concepts. But since it was extremely difficult for this mother to express the love she felt for her son and I'm sure, similarly difficult for him to put his feelings into words, we let this sweet song do the talking.

I guess I've always leaned toward the sweet and simple. This is probably why I love observing little ones. When they hear music they begin to dance. They don't give a lot of thought to how they dance. They just move to the music and smile a lot. When children recognize someone they love, their faces tend to light up and they frequently launch into a running hug offered with abandon, exuberance and honesty.

When my oldest son came home from preschool one day he wanted to tell me all about his favorite new friend. He told me about the games they played, the food they ate and the laughs they shared. Lastly, he told me the boy's name and that he had a brown face. This was just one observation amongst many, helping me to be able to identify his new friend when I met him the next day. My younger son had a similar experience, except the last piece of information that he provided was that his new friend was a girl.

Children make friends incredibly easily. They basically walk up to someone their size and say, *"Do you want to play?"* Their needs are not very great. They can make games out of sticks, dirt, sand and leaves. They do not try to hide their feelings. They stomp their feet when they are mad and stretch, yawn and say, *"I'm sleepy"* when they are tired. They are empathetic. When they see someone crying they want to cry also and the same goes for laughter. They like to wear comfortable clothes, eat only when they're hungry and stop eating when they're full. You tend to know where you stand with them.

It is no wonder that Jesus said, *"Let the children come to me, and do not prevent them; for the kingdom of heaven belongs to such as these."* (Matthew 19:14) The trip to the children's book store reminded me of this. It reminded me of what John the Baptist meant when he said, *"He must increase; I must decrease."* (John 3:30) The Holy Spirit that dwells in me must grow bigger and the other occupant, me, must get smaller. Then nothing will be able to blow this house down. I think I can! God willing, I surely can.

Day 1) Do you have a favorite children's story from your childhood that you find yourself quoting often? Are the lessons in the story still applicable to your life today? Reflect on a time when a childhood lesson helped you in an adult situation.

Day 2) Do you enjoy observing children? Have you ever found yourself, as an adult, wanting to ask another adult to come out and play? Have you ever wished you had the simplicity of a child to ask another to be your friend? Contemplate casting off sophistication and innocently approaching another you've been hoping to befriend.

Day 3) Have you ever noticed how children do not pay attention to color or gender? Is there a person of different origin whom you have been hesitant to get to know due to some unfounded apprehension? Contemplate the Eucharistic Prayer for Reconciliation: "In that new world where the fullness of your peace will be revealed, gather people of every race, language, and way of life to share in the one eternal banquet."

Day 4) Do you know someone who has built their house out of straw or sticks instead of bricks? Have you witnessed their house crumbling due to a poor foundation? What's the foundation like under your house? Pray to Jesus, the stone which the builders rejected who has become the cornerstone, for a cementing of your faith.

Day 5) Are you familiar with the song "I Hope You Dance" by Lee Ann Womack? If you get the chance "to sit it out or dance" which do you choose? Ask Jesus for a heart ready to embrace all of the joy that life can offer.

Day 6) Have you ever felt you are too "little" to handle the things life throws at you? Do you look at some of the hills you have to climb and simply feel you are not capable? Place yourself before the God of the impossible and yoked to Jesus rely on His strength to lead and guide you.

Day 7) Is there a "Chicken Little" in your life always yelling that the sky is falling? Do you know a "Boy Who Cried Wolf" whom no one listens to anymore due to too many false warnings? Do you identify with the "Little Red Hen" who did not shy away from the hard work necessary to make his bread? Choose the characters from your favorite children's stories you would most and least like to emulate.

The seeds of faith and love of God and His Church were planted in me at a young age by my loving parents. All of the religious traditions and holy days were carefully observed in our household. I learned my prayers by imitating my parents. The seeds of sense and sensibility were also being planted. But I've only recently begun to recognize the fruit.

My mom always wears sensible shoes. This thought flashed through my mind as I was standing in uncomfortable shoes at a social gathering with people from our club recently. The topic of conversation was performance anxiety. Specifically, two women were telling me how apprehensive they are about playing competitive golf. One said she is afraid of making a fool of herself.

My mind flashed to my mom because I had been similarly reluctant to become her bridge partner. Despite the fact that I learned to play bridge so that I could play with my mom, I was very nervous when I first accompanied her to the local senior center to play duplicate bridge. My mom is an excellent bridge player and I am a beginner. I had a dose of performance anxiety and visions of making a fool of myself.

The lessons learned by accompanying her to the senior center have been numerous. One woman's hands are so arthritic that she has to position her cards in a plastic holder. Another is legally blind and her partner has to call out the cards as each person plays them. A moderator fills in for people when they have to go to the bathroom. There is no such thing as a quick trip with the seniors. But they are all there each week, enjoying themselves immensely, with no thought given to resembling anything foolish.

In my circle of friends in our age group there is a tendency to take ourselves way too seriously. No wonder we have performance anxiety. We have so much of our identity wrapped up in how we will be perceived by others. Everyone's approval of how we look, what we do, where and with whom we do it, is constantly sought. Having to prove yourself is not very compatible with the "don't sweat the small stuff" concept. The ego sees it all as big stuff. "Vanity of vanities! All things are vanity!" (Ecclesiastes1:2)

This is why I love to be around senior citizens. Seniors wear sensible shoes. Seniors wear comfortable underwear and comfortable clothes. They seem to be way past trying to impress anyone. My mom's vanity license plate is as vain as she gets. It says "Mom of 13." She didn't even buy it for herself. It was a gift from one of my sisters. This is the one thing of which my mom is proud. She loves to talk about her family.

Mom's formal education stopped after high school. But she has something that they can't teach in school. It used to be called common sense. It is frequently referred to as uncommon sense now because it is so rare. Those who lived through the great depression seem to have it in abundance. They live within their means and always seem to be prepared. What their earnings won't cover they trust that God will provide.

Mom clips coupons and stocks up on things on sale. She came of age before credit cards or ATM cards and always has cash on hand. The cash is in small bills: ones, fives, tens and twenties. She loves to have exact change. Her purse is stocked with a Rosary, tissue, cough drops, snacks, safety pins, pens and anything that you might need at any given moment. She always carries holy cards and a picture of her family.

When mom is venturing out to a place she's never been before she usually does a dry run during the day so she's sure to know where she's going. She allows plenty of time to get to her destination and keeps all of her appointments on a very organized calendar. She has an extensive list of people that she prays for everyday, and if she tells you she will pray for your special intention, you can count on it. She seems to have a direct line.

The "common sense" commandments must have "waste not, want not" at the top of the list. "You never know when that might come in handy," "an ounce of prevention is worth a pound of cure" and "necessity is the mother of invention" were expressions heard often in our household. I have frequently seen mom make something out of almost nothing. She recycled before recycling was popular.

Pieces of wax paper, tin foil, plastic bags and paper towels pepper mom's kitchen. Boxes, wrapping paper and ribbon are saved from year to year. Same goes for plastic containers, glass jars, lids, rubber bands and paper clips. Nothing is thrown out that can be used again. She makes things out of scraps. Leftover food items become a stew, soup or casserole. Scraps of cloth become patches and yarn gets crocheted into potholders.

There was a time when I did not find this all so endearing. My father used to love to go to garage sales and was always bringing home some new treasures. At one point when I was in high school our enclosed front porch was decorated with different size bottles filled with colored water, statues of native dancers, a collection of rocks, an old Barbie case complete with clothes and various old dolls with crocheted outfits mom had made for them. Many of the dolls' hair had been cut off and their eyes were half shut.

The crochet theme was carried throughout the house. There were crocheted rugs, afghans, curtains, doilies, hats, scarves, potholders and balls amongst other things. My adolescent sense of longing to be like everyone else, overrode a sense of pride in my mom's domestic abilities. I had no idea how awesome it was that, instead of store bought birthday gifts, my mom typically provided a hand sewn item for a friend.

I know how awesome it is now. I proudly carried a navy crocheted purse up the aisle at my son's wedding, made with love by mom. When I sat down next to her in the pew she smiled at me and patted the purse in my hand. It meant a lot to her that I had chosen my dress specifically to match that handmade purse. It meant a lot to me that my beautiful, ninety year old mother was at my side watching her grandson get married. I knew she had a tissue in her purse in case I needed it. And in honor of her I had also worn sensible shoes. Maybe the common sense is to follow. God will provide.

Day 1) Reflect on your religious upbringing. Was there a particular person or persons who planted the seeds of faith in you? Are those individuals still watering the seeds or are they nourished elsewhere? Have you planted the seeds of faith in others? Say a prayer of gratitude for those persons responsible for teaching you about God and ask how you might be used to spread knowledge of Him.

Day 2) Have you experienced performance anxiety in your life? Have you overcome this or does it still rear its ugly head from time to time? Cast all of your anxiety before the Lord because He cares for you and pray for a confident and courageous spirit.

Day 3) Do you spend much time with the elderly? Are there lessons you have learned from those older and wiser than yourself? Consider how the priorities of life become greatly simplified as one ages and what this simplification might teach you.

Day 4) Is there something which caused a sense of embarrassment during your upbringing which instills a sense of pride now? Do you see yourself becoming more like your parents than you ever thought you would? Consider the ways in which you desire to age as your parents aged and the ways in which you hope to differ.

Day 5) Is there a person you know who seems to have a great deal of common sense? Is there someone who comes to mind greatly lacking in this attribute? Do you tend to avoid people who just can't seem to get their acts together? Does having a lack of common sense describe you? Ponder James 1:5 which tells us "if any of you lacks wisdom, he should ask God who gives to all generously and ungrudgingly, and he will be given it."

Day 6) Consider the commandment "Honor thy father and thy mother." Reflect on your treatment of your parents and ask forgiveness for any time you neglected to honor them as instructed by our Lord.

Day 7) Reflect on any advice given to you by your parents which stands out in your mind. Consider a time when you followed or neglected to follow this advice and the resulting consequences. Say a prayer of thanksgiving for the gift of your parents and any and all sense and sensibility passed on to you.

I like signs. I have them all over the house. "Try our famous peanut butter and jelly sandwich," "Live well, laugh often, love much" and "Thou shalt not whine" grace my kitchen walls. "If friends were flowers I'd pick you," "How did everybody end up in my kitchen?" and "Please don't mess with the cook's buns" are in the pantry area. "There comes a time in the day that no matter what the question...the answer is wine" hangs right next to my current favorite "Because nice matters." Nice does matter, though sometimes it seems like the exception rather than the rule.

Several years ago, my husband and I were in New York City at Christmas time and decided to visit F. A. O. Schwartz. Everyone had told us that we had to buy the kids something at this famous toy store and that there was nothing like it in December. We walked through the front door and felt like cattle being herded along as we shuffled, shoulder to shoulder, from one end of the store to the other. We managed to find gifts for our three children and then got in a long line to pay for them. The entire transaction took place without the salesperson uttering a single word to us. She rang up the gifts, took our credit card, handed back the card and purchases and never established eye contact.

We had exactly the opposite experience in northern Michigan recently. During our drive up north my husband and I both commented on how nice the woman working at Subway was to us. We stopped in a little after nine p.m. at the last fast food hub before completing the final hour of our drive. This woman was working solo, and there was a line, but she was cheery as could be. She welcomed us to Subway, made friendly small talk while preparing our sandwiches and ringing us up, thanked us for choosing Subway and encouraged us to come again. We felt welcomed and valued.

When we arrived at our cottage our next door neighbor headed over at his first opportunity and gave us a great big hug and welcome back. The lady that works at the shack at the golf course did the same thing the next day between nines of our round. She always has fresh coffee made for us and warms up the muffins she knows we will be ordering at the turn. The lady at the corner restaurant made her usual inquiries about our golf games when we went in to pick up our carry-out order. The owner of the pizza place thanked us profusely for our business and smiled broadly while telling us of a recent several star rating his restaurant had received in a magazine. People are nice up north. They seem to be quick with a smile, a handshake and a hug.

During this same trip we randomly chose a roadside church at which to attend weekend Mass because the timing fit in well with our plans. At the end of the service the priest led a chorus of Happy Birthday to those born in June. He then asked the visitors to identify themselves and to share where they call home. He implored the congregation to give us a hearty welcome. This resulted in two parishioners walking us out to our car excitedly sharing that they had once lived across from our church down state. They were pleased to hear that we are friends with the family currently residing in their former home.

There is a sign we pass on the way to and from our cottage, in front of a small Christian church, which reads "Come as you are." This theme seems to be prevalent in the small towns of northern Michigan. Folks tend to be pretty casual. We got paired with another couple for eighteen holes of golf who were wearing denim shorts, socks and sandals. He was a retired truck driver who smoked nonstop and played from the red tees. She had difficulty walking the course due to foot and knee problems. But they were an absolute delight on the course. They played quickly, kept the ball in play and laughed a lot. The round ended with a firm handshake and lots of warm wishes.

Our weekend of northern Michigan bliss ended prematurely as we had agreed to play in a couple's golf event back home on Sunday afternoon. The traffic increased as we neared suburbia but the smiles decreased. Driving down our street we waved to a neighbor we have met several times who always acts like he doesn't know us. He didn't wave back. We changed into our golf attire and headed to the club only to realize that we were supposed to have dressed in a Jimmy Buffet *Margaritaville* theme. Everyone was sporting bright tropical colors and we were wearing black and dark blue. Needless to say we were not in the running for the prize for best outfits. We didn't come close to best in golf either. The "come as you are" world had been left miles behind.

We keep old clothes at our cottage and that is what we wear every day. We eat very simple meals and are repeatedly amazed at how little we pay for what we consume. There is a bakery we frequent in a small town near our cottage where we continually question whether they have charged us enough. We will order two sandwiches, chips, two drinks, a couple of donuts and a muffin and be told we owe seven or eight dollars the same price we pay for a fancy coffee and a scone at home.

There is a man who does work for us at the cottage who has submitted drawings of his plans on loose leaf paper with an ink pen. He has fixed our roof, sanded our deck, refinished our bathrooms, replaced our counters, painted, built a bar, selected and installed wooden blinds and refinished our hardwood floors. He does excellent work and charges very reasonable prices. Yet, he nervously calls after we arrive each time to ask if everything is to our satisfaction. It is almost as if our praise of his work means as much to him as the payment. He really wants to please and takes tremendous pride in his craft.

My husband has an old wooden boat that a northern Michigan man refurbished for him. This man videotaped the entire refurbishing process explaining every step taken and part chosen. This was truly a labor of love. This same man winterizes and stores our boat for us and returns it to our shore station every summer. He talks about our boat as one would speak of an old friend. We gladly pay his very detailed bill each year because he has begun to feel like family. He really cares and it shows.

A church just up the road from us in suburbia has a sign with clever sayings that change monthly. Last month it said "No matter who you work for, God is your boss." This month it says "If you don't have time for God, you are too busy." I think our handyman, our wooden boat expert, and all the small business owners we have encountered up north know that God is their boss. They understand that making time for their neighbors and customers is making time for God. The genuine spirit of their smile, greeting, hug or handshake demonstrates their conviction that nice matters.

I must learn to capture that up north "come as you are" spirit and transport it to this down state bustling metropolis. I must be quick to offer a smile, a handshake and a hug. I must remember that whatever I do, I do for the Lord. I must not be too rushed, too distracted or too busy to be kind because that would not be nice. And nice definitely matters.

Day 1) Do you have a sign in your home or one that you encounter during your daily travels which particularly speaks to you? I am gazing at one near my computer which says "The most important things in life...aren't things." Ponder a favorite expression and why it speaks to you.

Day 2) Does "come as you are" aptly describe any of the arenas of your life? If you were invited to a "come as you are" party right now would you feel comfortable attending? Do you feel you have ample opportunities to truly be yourself? Explain.

Day 3) What kind of a relationship do you have with the people who provide services for you? Do you take time to consider the person behind the name tag, the counter or the uniform? Are you willing to compliment good service and express gratitude for a job well done? Reflect on persons in your life you may have neglected to acknowledge and make a plan to correct any omissions in the future.

Day 4) Do you agree with the expression "because nice matters?" How hard do you try to be nice to those you encounter daily? Can you think of a time recently when you were not as nice as you should have been to another? Contemplate any needed reconciliation.

Day 5) Deuteronomy 8:17-18 tells us to remember the source of all we have: "Beware lest you say in your heart, 'My power and the might of my hand have gotten me this wealth.' You shall remember the LORD your God, for it is he who gives you power to get wealth." Ponder the source of all that you have and consider for whom you work.

Day 6) Do you frequently feel you are too busy for God? Do you ever feel that you don't have time to be thoughtful? Take time out now to sit with the Lord. Ask Him to help you to reassess your priorities.

Day 7) Make a list of the things that matter most to you. Now ponder 1 Thessalonians 5:16-18 "Rejoice always. Pray without ceasing. In all circumstances give thanks, for this is the will of God for you in Christ Jesus." Rejoice. Pray. Give thanks.

A catalogue arrived in the mail this week entitled *As We Change*. From the picture of the woman on the front, as well as a quick flip through the pages, it is clear that this is a catalogue for the mature woman. Products promising to "Reverse aging for youthful eyes," "Erase vertical lip lines" and "Turn back the hands of time" are on every page. There is even a pillow to keep your chest free of creases and revitalize your décolletage. This week's mail also included an AARP card application and a copy of *More* magazine which caters to woman over forty.

It seems like the hands of time have been assaulting me lately. My husband and I stopped into a restaurant on our way to a local Carole King-James Taylor concert and were dismayed to discover that our young waitress had never heard of them. Her reaction somewhat mitigated our shock at discovering an audience of grey haired people in khakis when we entered the stadium later. As we stood to clap and dance to a rousing rendition of *I Feel the Earth Move* the people behind us yelled, "*Down in front!*" We were supposed to sit in our seats and tap our toes to the music like decent, mature people.

At a recent dance audition for a local community theatre production, I found myself huffing and puffing after a relatively simple routine. The combination was a series of basic Charleston moves with some leg flicks and kicks. There were maybe twelve different steps taught which would have been very easy for me to memorize just a few years back. Remembering the sequence was no longer easy. At this same audition a young, flat belly told me that she hoped to have a figure like mine when she was my age. I guess this means that if she had my figure now it would not be so great but it would be alright when she is much older.

A question I get asked frequently now is, "*Do you have any grandchildren?*" This obviously indicates that I look old enough to be a grandma, and with two children married I am definitely in that ballpark, but I guess I am somewhat in denial about the outer me. The inner me still feels young, energetic and carefree. The inner me still wants to buy jeans that belt at the hip and not at the waist. The inner me still wants to shake a tail feather on the dance floor to young people's music, even though most of my moves have that 70s disco flavor. *Saturday Night Fever* and the "Bump" were big in my day.

The outer me occasionally demands to be noticed and will not be ignored. About a week ago I was looking in the rear view mirror checking traffic for my husband who was driving and caught a glimpse of my neck in the sunlight. It was scary. I also have to use tweezers to remove hair in odd places and have very sun damaged old lady hands. Since aging happens gradually and I don't spend as much time looking at myself in the mirror as I once did, the inner me likes to think that I still look on the outside the way I feel on the inside. Sadly, the inner me is wrong.

At that same audition a few weeks ago came the realization that I did not know many of the people trying out at my local theatre group. I have been a member of this group for about twenty five years and have done more than a dozen memorable roles. But now there is a whole new crop of people in the mix and I have not been around enough lately to be familiar with most of them. This same situation has occurred at the club where we play golf and at the parish where we worship. My husband was president of our club less than five years ago but there has been a lot of turnover in the membership since then. The club tables, as well as the church pews, seem to be full of new young families we do not know.

The cast list of the show for which I was auditioning is also filled with lots of new young people that I do not know. I did not get cast. I was not as prepared as I should have been and had many rehearsal conflicts due to time my husband and I plan to spend up north. A friend auditioning alongside me commented that I did not seem "hungry" for the role. She was right. As the call back went late into the evening and I was asked to sing a third time I could not seem to dig deep enough to give the director what he wanted. He chose a younger woman with an incredible belt. Out with the old and in with the new.

When the going gets tough the tough go up north. At least that is where members of this family go to get over rejection, setbacks and stress. A change of scenery does a body good when the old scenery causes a bad tape to be replayed in the brain. My kind husband took his aging wife up north to our happy place to initiate an attitude readjustment. It worked. We got up when the sun came up and went to bed when the sun went down. We played golf, weeded, planted flowers, put the boat in the water and walked and ran along the lake. I wore my flip flops that don't hurt my bunions and my old warm up pants from the eighties. We both enjoyed a good read and good wine.

One of the books I was reading was *God's Words of Life for Catholic Women.*" Its chapters on pride and humility particularly spoke to me. The more prideful we are the more difficulty we have watching our looks and talents fade. This stems from having too much of our identity wrapped up in the exterior. Concerns about the outer me had been given much more priority than concerns about the inner me. It was definitely way past time to begin focusing on inner beauty.

The opening hymn at Mass that Sunday was *We Are Called*. The priest then addressed the four ways that we are called in the song: to act with justice, to love tenderly, to serve one another and to walk humbly with God. He used these words to initiate an examination of conscience to call to mind the times that we had not walked humbly with God that week. It was clear to me that most of my decisions and actions as of late had been lacking in this humility. It was time to start focusing on what God sees as beautiful. I don't think that wrinkles, bunions, chin hairs or age spots have anything to do with it. I also don't think it has to do with how long I can hold a note or how loudly I can sing. It certainly has to do with whether or not I act justly, love tenderly or serve another. This is the way in which I hope to grow beautiful. Aging cannot decay the inner me.

Day 1) How have you been handling the aging process? Is there any particular aspect of aging which you have found hard to accept? Separate those things which are beyond your control from those over which you have control. Ask God to help you to age well.

Day 2) Has your spiritual maturation kept pace with your physical maturation? Do you purchase as many products to enhance your spiritual growth as you do to combat the negative effects of aging? Are you as concerned with the parts of you that are unseen as you are with those that are seen? Reflect.

Day 3) Has your definition of beauty changed with age? Is there someone whom you once found lacking in beauty you now find beautiful? Is there someone whom you once found beautiful you no longer see as so? Ask God to give you eyes for real beauty.

Day 4) Consider the song "We Are Called" and the four ways in which it instructs us: to act with justice, to love tenderly, to serve one another and to walk humbly with God. This lyric is taken from Micah 6:8: "What does the Lord require of you but to do justice and to love kindness, and to walk humbly with your God." Speak to the Lord of this requirement and how He desires you to personally answer this call.

Day 5) Have the hands of time been assaulting you lately? Have you had to confront specific limitations which correspond to your age? Have you had a rude awakening over something you could once do easily which now proves difficult or impossible? Pray for an appreciation of all the things you can do and acceptance of those you cannot.

Day 6) When you read an obituary for someone your age does it startle you? Do you realize that time is a gift from God and that the alternative to birthdays is death? Consider any relationships in need of healing, unfinished business in need of closure and things left unsaid which need to be said. Contemplate being ready to meet your maker.

Day 7) Do you attempt to recognize the beauty of God's creation? Do you appreciate the changing seasons and the offerings of each? Have you ever sat mesmerized by rain hitting a window, wind blowing leaves off of a tree or the sun or moon lighting an object just so? Compose a song of praise to God the artist painting such beautiful pictures for our viewing pleasure each day.

A gentleman held a door open for my daughter and me recently when we were entering a building and my daughter returned the favor by opening the inner door for him. She smiled at me and said, "*One good turn deserves another.*" I smiled back knowing that she has heard me say that many times and that I have also heard my mother say that many times. These are the little things we pass on to our children without even realizing it.

Kindness seems to breed kindness. At a high school musical I attended this spring one of the females in the chorus spent an entire scene holding up a Christmas tree. This was the final scene of the musical *Annie* and during the change of scenery it was clear that the Christmas tree was going to fall over, lights, ornaments and all unless a cast member hung on to it. Rather than ruin the moment for the lead actors attempting to sing and dance their way to happily ever after, this performer stood in the background exerting force on the 15 foot tree. She missed out on her own choreography to let them have their moment.

This young lady's selflessness prompted me to offer a hand to a struggling young woman at the mall. This woman was carrying a child in her arms and had another toddler at her side while attempting to carry a floor lamp up the escalator. The way her arm was extended with a firm grip on the lamp reminded me of the Christmas tree incident and inspired me to ask if I could carry it for her. She said yes gratefully, without hesitating, and we managed to find "Pottery Barn for Kids" and make the return. The lamp was heavy and the store was not close but I was moved by the actress from the musical.

"What goes around comes around" is another familiar expression generally referring to unkind people getting their just rewards. But it applies equally well to good deeds begetting other good deeds. When I was waitressing years ago I accidentally dropped a piece of red snapper in a woman's lap. The entrée slipped off of the plate as I leaned in to set it in front of her and landed on her beautiful silk suit. She took one look at my horrified expression and said it was nothing that a trip to the dry cleaners couldn't fix. I fought tears as I apologized and thanked her repeatedly for her understanding.

Years later I was attending a fancy charity party in a brand new white suit that was probably the most expensive ensemble that has ever graced my closet. My husband was the president of our club at the time and I had been trying to upgrade my clothing purchases to appear more presentable on his arm. I was standing at one of those cabaret style tables nibbling on an appetizer when a waitress accidentally knocked a diet coke down the front of me while clearing. You would have thought she had just mortally wounded someone from the look of horror on her face. I took one look at her eyes welling up with tears and said what the woman in the silk suit had said to me years before: it was nothing that a trip to the dry cleaners couldn't fix.

There are plenty of statistics on how children from abusive families, alcoholic families and other types of dysfunctional families pass on these traits to the next generation. But it is harder to quantify the effects of positive influences and good examples. "Practice random acts of kindness" seems to speak to the difficulty of statistically proving how much good comes from good: it is random. But like little ripples on a pond the effects of kindness can be far reaching. The initiator of the kindness rarely gets to see beyond the immediate effect of the action but like the energizer bunny it keeps going and going.

Our boat broke down on Houghton Lake once when the kids were small and a kind boater towed us miles back to our rented cottage. The journey consumed over an hour of time and several gallons of gas. We urged the gentleman to take money for his time, expenses and inconvenience. He refused payment and simply suggested that we do the same thing for a boater in trouble someday. We had the opportunity to do that very thing years later when a boater ran out of gas in front of our cottage and requested help. Chances are pretty good that the rescued family in front of our cottage will have a similar opportunity to help another in the future.

A wise person once said that you can distinguish a good act from a bad act by how you feel afterwards. I find this to be incredibly true. There is a sense of peace that seems to come over me when I choose the good. Conversely, when I don't take the time to help another and choose to act like I don't see the need it haunts me. Every time I think I am going to feel better when I unload on someone or give them a piece of my mind I don't. I feel worse. I see the hurt in their eyes that I have caused and realize that some things are better left unsaid. I also realize that some things, even though they are difficult, need to be endured.

Jesus demonstrated the importance of serving one another throughout the gospels, but one of the most memorable occurrences was when He washed His Disciples' feet. He did this at the last supper much to the dismay of His followers telling them: *"Do you realize what I have done for you? You call me 'teacher' and 'master' and rightly so, for indeed I am. If I, therefore, the master and teacher have washed your feet, you ought to wash one another's feet. I have given you a model to follow, so that as I have done for you, you should also do.*" (John 13:13-15) Jesus followed this selfless act with the ultimate selfless act. He laid down His life for His friends.

We have the perfect model to follow in Jesus. We are called to be imitators of Christ, to be perfect as He is perfect. This is a tall order and can seem overwhelming at times. When I am overwhelmed by the tasks at hand I tend to break things down to one task at a time. Today, in this moment, I will ask God how He can use me this day. I will tell Him that I am willing to serve and ask Him to open my eyes to the need around me. It may be as simple as carrying a lamp or opening a door for a stranger. But with my eyes and heart wide open I will remember all of the things that God has done for me. One good turn deserves another. It is my turn to carry the lamp and open the door. And it will feel good afterwards.

Day 1) Call to mind a time when someone's act of kindness inspired you to imitate them. Did you tell the person that their act of kindness inspired you? Have you been told recently that your behavior has inspired another? Ask the Lord to provide you with opportunities to serve others and to give you eyes to see and courage to respond.

Day 2) Have you ever unloaded on someone in the hope that it would make you feel better only to discover that it made you feel worse? Have you ever been the recipient of someone's venting with no forewarning that the venting was coming? Pray for a spirit of discernment and a voice to be used to build up rather than tear down.

Day 3) Consider the positive role models in your life. Have they changed or remained the same? What are the common attributes which all of them possess? What type of role model would you like to be to others? Explain.

Day 4) Do the stories of Jesus washing another's feet, dining with prostitutes or embracing lepers disturb you? When you hear the story of a poor man named Lazarus, covered with sores, lying at the rich man's door and "dogs even used to come and lick his sores" (Luke 16:21) can you feel compassion rather than disgust? Ask Jesus to reveal to you those in need outside of your door and to give you the strength to open and minister.

Day 5) Jesus said "as I have done for you, you should also do." (John 13:15) Jesus always practiced what He preached. Can you think of a time when you have not practiced what you have preached? Ask Jesus to enlighten you about a time when your words and behavior have been incongruous and to help you to overcome this tendency.

Day 6) Opening a door for a stranger, holding an elevator, allowing another car to merge into your lane, offering someone your seat, picking up an item that was dropped or plunking extra coins in an expired parking meter are just a few examples of ways you could brighten another's day. Make your own list and then put them into action.

Day 7) We all make choices everyday about which doors to enter and exit, open and close, investigate or avoid. Is there a door you have closed which you need to consider reopening? Is there someone knocking at your door whom you need to let in? Ponder "Behold I stand at the door and knock." (Revelation 3:20)

There are many different types of loss. The first definition of "lose" in *The New American Webster Dictionary* says "miss and not know where to find." This is the simplest form of loss and tends to happen to keys and glasses. This is generally not serious as most things are replaceable. If it is your mind or yourself which you cannot find, that is altogether a different story. The second definition says "be deprived of; be parted from." The third says "cease to have." These are the more serious forms of loss. *"I am sorry for your loss"* is a condolence I uttered recently at a funeral for the husband of a friend. Her "cease to have" put my own recent losses in their proper perspective.

This has been a season of letting go. My oldest son has a wife now and doesn't need his mommy anymore. He actually hasn't needed me for awhile but the marriage certificate spells it out clearly for me. The same goes for my daughter. I know they say that you're not losing a son, you're gaining a daughter and not losing a daughter, you're gaining a son. But the relationships definitely change. There is a letting go in the process.

I also had to say good bye to my youngest son recently. It was not a final good bye and he was not going off to war or involved in anything concerning life and death. He was just heading to the other side of the country to start a new job and I was his ride to the airport. But giving him that last, lingering hug and then watching him walk away with his bags packed really tore at my heart. I got into the car and began to sob in a more violent way than I can remember doing in a long time. I felt like I was losing him.

The silence of the empty nest and the desire to fill the void that family activities once occupied led me into two competitive situations recently which brings me to the fourth definition of "lose:" "cause or suffer defeat in a game, suffer loss; be defeated." I signed up to play in a golf match play tournament and I auditioned for a role in a local theatrical production. I lost at both. I have been feeling like the biggest loser and the losing does not involve weight. Weight loss would be exciting.

Like losing rejection hurts. Yet the only way that one can win is by entering the competition. We all know that the barker from the amusement park yelling "everybody's a winner!" can't be trusted. Sometimes you win and sometimes you lose. And losing hurts. I encountered a teary-eyed friend at church last week attempting to come to terms with the fact that her husband is likely to lose an important election. He is a candidate we have supported personally and financially. As the stakes get bigger so does the loss. The cloud of competition and loss seems to be following me.

St. Paul instructs us to compete well. He reminds us that the runners in a stadium all run in the race but only one wins the prize. In verse 10:24 of 1 Corinthians he urges us to "Run so as to win." The whole notion of competition has always been unsettling to me. I am frequently in competitive situations and yet would prefer not to be. I do not relish beating someone at something but also do not relish losing. I prefer to avoid the whole scene altogether. But unless one enters it one will never land a role, win a game or get elected. You have to put yourself out there in order to win. So the competing continues.

Even the apostles competed. Luke 22:24 discloses "Then an argument broke out among them about which of them should be regarded as the greatest." Mark 10:37 reveals James and John asking Jesus for the best seats in heaven: *"Grant that in your glory we may sit one at your right and one at your left."* Peter, also, after being given the keys to the Kingdom and told he was to tend Jesus' sheep, directed his concern to the disciple whom Jesus loved. John 21:21 says "When Peter saw him, he said to Jesus, 'Lord, what about him?'" Jesus responded to Peter, *"What if I want him to remain until I come? What concern is it of yours? You follow me."* (John 21:22)

So when my question to the Lord is, *"What about him?"* as in why does that person always win, always get what he wants or always come out on top I must look to how He responded to Peter. He reminded Peter simply not to be concerned with another's position. His response to Peter included a directive: You follow me. Whether we win or lose, are happy or sad, healthy or ill, rich or poor we are to follow Christ and do His will.

"Take Lord and receive all my liberty, my memory, my understanding and my entire will, all that I have and possess. You have given all to me. To You, O Lord, I return it. All is yours. Dispose of it wholly according to Your will. Give me Your love and Your grace, for this is sufficient for me." (Saint Ignatius) This prayer, which I say frequently, reminds me to give it all away. I am to give it all to the Lord requiring only His love and His grace. The Gospel writers tell us that "whoever loses his life for my sake will find it." (Matthew 10:39) The Gospel of John reminds us: "Whoever serves me must follow me, and where I am, there also my servant will be." (John 12:26)

If you want to gain your life you must lose it. What you lose in this world you will gain in the next. "I even consider everything as a loss because of the supreme good of knowing Christ Jesus my Lord. For his sake I have accepted the loss of all things and consider them so much rubbish, that I may gain Christ." (Philippians 4:8) Here Paul is not referring to losing a game, a role or even an election. Paul understands that most of us find it difficult to put up with it if someone "gets the better of you, or puts on airs or slaps you in the face." (2 Corinthians 11:20) But what he considers rubbish includes imprisonments, beatings and brushes with death. He reports that "three times I was beaten with rods, once I was stoned, three times I was shipwrecked" and he confronted forty lashes minus one (five times), robbers and hardships. (2 Corinthians 12:23-27) Clearly when Saint Paul speaks of loss, he knows what he is talking about.

Saint Ignatius, also, is willing to give up his liberty, memory, understanding and entire will. All Saint Ignatius asks for in return is the love and grace of the Lord and Saint Paul is willing to accept the loss of all things if only he may gain Christ. That certainly silences all of my whining and complaining. So I've lost a few things. I have to be willing to lose it all on earth to be a big winner in heaven. This applies to everyone. "What profit would there be for one to gain the whole world and forfeit his life?" (Matthew 16:26) There is no profit in gaining the whole world if you lose your soul in the process. But we can gain Christ and save our souls if we are willing to give everything else away.

Maybe there is truth in the carnival barker's shout "everybody's a winner!" Everybody can be a winner if they are not afraid of losing. This is the ultimate game and the stakes are high. We must compete well and run, so as to win. Jesus is out in front and it is He whom we must follow. Even better, He tells us that we can take His yoke upon our shoulders. He is going to help us cross the finish line. I have to ask myself why I would want to be in any other game in town when I can be the biggest loser in this game and still win. The answer is that I do not. I'd better stop whining and get off the bench.

Day 1) Has there been a season of your life when you felt like the biggest loser? How did you get through this period? Was there a particular person who helped you through? Was there a Scripture passage which helped you put your losses in their proper perspective? Reflect on your experience with loss.

Day 2) Do you ever find yourself asking "what about him?" as in why does that other person always seem to get what they want? Reflect on the commandment "Thou shalt not covet thy neighbor's goods."

Day 3) Have you ever lost out on something only to look back and realize that it actually worked out for the best? Consider a time when a loss in the short term turned out to be a gain in the long term.

Day 4) Do you have a hard time letting go of things? Examine your life for something you have been hanging onto which you need to set free.

Day 5) Do you know a person who seems to be piling up gains on earth yet losing his or her soul? Reassess your own profit and loss columns and determine if there is anything you are forfeiting which heaven would see as gain.

Day 6) How comfortable are you in competitive situations? What is your reaction to St. Paul's instructions to compete well and run so as to win? Are you keeping your eyes on the prize? Contemplate your place in the race.

Day 7) Ponder the last line of the Prayer of St. Ignatius: "Give me your love and your grace for that is sufficient for me." Is the love and grace of God sufficient for you? Consider anything that might be standing in the way of returning all God's gifts to Him.

I passed a garden lined with rocks on one of my walks recently and was reminded of my dad. He loved rocks. He referred to himself as a "rock hound" and spent many hours walking the beaches of the Great Lakes looking for special ones. He would polish the smaller, pretty stones in a rock tumbler and put them on display in his home. The Petoskey stones, geodes and larger rocks would line his yard, garden and porch. Books on rocks and minerals lined his shelves.

He loved old books. He had a shirt that said "so many books, so little time." He made a hobby out of searching old book stores for rare books and first editions. He was always giving my husband books on golf and my children books about sports. Once you expressed an interest in a particular subject, dad made it his mission to supply you with plenty of good reading material on that subject.

Dad enjoyed simple things. He liked going for long walks. I still occasionally think I see him when catching a glimpse of an elderly gentleman walking through town. Then I remember that he's walking in heaven now. He's probably enjoying crisp, golden delicious apples while admiring a perfectly manicured lawn. His idea of relaxation was picking up twigs in the yard and sweeping the sidewalk. He always mowed his own lawn and shoveled his own snow. He would shovel several times during a continuous snow fall trying to stay ahead of the accumulation game. He usually won.

I felt as if dad were walking with me on my recent trek along the lake up north because I kept seeing things through his eyes. He loved trees and birds. He referred to Northern Michigan as "God's country." We would always stop at scenic look-outs on our trips up north and linger especially long at the lake views. He would also stop at all sidewalk sales, thrift shops and yard sales. That was why one yard sale sign caught my eye. It said "Treasures!" Dad was always bringing home treasures.

Dad loved bargains, as do I. He passed away over ten years ago but I still think of things I want to tell him. The dress I wore to my son's wedding was a bargain. Originally priced at two hundred and something, the dress was reduced to one hundred and something, then eighty three bucks and still on the sale rack. I added a rewards card to the purchase and walked away paying a little more than ten dollars. Dad would have been proud of that.

My husband and I often refer to our lives as "The tale of two worlds." We will order a large antipasto salad and a loaf of hot, fresh bread up north for carry out and pay $11.61. Then we will be invited to meet friends at a fancy restaurant for dinner down state and be charged sixteen dollars for one glass of chardonnay. One glass of wine will cost more than our entire meal up north. Even though we can afford to pay for the pricey wine and the pricey meal it just doesn't feel right. It feels obscene.

We are torn between the worlds of simple and fancy. It is said that things tend to come full circle and I am beginning to realize the truth in that saying. We are born into this world dependent on others, work hard to develop and establish our independence and then are likely to return to being dependent on others again before we die. Similarly, I was raised to appreciate simple things, then went through a phase of craving everything fancy and am now returning to the keep it simple philosophy.

Our most recent desire to simplify was prompted by cleaning my husband's closet. He was attempting to put his Christmas gifts away this past winter when he realized that in order to make room for the new he had to get rid of the old. He spent an entire weekend stuffing clothes into bags to be given away. He confessed to actually being embarrassed by the amount of clothes he had accumulated and found things he had purchased but had never worn that still had the tags on them.

I proceeded to do the same thing to my side of the closet. The most painful moments of stuffing clothes into the giveaway bags came from those items for which I had paid too much and worn too seldom. Both my husband and I have occasionally succumbed to grown-up peer pressure to buy such and such an item from such and such a clothier. My husband was the butt of some jokes at one social gathering because the crowd felt that his sweater was outdated and that only their chosen clothier could help. I have also been ridiculed for my willingness to purchase knock-off purses and costume jewelry.

But, like my father, my husband's mother was a bargain shopper and bargain blood runs deep in our veins. We have an aversion to being overcharged or oversold. Like the child viewing the emperor's nonexistent fancy new clothes we both frequently want to yell out "the emperor is naked!" Your $300.00 face cream is not going to prevent you from getting wrinkles and your cutting edge designer outfit is not going to prevent you from growing old. Your dog definitely does not need jewels or an expensive coat.

Determining wants from needs takes me back to a tour my daughter and I once took of an historic cabin in a neighboring suburb.

There were two dresses on hooks on the wall of the pioneer girl's bedroom. The tour guide explained that one was her everyday dress and one was her Sunday dress. That was it. That was all she needed. She also had a pair of shoes, boots and a coat. The tour guide asked the group how they would feel about only owning two dresses. The children seemed horrified but I remember thinking that it would certainly simplify things.

This household has agreed to a moratorium on spending since the closet cleaning incident. We want for nothing and are redefining our concept of treasure. The new definition embraces the concept "for where your treasure is, there also your heart will be." (Luke 12:34) Dad always knew it was the simple things that had the most value. Like him I treasure a good book, a long walk and a crisp apple. Like him, I am coming to understand that love of God and love of neighbor are treasures far more precious than silver or gold. This is how I plan to fill my treasure chest with "an inexhaustible treasure in heaven that no thief can reach nor moth can destroy." (Luke 12:33) I might save a few mothballs and a tiny space for the $10.27 dress.

Day 1) List some of the things that you treasure. Has your concept of treasure changed over the years? Is there something you used to treasure which you no longer value? If you could choose one thing to pass on to a child or loved one, what would it be?

Day 2) Are the things you treasure different from those of your parents? Have your parents influenced your concept of treasure? Compare and contrast your "treasure chest" with that of your parents.

Day 3) Do you ever feel you are living a "tale of two worlds?" Compare any memorable small town and big city experiences or other contrasting experiences. In which environment are you most comfortable? In which environment do you find it easiest to live out your faith?

Day 4) Can you think of a way in which your life has come full circle? Have you been aware of the movement along the curve or has the journey taken you by surprise? Do you view this journey in a positive or negative light and why?

Day 5) Do you ever feel you are becoming your mother or your father? If yes, do you see the resemblance as something positive? If no, have you made a conscious effort to be your own person? Explain.

Day 6) When was the last time you experienced sticker shock? Are you comfortable walking away from an intended purchase after realizing that an item is overpriced? Have you ever succumbed to peer-pressure and spent more than you should on something merely to fit in or not make a scene? How do you determine value?

Day 7) Is there an area of your life in need of simplification? Do you enjoy simple things and try to keep all as simple as possible? Would you appreciate or resent a sign that said "simplify" in your home? Ponder the phrase "'tis a gift to be simple."

Love is not jealous. Whenever I hear that line from *Corinthians* I feel a little guilty. Because even though I am a grown, middle-aged woman, immersed in blessing, I still find myself confronting jealousy from time to time. It usually appears when I begin to compare myself to someone else and my internal scoreboard tells me that the other person is winning. I really need to turn the scoreboard off and grow up.

I experienced a slight flash of jealousy recently when my daughter was telling me how much her new mother-in-law loves to cook. Her mother-in-law spends her happiest moments in the kitchen, preparing meals for her family and friends. She simply loves to entertain and does so often. The bigger the group she has to feed the more joy she seems to derive from the process. My daughter is an attentive student and anxious to learn as much as she can from her new mom. Her old mom is not much of a cook.

My son has married into a family of doctors. My husband is a doctor, my son and his wife are doctors and both of her parents are doctors. When the medical jargon begins I start to sing "the cheese stands alone" to myself, as in little cheese in the land of big cheese. At the Baccalaureate Mass at their recent graduation all of the doctors in attendance were invited to participate in a candle-lighting ceremony. Then all of the doctors were invited to take the *Hippocratic Oath*. All of the doctors certainly got the medical jokes delivered by the guest speakers. This undereducated cheese did not.

When I was a sports mom I knew how to do that. When I was a theatre person I knew how to do that. Now as an empty nester I am learning how one does that. My son and daughter-in-law have asked me how I would like to be addressed. The choices appear to be Mom, Mrs. Ward or Patty. Since they each already have a mom whom they dearly love and Mrs. Ward is too formal I have opted for Patty. I am 52 year old Patty, wife of one, mother-in-law of two and mom to three still trying to figure out what I am going to be when I grow up. I emphasize "when" because I do not feel that it has happened yet.

Jealousy is just one of my childish behaviors. Not liking to share is another. Allowing my feelings to be hurt too easily is also on the list. Coveting other people's intimacy occurs often. Deciding that I don't want to go out and then wondering what everyone else is doing happens frequently. I compare myself to others, come up short and then pout. This tendency probably heads the list. I am definitely in process and still have much to learn and many things to scratch off my "to do" and "get over" lists.

Reflecting on those things I still want to conquer and accomplish prompted me to ask my husband the "bucket list" question recently. A bucket list identifies those things you still want to do before you kick the bucket. He was looking at a coffee table book of famous golf courses from around the world and I expected him to name several travel destinations and list other goals and dreams. He answered simply, "*I would like to grow old gracefully with you.*"

Wow. How mature. How succinct. He likes our life and the way we are living it and wants to keep living it this way until we die. This is a man who is comfortable in his own skin. He is comfortable with the choices he has made and his lot in life. He is not the least bit concerned with what other people are doing. I think this means that he has already grown up. I definitely have some catching up to do.

While I sit around thinking about how I am going to live my life he is actually living his. As a physician he has a vocation. He is a healer. As a mother I was a caregiver and a nurturer. But the birds have flown out of the nest and I now have no one to teach to fly.

My husband gives of his time and talents to his patients day after day, year after year, and will continue to do so for many years to come. He is content. I now have too much time on my hands and must find a vehicle for giving back. Constructive behaviors would certainly reduce my childish behaviors.

One way to practice more grown up behaviors would be to practice a more grown up faith. 1 Corinthians 13:11 explains "When I was a child, I used to talk as a child, think as a child, reason as a child; when I became a man, I put aside childish things." It is time to put aside childish things. It is time to move from milk to solid food. "I fed you milk, not solid food, because you were unable to take it. Indeed, you are still not able, even now, for you are still of the flesh. While there is jealousy and rivalry among you, are you not of the flesh, and behaving in an ordinary human way?" (1 Corinthians 3:2-3) Jealousy, rivalry, insecurity, coveting, pouting and other childish behaviors must cease.

The opposite of coveting, hoarding and envying is giving. A grown-up faith is one of generosity. *The Prayer of Generosity* attributed to Saint Ignatius conveys this beautifully. "Lord, teach me to be generous; teach me to serve you as you deserve; to give and not to count the cost; to fight and not to heed the wounds; to toil and not to seek for rest; to labor and not to ask for reward save that of knowing that I do your will."

These words tell us how to not only grow old gracefully, but in a grace-filled way.

We are instructed not to count the cost. This requires not keeping score. I am to turn off the scoreboard in my head that says she is a better cook than I am, she is smarter and more accomplished than I am, she is holier than I am, she is more talented than I am, she is preferred. I just serve the Lord. I just keep toiling. I do not ask for my reward. I do not seek for rest. I remember that love is patient and kind. I remember that love is not jealous. I put aside childish things and live a grown up faith. I will grow old in a graceful and grace-filled way. It's time to grow up.

Day 1) Regardless of your age, are there childish behaviors you have yet to leave behind? Lay your concerns before the Lord and ask Him to help you to put aside childish things.

Day 2) Do St. Paul's instructions about love elicit any particular reaction from you? Read 1 Corinthians 13 paying close attention to what love is and what love is not. Ask the Lord for opportunities to put love in action in your life this day.

Day 3) Reflect on the Prayer of Generosity cited above. Is there a particular line of this prayer that speaks to you? Contemplate generosity in terms of giving and not counting the cost.

Day 4) Have you ever put together a bucket list? Consider what might be on your bucket list if God was compiling it for you. Pray that your will be united with His will.

Day 5) Jealousy and rivalry among us indicates that we are of the flesh and not of the spirit, behaving in an ordinary human way. Admit any jealousy you are experiencing to the Lord. Ask Him to take you beyond the ordinary and to do the extraordinary.

Day 6) Call to mind a person you know who has aged gracefully and in a grace-filled way. Consider what it is about this person that makes them exemplary. Pray for the courage and discipline to follow this example.

Day 7) Consider the words of Psalm 139:1-3: "O Lord, you have probed me and you know me; you know when I sit and when I stand; you understand my thoughts from afar. My journeys and my rest you scrutinize, with all my ways you are familiar." The Lord knows you personally and intimately. Share the concerns of your heart with Him.

Attending noon Mass last week, I learned that it was the feast day of Saint Maria Goretti. Maria Goretti died a martyr's death on July 6th, 1902, when she refused to succumb to the sexual advances of a neighbor boy. She died from multiple stab wounds inflicted by her attempted rapist at the age of 11 years, 9 months and 21 days. She is the youngest officially recognized Roman Catholic saint and is the patron saint of chastity, rape victims, youth, teen age girls, poverty, purity and forgiveness. Maria forgave and prayed for her perpetrator in the painful hours before her death.

Her feast day prompted the priest to discuss purity and the vast array of temptation assaulting our youth today. He suggested that we pray fervently for our youth and for ourselves, that we might be better role models and examples for them. He happened to be a visiting priest with an accent suggesting that he was not from the United States. I found this noteworthy because just a few weeks prior, at another parish where I attended Mass, a foreign visiting priest had discussed the sin of fornication. I sat up and took notice because the sin of fornication, to consummate a love affair when not married, is rarely addressed from the pulpit. Actually, I have never heard it addressed.

Here in the good old U.S. of A. there seems to be little we find shocking anymore and little of which we are in awe. Married persons having multiple affairs, juveniles having multiple sex partners and young girls having multiple abortions barely raise a collective eyebrow. There is even a film entitled "Zoo," short for zoophile, signifying a person with a sexual interest in animals. This film debuted at the Sundance Film Festival in January 2007 where it was one of 16 winners out of 856 candidates. About a man who died after a sexual encounter with a horse, it was reviewed as "tender beyond reason" and "gorgeously artful." (Wikipedia)

I happened to find Maria Goretti's story tender beyond reason and was inspired to search the Web to learn more about this courageous young saint. There I discovered that some members of the feminist movement have criticized the veneration of Maria Goretti. They object to these martyrs of chastity insisting that they reinforce misogyny, sexism and violence against women by supporting a "better dead than raped" adage. There was also a book written about this controversy wherein the author argued that "irrespective of whatever happened, it was not worthwhile for Maria Goretti to let herself be killed for a stupid insignificant value such as virginity, and that the Church had done even worse by projecting her as an example."

Unfortunately, the view that virginity is a stupid, insignificant value seems to be shared by many. Modesty is also viewed as stupid and insignificant by this same faction. Exposed cleavage and buttocks are in. Even in the golf world where Bermuda length shorts and modest blouses were once required one now finds skimpy skirts and revealing tops. A female guest was observed on the driving range last year in thong underwear under an extremely short, pleated skirt. The other golfer's efforts to keep their eyes on the ball and mind on the game were being greatly challenged by her exposed derriere.

Purity is being challenged on every front. The sexual revolution has left us with rampant promiscuity, venereal disease, grossly immodest fashions, abortion, adultery and a high divorce rate amongst other things. In Peter Kreeft's book *Back to Virtue*, after chapters on the four cardinal and three theological virtues, he contrasts the beatitudes with the seven deadly sins. In chapter twelve *Pure of Heart vs. Lustful of Heart*, he contrasts the beatitude "Blessed are the pure of heart for they shall see God" with its opposite: lust. He explains "Lust is like mud. Its opposite is like clear water, or clean air. It is called purity of heart. Purity's most obvious aspect is sexual, as confronting sexual lust. But it is much more than that. It must be for its reward is much more than only the reward of sexual purity." It is the greatest reward of all: to see God.

What the two visiting priests and Peter Kreeft have in common is a willingness to discuss virtue and sin. The definition of virtue found on the inside cover of Kreeft's book is as follows: "virtue (n.) 1. Moral excellence; right living; goodness. 2. A particular type of moral excellence. 3. A good quality or feature. 4. Purity, chastity. 5. Effectiveness." Sin is the opposite of these: immorality, transgressions, offenses and missing the mark of right living and goodness. But this concept of sin does not sit well with the anything goes mentality prevalent in our world today. Sin, as well as virtue, seem to be regarded as outdated concepts corresponding to the "nothing is shocking" and awesome is a word synonymous with "cool" crowd.

As a Catholic, I am asked to confront my sin at the beginning of every Mass during the Penitential Rite. It is important that I recognize myself as a sinner in order to be able to welcome the forgiveness of Jesus. This prayer begins "I confess to almighty God, and to you my brothers and sisters, that I have sinned through my own fault in my thoughts and in my words, in what I have done, and in what I have failed to do." The phrase which jarred me, after the priest's comments about Saint Maria

Goretti, was "what I have failed to do." He was imploring us to be better role models and examples for our youth. I had to ask myself how many times I have failed to do this. My choice of dress, behavior and speech does not always reflect purity.

The Psalm spoken at Mass a few weeks ago also stung my conscience. Psalm 50 warns "Remember this, you who never think of God. Why do you recite my statutes, and profess my covenant with your mouth, though you hate discipline and cast my words behind you? When you see a thief you keep pace with him, and with adulterers you throw in your lot. To your mouth you give free rein for evil; you harness your tongue to deceit." This psalm ends "to him that goes the right way I will show the salvation of God." I began to think about my resistance to discipline, the words that come out of my mouth and my behavior around the company that I keep. I began to think about how we, as a society, are robbing our children of their innocence and their youth. I decided that it was time for me to clean up my act.

I am in awe of Saint Maria Goretti and all of the other martyrs and saints who were pure of heart and are now spending all of eternity seeing God. Some may find it shocking, but I find this purity worth emulating. God finds this pleasing and the rewards will be awesome. Blessed are the pure of heart for they shall see God. I must clean it up.

Day 1) When was the last time you found something shocking? Would you say that you are frequently or infrequently shocked? If you discussed whatever you found shocking with another did they share your feelings? Rate yourself with respect to "shockability" and explain why you feel you are in the majority or a minority.

Day 2) Reflect on the beatitude "Blessed are the pure of heart for they shall see God." Consider the role of purity in your life and pray for a clean heart and steadfast spirit.

Day 3) Have you been in a position to serve as a role model for youth? Did you take this responsibility seriously? Are there any behaviors you would change if you knew you were being observed by little ones? Do an examination of conscience and consider your choice of words and deeds as witnessed by a youthful audience.

Day 4) Have you given much thought to the martyrs of the church? Can you envision yourself as one who chooses to suffer, even to die, rather than renounce his or her faith or Christian principles? Say a prayer of thanks for the martyrs of the church and lay all of your fears about suffering before the God who loves you.

Day 5) Have you personally taken a stand against immorality and paid a price? Have you ever avoided taking a stand and later regretted your decision? "For God did not give us a spirit of cowardice but rather of power and love and self-control." (2 Timothy 1:7) Pray to the God of the impossible about your challenges and weakness.

Day 6) "Awe" is defined as "fear mingled with admiration or reverence." When was the last time you were awestruck? Think of something truly "awesome" as in inspiring awe. Ask the Lord for eyes to see as He sees and senses open to the awesome in the world.

Day 7) Are you named after a saint? Are you aware of various feast days, set apart by the Church giving special honor to God, the Savior, angels, saints and sacred mysteries and events? Do you recognize that we are in communion with the saints in heaven, honoring them as glorified members of the church, invoking their prayers and aid and striving to imitate their virtues? Ask for the intercession of your favorite saint.

"My do it!" is what my children used to say when they were little and wanted to do something by themselves. Although I admired this desire for independence, quite frequently they weren't yet ready to handle the task in question by themselves. This is when the milk ended up all over the counter, whatever they were carrying crashed onto the floor, clothing got put on backwards and shoes wound up on the wrong feet. They would even hurt themselves occasionally in the process. Some assistance would have been beneficial but they were more interested in going it alone. I, too, have a hard time asking for help. I prefer to do things by myself.

This preference for self-sufficiency developed over time in direct response to disappointments. The few times I have asked for help and it was not forthcoming left me disappointed, resentful and sad. I had requested assistance or admitted my needs to someone with the hope that they could help me and they were either unwilling or unable to help. I would make a mental note to ask for help as seldom as possible, and above all else try not to be needy. Low maintenance was definitely preferable to high maintenance.

However, I also began to notice how those friends, who don't hesitate to ask other friends for help, seem to share a special closeness. The opportunities to help each other out seem to draw them together. This applies to family as well. The old adage "the squeaky wheel gets the grease" comes to mind. The squeaking sibling who is not afraid to ask the parent for what they need ends up getting all the nurturing grease. The parent wants to nurture and be needed and the "child" desires nurturing and has needs. The wheel and the grease roll happily along. Of course, I want some of that nurturing grease also but not badly enough to start squeaking. I refuse to be a squeaker.

This internal struggle between independence and dependence, alone and together, selfish and unselfish has been going on for some time. I don't like to be needy. I resist being vulnerable and prefer not to be indebted to others. I am a social person but also crave my alone time. I continually strive to strike a balance between solitude and companionship. I am not always as hospitable as I might be. This struggle came to mind as I was reflecting on a sermon I heard recently. The Scripture readings for the past few weeks have revolved around the theme of hospitality. The story of the Good Samaritan, Martha and Mary entertaining Jesus in their home, and Abraham providing nourishment for three strangers raised the question of how hospitable we are.

Coincidentally, my daughter had asked me the same question while hanging out at our cottage during a recent visit up north. She noted that when we first purchased our cottage, over a decade ago, we had a steady stream of visitors and guests. During the past few years the number of people we have entertained has greatly diminished. She wondered why we don't have more groups of people up to the lake for fun and frolic. She asked if this was a concerted effort to have more alone time or simply the result of fewer close relationships as time goes by.

Hmmm. Here was that hospitality question again. I have been reflecting on this quite a bit lately trying to determine when and how our socializing changed. We used to have frequent parties at our home and numerous gatherings at the cottage. We had family get-togethers, golf outings, bonfires and game marathons. We purchased jet skis and a ski boat to provide hours of lake fun. We encouraged friends and family to use our place and rented it frequently to strangers. And then we got older.

We have settled into a nice routine at the cottage that we find relaxing but others might consider dull. We don't party late into the evening any more. We try to limit our sun exposure and don't eat a lot of junk food or drink a lot of beer. A day of waterskiing makes for very sore muscles the following day and tubing is very hard on this old girl's back. We go to bed early, get up early and spend lots of quiet hours reading and looking at the lake. All of the decisions that get complicated when you have a group are very easy to make when it's just the two of us.

"What are we going to do today?" "What are we going to eat?" "What are we going to drink?" "What are we supposed to wear?" "What are we going to do tonight?" Being the hostess means taking care of your guests' needs and planning the entertainment. My husband and I have peanut butter and jelly sandwiches for lunch and salads for dinner. We obviously feel the need to improve the offerings when we have guests. We are also very comfortable with long periods of silence. When we have company we feel compelled to be more lively conversationalists. It definitely changes the routine.

I often joke that I only have so much "charming" in me. It's like a switch goes off at a certain point in the evening when the charming well runs dry. When you are visiting someone else and your charming supply is exhausted you can make excuses and head home. Even when you are entertaining guests in your home, you can hint about having to get up early the next day, begin to suppress a yawn and most guests catch on and say their good byes. But this gets trickier when folks are staying with you. The charming time begins at breakfast, extends past dinner and begins again the next day.

A table for two is definitely easier. But it can also get lonely. There is a fine line between tranquility and isolation. I do desire to be connected to others, to converse and interact with others and to be involved in other's lives. We are called a "community of faith" for a reason. The scripture passage on "One Body, Many Parts" describes this well. "But as it is, there are many parts, yet one body. The eye cannot say to the hand, 'I do not need you,' nor again the head to the feet, 'I do not need you.'" (1 Corinthians 12:20-21) We are interconnected. We are here to lift each other up and help each other out. When we see someone hurting by the side of the road we are to stop and offer assistance. When visitors knock at the door and need refreshment we are to give generously.

I am reminded of why my husband wanted to buy our cottage years ago. Neither of our families owned cottages or boats when we were growing up but my husband's family was invited to his aunt's cottage several times during his childhood. He learned to water ski in response to the kindness of a boater on the lake who was willing to invite the neighbor kids along and patiently pull them up until they had mastered this water sport. He wanted to do the same thing for our children and the children of our friends and family. In the early years of owning our cottage we did this quite a bit.

It is time to return to the practice of hospitality. My tendency to prefer solitude in recent years stems more from laziness and selfishness than anything else. It takes effort and energy to play the gracious hostess and to concern myself more with other's needs than my own. But if I keep sending the message that I prefer to be left alone and do things by myself I may just get my wish. My desire to be self sufficient, low maintenance and rarely indebted to others may come back to haunt me. Especially since it is the imperfections and vulnerability in others that tend to draw us in and bind us together. I don't hear a lot of clamoring amongst my peers for perfect friends. Those that appear to have it all together rarely do anyway. They just don't want to expose their flaws.

This brings me to the toughest segment in the sermon about the Good Samaritan. The priest asked us to envision ourselves as the needy one. He asserted that when most hear this story they place themselves in the position of those walking by the wounded man or helping the wounded man. One rarely imagines himself as the victim, suffering by the side of the road, dependent upon a stranger's kindness to live. He asked us to imagine that we are the victim and the person approaching us to offer help is our enemy, the last person in the world before whom we would wish to appear vulnerable.

I began to squirm in my seat a little. I would have to be willing to accept this assistance. I would have to be willing to squeak and receive the nurturing grease or die. His point was that we should not only strive to be the Good Samaritan but that we must also allow others the opportunity to be the Good Samaritan to us. We must be willing to provide hospitality and accept hospitality, to give and to receive. If I choose to do neither than I may end up all by myself. This wheel had better start squeaking.

Day 1) Do you consider yourself to be a hospitable person? Have you become more or less hospitable with age? Consider any factors which might be preventing you from being as hospitable as you would like to be.

Day 2) Do you prefer to do things by yourself or are you more likely to seek the companionship of another? Do you have difficulty asking another for assistance? Do you consider yourself to be high maintenance or low maintenance and why?

Day 3) Are you more likely to entertain others in your home or be entertained by others in their homes? Which scenario do you enjoy more and why? Do you try to strike a balance between staying home and going out, solitude and companionship, giving and receiving? Are the scales of your life in balance or tipping?

Day 4) When you hear the Good Samaritan story where do you usually see yourself? Take a moment to envision yourself as each of the characters in the story: the injured person by the side of the road, one passing by without assisting, one who stops to help and one at the inn who receives the injured person. What do you learn from each?

Day 5) Reflect on the Scripture passage which describes the church as many parts yet one body. Do you truly feel that you are a part of a community of faith? Does the notion of spiritual connective tissue speak to you? "For in one spirit we were all baptized into one body." (1 Corinthians 12:13) Pray for unity in your family, community and world.

Day 6) Do you have difficulty being a squeaky wheel? Do you ever find yourself resentful when other squeaky wheels get the grease? Is there a particularly needy person in your life who does a lot of squeaking? How do you respond to the "squeaks?"

Day 7) "Do not neglect hospitality, for through it some have unknowingly entertained angels." (Hebrews 13:2) Call to mind a time when you were able to see a heavenly messenger speaking to you through the eyes of a stranger. Pray for the ability to recognize the light of Christ in those you encounter.

Contradictions have always bothered me. We are told that haste makes waste but also that he who hesitates is lost. We are frequently warned to look before you leap but also that analysis is paralysis. Obviously this is all a matter of degree and like Goldilocks in *The Three Bears* we want everything to be just right. We don't want to dress too young or too old for ourselves. We want to be appropriate, or more specifically, we do not want to be inappropriate. If brown is the new black then inappropriate is the new bad. Appropriate is the new just right.

Even in Scripture there seem to be contradictions. We are told that unless we turn and become like children we will not inherit the kingdom of heaven. But then we are told to put aside childish things. We are told that the Lord has hidden these things from the wise and are then instructed to be wise as serpents. Jesus is called the Prince of Peace and then tells us not to think that He has come to bring peace upon the earth. Fear is the beginning of wisdom and yet we are repeatedly told to fear not. The boldness of the disciples is applauded but the beatitudes tell us blessed are the meek.

I will leave it to biblical scholars and theologians to explain these apparent contradictions. I trust that there are perfectly reasonable explanations which have to do with context, translation and interpretation. I am simply trying to make sense of it all. Jesus wants to spread the good news and yet instructs those that He has healed to "see that you tell no one." (Matthew 8:4) Jesus states, "*When someone strikes you on your right cheek, turn the other one to him as well.*" (Matthew 5:39) Then Jesus instructs His disciples, "*Whatever town you enter and they do not receive you, go out into the streets and say, 'The dust of your town that clings to our feet, even that we shake off against you.'*" (Luke 10:10-11) He also says don't throw pearls before swine. (Matthew 7:6)

Wisdom is a gift of the Holy Spirit and I pray for this gift often. I so want to understand Holy Scripture and to apply the messages to my daily life. Some of them are easier to decipher than others. I can grasp the difference between being childlike, innocent and open, and childish, immature and silly. I can comprehend the difference between desiring to be wise in spiritual matters and being wise, resembling arrogant, in earthly matters. I believe that the kind of peace that Jesus gives is not as the world gives and that shaking off the dust from one who doesn't receive you is different than striking back.

I also recognize the sin of pride in my desire to try and find just the right answer to everything. I feel like an annoying child asking a parent "why?" and "how come?" over and over again. I get some relief from the scripture stories about the persistent woman before the judge and the persistent neighbor asking for bread. The persistent one who asks shall receive and the persistent one who seeks shall find. It may simply not happen in the way one expects or as quickly as one would hope. This is an instant gratification society however and this inquiring mind wants to know the right answers right now.

Scripture tells us to make straight our paths but mine seems more like a long and winding road. I think a heavenly navigation system would be nice. I would love to be able to push an "on star" button to reach the heavens and ask for directions. Jesus says that He is the Way, the Truth and the Life and no one gets to the Father except through Him. I believe this but in day to day life it is easy to get misdirected. It would be nice to see a sign that says "narrow gate...enter here." We have access to "mapquest" and GPS systems at the touch of a button to navigate our earthly routes. This instant gratification seeker with her fast food mentality likes the idea of a quick text message for Divine navigation.

The heavenly navigation system definitely exists but it is not instantaneous. We are to work out our salvation in fear and trembling. We are to practice the presence of God and pray without ceasing. We develop this relationship over time with lots of asking and waiting to receive. God is always there wanting to direct our paths and be our guide. The system exists but too often we forget to turn it on or even remember it is there at all. Even worse we hear the directions but simply choose to alter our path because we want something down a different road. It isn't on the map but it sure looks good and we want it now. We mute the system and go after it.

So, yes, I am a contradiction myself. I pray for peace but can't always get along with my own family and friends. I know that physical health is important but often eat and drink too much and exercise too little. I try to walk the walk of faith but frequently it is one step forward and two steps back. I abhor materialism but then find myself buying things that I don't really need. I am aware that I am to practice what I preach and let my conscience be my guide but too often I just turn off the navigation system and throw caution to the wind. Instead of being a person of extremes I could stand to be a little more moderate.

"Everything in moderation" is one of my husband's favorite expressions. This is probably because he is a physician and sees the effects of a tendency to either overdo or under-do. Alcohol, sweets, work, play, exercise, shopping, socializing are all examples of things one should do moderately rather than excessively. Reading, studying and theorizing top my personal list. I spend too much time studying God and talking at God and not enough time listening and following directions. It is true that an unexamined life is not worth living but an overly examined life may end up going nowhere.

"Thy word is a lamp unto my feet and a light unto my path." I will follow the light and stay close to your word. I will walk boldly when necessary but be blessed in my meekness. I will try not to be too hasty or too hesitant and to examine rather than overanalyze. I know that awe of God is the beginning of wisdom and that only the spiritually wise can understand heavenly things. I accept that I will occasionally contradict myself and that my words and my behavior will not always be appropriate. But like Goldilocks in The Three Bears every now and then I will get it just right.

Day 1) Can you comprehend the difference between the wisdom of God and human wisdom? Are you open to the Holy Spirit who helps us to understand the truths revealed in Scripture, tradition and the deep mysteries of God? Pray for true wisdom, the kind bestowed on you by the spirit of God not the spirit of the world.

Day 2) Have you ever turned off a navigation system because the voice was annoying or you did not like or understand the directions being given? Are you generally the person reading the map or driving the car? Do you hesitate to ask for directions and prefer to stumble upon your destinations by trial and error? Compare a typical earthly journey with your heavenly journey.

Day 3) How contrary of a person are you? Do you have a tendency to contradict yourself or others? Is there something you once considered a contradiction which now makes sense to you? Is there something you once saw as folly you now view as wise?

Day 4) Consider the role of moderation in your life. Do you see yourself as more of a moderate person or a person of extremes? Do you view moderation in a positive or negative light? Explain.

Day 5) Is there a particular passage from Scripture that has never made sense to you? Are you willing to take the time to research this passage and study commentaries which may shed light on this for you? Can you take this in prayer before the Lord and ask for enlightenment or merely to accept what you can't fully understand? Ponder "My thoughts are not your thoughts, nor are my ways your ways." (Isaiah 55:8)

Day 6) In our fast-paced world do you find it difficult to wait for answers from the Lord? Do you pray with instant gratification hopes for lightening fast responses? Call to mind a time when a prayer was answered later than you had hoped in a way you didn't expect and yet perfectly.

Day 7) Recall a recent Goldilocks moment when everything turned out just right. Do you take the time to savor perfect moments and say a prayer of gratitude for the ways God is at work in your life? Can you find something perfect in this very moment: the room in which you are sitting, the roof over your head, the clothing on your back, your eyes, your mind, your hands, your legs? Thank the Lord for making everything just right.

Another summer is winding down and fall is approaching. I love fall. My birthday is in the fall and is always a time for reflection. I look back at the past year and try to assess how I have lived my life and in what ways I need to improve. Chapter 52 is being written at the end of my 52nd year. I am most likely in the fall of my life and as the trees begin to shed their leaves I have a few things I need to shed also. Rereading these essays has made that painfully clear.

Dead leaves, like cobwebs on my tree, were definitely obstructing my view. I was very aware, for example, of the other somber faces at the mall, refusing to smile at me when I passed by. I then brought my sister mall-walking with me one day and was forced to walk at a slower pace. I noticed how many people were smiling at her and greeting us as they walked by. I told her how surprising this was to me as many of these folks were the stubborn "non-smilers" I had referred to in my earlier essay. Her response shook a few leaves off of my tree.

"Patty, you have no idea how you look when you blow by these people. You are quite intense. You are in your all black outfit, with your hair pulled back in a ponytail under your black hat, with your eyes hidden behind your dark sunglasses. Your arms and feet are pumping so fast that the other walkers barely have time to acknowledge you before you charge by." My body language definitely was not communicating approachability or welcome." "Oh," I replied. "I never thought about it like that."

I then discovered that there is a mall-walking club, complete with a newsletter and organizer that counts most of these walkers as members. They all know each other by name because they belong to the club and have taken an interest in each others' lives. I have since joined and introduced myself to a few of the regulars and have learned some enlightening things about my fellow walkers. I discovered that the one woman who is there most frequently began walking after the death of her son years ago. She took to mall-walking as a means to work through her grief. I thought she was obsessed with exercise but she is actually just focused on healing.

Rereading my essay on breakups always stings and made me rethink my decision about leaving the birthday lunch group. I chose to walk away from something because it was not working for me but it seemed to be working well for everyone else. I should have been willing to put other's needs ahead of my own. I didn't like being the weakest link in the chain so I broke the chain. I voted myself off of the island. But now the severed chain and empty space on the island haunts me. As of this writing I have asked to reunite with the group and have been welcomed back. I look forward to the celebration of the late summer birthdays.

The dead leaves of hypocrisy must also be shed. I have questioned how many cleft palates could be repaired, or homeless could be fed, with the price of an expensive watch or purse after writing an essay about my husband purchasing a new Corvette. I talk about being bold with respect to faith-sharing but then walk away from an interfaith book club, which may have provided a rare opportunity for dialogue, after a few criticisms of the Catholic Church. I express disdain for wine snobs and then admit that I must have Starbuck's French Roast Coffee each morning. This tree really needs a good shaking.

But this is how the walk of faith goes. It is a cycle of dying and rebirth. I continually shed the old self and put on the new self. Colossians 3:9-10 explains that one can become a new creation "since you have taken off the old self with its practices and have put on the new self, which is being renewed, for knowledge, in the image of its creator." I cannot do this on my own. I need grace, constant grace. As Brother Lawrence says in The Practice of the Presence of God when he neglects to be aware of God's presence, "See that is what happens to me when I am left on my own. I fall into my sinful ways. Lord, you must stay with me." Be with me, Lord. Keep calling me.

I continue to write stories in my head about persons and circumstances that I encounter daily. Maybe a sequel will have to be written entitled *Playing Phone Tag with God*. He calls. I don't pick up. I call back and He seems not to answer. We finally connect and catch up, having a most pleasant conversation, and then our chat is interrupted by call waiting and I must place Him on hold. I then forget to get back to Him. He calls, I don't pick up and the cycle repeats. Maybe I just need to be still more often to hear His call or simplify His message. Be still and know that I am God. Be still and know that I am. Be still and know. Be still. Be.

Looking back has made me aware that the call is actually not coming from outside of me but from inside. Mark 12:34 assures that "You are not far from the kingdom of God." It is very close. A favorite passage from Deuteronomy, about God's commands and the voice of the Lord, explains that it is not up in the sky and it is not across the sea. It "is something very near to you, already in your mouths and in your hearts, you have only to carry it out." (Deuteronomy 30:10-14) A song from our church hymnal, *Deep Within*, conveys this well: "Deep within, I will plant my law not on stone but in your hearts."

There is a voice planted deep inside this tree. It is very near to me and I don't have to travel far to answer the call. It is an ongoing call taking place on the open line in my heart. It rings continuously. All I have to do is pick up.

Day 1) Is there a certain season or month which spurs you into a reflective mode? How honest are you with your assessments of personal and spiritual progress? Is it easier for you to find fault with yourself than to recognize growth? Consider that we are to love our neighbors as ourselves and be kind to yourself as you make your appraisals.

Day 2) Has a friend ever opened your eyes to culpability in a situation which you had neglected to recognize? How receptive were you to this insight? Have you been the bearer of some eye-opening news to another? Consider the role of friends and loved ones in admonishing harmful behaviors.

Day 3) Ponder Psalm 145:18 which says: "You, Lord, are near to all who call upon you, to all who call upon you in truth." How near do you consider the Lord to be? How often do you call upon Him? Do you call upon Him in truth? Call upon Him now.

Day 4) Have you severed a relationship in recent months that has left you with an unsettled feeling? Is it possible that you are being drawn back into a relationship with this person? Pray for healing of the brokenness you may have caused and ask for direction as to how to proceed.

Day 5) Have you reread old journal entries or replayed conversations in your mind and detected bitterness or negativity you were not aware of at the time? Do you have dead leaves which need to be shaken from your tree? Every day you have the opportunity to shed the old self and put on the new self being renewed in the image of your creator. Let the shedding begin.

Day 6) While it is not advisable to dwell on the past, history can teach important lessons and prevent us from repeating mistakes. What are some of the recurrent themes, battles fought, territories expanded and fun facts to know and tell about the history of you. Take a brief moment to look back and be a student in your own History 101 class.

Day 7) Take a moment now to look forward. Write your desired ending to your story. Remember that God's plans for us are always better than our own and be prepared for some rewrites. Reflect on the lyrics "Be not afraid, I go before you always, come follow me and I will give you rest."

LaVergne, TN USA
18 February 2011
216948LV00005B/7/P